GLENCOE AND THE INDIANS

GLENCOE AND THE INDIANS

*A real-life family saga which spans two continents,
several centuries and more than thirty generations to
link Scotland's clans with the native peoples of the
American West*

JAMES HUNTER

MAINSTREAM
PUBLISHING

EDINBURGH AND LONDON

In memory of
Charles Duncan McDonald,
1897–1995,

and in tribute to all those peoples, right
across the world, who are grappling with
the consequences of their having got in the
way of what history's winners invariably
call progress

First published in 1996 by
MAINSTREAM PUBLISHING COMPANY (EDINBURGH) LTD
7 Albany Street
Edinburgh EH1 3UG

ISBN 1 85158 829 9

Subsidised by

THE SCOTTISH ARTS COUNCIL

A catalogue record for this book is available from the British Library

Typeset in Monotype Perpetua

Printed and bound in Great Britain by Butler & Tanner Ltd

Contents

Note on nomenclature

There is no 'proper' way of spelling Highland surnames. The family featured in this book have variously spelled their name MacDonald and McDonald. Both forms are used here – in accordance with the preferences of different individuals.

Neither is there any 'proper' way of referring to those human beings who, in the ensuing pages, are called Indians or Native Americans. The latter term is widely regarded nowadays as the politically correct one. The McDonald family, however, mostly call themselves Indians or Indian people. This book tends to follow their example.

Acknowledgements

Some four or five years ago, when researching an earlier book about the many links between the Scottish Highlands and North America, my attention was drawn to the career of a man called Duncan McDonald. Despite his wholly Highland name, it appeared, Duncan considered himself Nez Perce. And when this Indian people found themselves embroiled in fighting with the United States army, it further appeared, Duncan made it his business to publish an account of the ensuing war as that war seemed to the Nez Perce.

Duncan's father, I learned, was a fur trader, Angus McDonald, who had been born in the Scottish Highlands and who, as a young man, had left Scotland for the American West.

Little additional information was readily available. But these few facts were so intriguing that I decided to make some reference to this Indian-Highland connection in my planned book. I duly mentioned my intention to Jim McLeod, the friend from whom I had first heard of both Duncan and Angus McDonald.

Jim lives in Idaho and I was due to spend some time with him in the course of my researches. Since Angus McDonald had traded in Idaho, I remarked to Jim during one of the transatlantic telephone conversations which preceded my Idaho trip, it would be good if we were able to visit together some of the places where Angus had been based.

There the matter would have rested but for a telephone call which Jim now got from an acquaintance. This acquaintance, a forester by profession, knew of Jim's own longstanding interest in the Highland fur traders who were among the first whites to venture across the Rocky Mountains into the region nowadays consisting of British Columbia, Washington State, Oregon, Idaho and Montana. At a forestry conference which he had been attending, Jim's acquaintance told him, he had met a young man, also a forester, who, it seemed, was descended from just such a fur trader.

The young man in question is Tom Branson. He lives on the Flathead Reservation in western Montana where he is employed as a forest manager by the Confederated Salish and Kootenai Tribes. Tom is a Salish tribal member. He is also Angus McDonald's great-great-grandson.

Tom kindly agreed to meet Jim and me. Our meeting took place in December 1993 on the Flathead Reservation – where Tom introduced us to his great-uncle, Charlie McDonald, nephew of Duncan, grandson of Angus and one of the Flathead Reservation's tribal elders.

What I heard that day from Charlie McDonald, a most welcoming man who was then in his nineties and who died just over a year later, convinced me that I ought eventually to make more detailed enquiries into the McDonald family story. This book is the result of these enquiries. It would not exist, however, but for the very generous help I have had from very many individuals and organisations.

For financial assistance with my research and travel costs in Scotland and North America, I am grateful to the University of Montana, Comataidh Telebhisein Gaidhlig, Scottish Television, Comunn na Gaidhlig and the British Council.

Equally crucial has been the help extended to me by other historians, writers and researchers in Scotland, Canada and the United States.

In Scotland, Iain S. Macdonald, Falkirk, permitted me to draw on the results of his work on the sheep-farming activities of a number of Glencoe families. Alasdair MacLeod, family historian at Inverness Public Library, helped me make a number of important genealogical connections. Margaret MacDonald, archivist at Skye's Clan Donald Centre, did likewise. Norman H. MacDonald, honorary secretary of the Clan Donald Society of Edinburgh, commented constructively on the results of my initial forays into MacDonald history. So did John Bannerman and W. David H. Sellar of Edinburgh University. And I was supplied by Charles MacFarlane, of Glenfinnan House Hotel, with material I should not otherwise have found.

In Canada, Marianne McLean and her husband, Philip Goldring, both of whom it is my good fortune to count among my friends, gave me valuable assistance. Marianne provided me with information drawn from her path-breaking research into emigration from the Highlands to North America. Philip supplied equally informative material deriving from his work on the history of the Hudson's Bay Company.

In the United States, where I spent several weeks working on this project, I was hosted, so to speak, by William E. Farr of the Center for the Rocky Mountain West at the University of Montana in Missoula. I could not have been in better hands. As something of a blundering amateur in the history of the American West, I was tremendously lucky to have had the chance to talk over my ideas with Bill Farr who was unstinting with support, advice and information.

Tony Incashola, of the Salish Cultural Committee on the Flathead Reservation, kindly gave me access to the committee's video-recordings of Charlie McDonald. Tom Smith, who made these recordings, was equally helpful.

My protracted quest for documentation relating to the McDonald family brought me into contact with the staffs of the various libraries and archives listed at the start of this book's bibliography. Their help is much appreciated. So is the assistance I got from Morna MacLaren and David McClymont of Portree Public Library. By testing almost to destruction the inter-library loan system, Morna and David supplied me, in my Isle of Skye home, with dozens of books which I did not expect to obtain on this side of the Atlantic Ocean.

I am profoundly grateful to my wife, Evelyn, both for tolerating my long absences in the United States and for putting up with my inexcusable tendency to be mentally in nineteenth-century Montana even at times when I was physically in twentieth-century Skye.

It remains for me to thank – however inadequately – the many members of the present-day McDonald family who have taken a close interest in, and helped greatly with, this project. The tremendous friendliness and hospitality which I encountered in McDonald family homes on the Flathead Reservation were such as to enable me to overcome my initial trepidation about raising and exploring issues which – because of the way our planet continues to be plagued by racial divisions and animosities – are necessarily sensitive and difficult. My debt to the McDonald family, then, is huge. But her McDonald relatives, I think, will understand why I single out Ellen Swaney for particular mention at this point. Ellen, Director of American Indian Achievement in the Office of the Montana University System's Commissioner of Higher Education, was my point of contact with the McDonald family over the many months it took to research this book. To her, I am grateful for much help and much encouragement.

I return, at the end of these acknowledgements, to Charlie McDonald. Sadly, Charlie did not live to see the completion of the project which resulted from my meeting with him. But the McDonald family have graciously allowed me to dedicate my book to Charlie's memory. This I do with the greatest respect.

THE AMERICAN ROCKY MOUNTAIN WEST

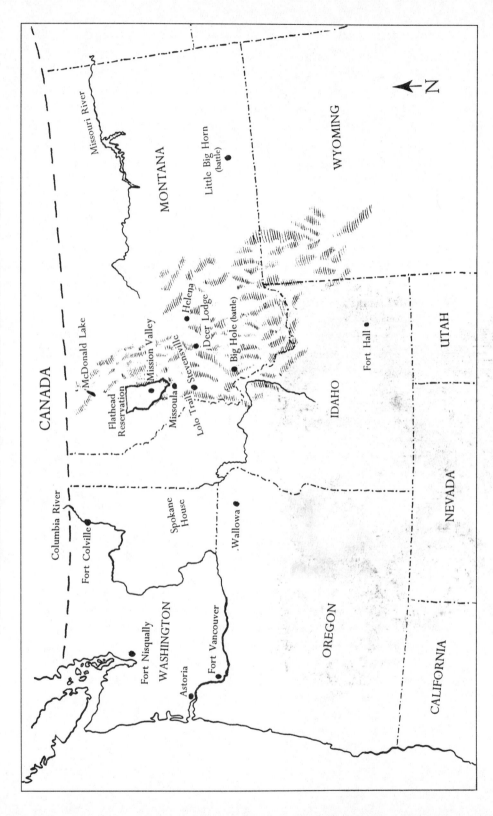

CHAPTER ONE

Nez Perce outriders!

In the Montana town of Missoula, then barely ten years old and home to no more than about 400 people, the afternoon of Saturday, 28 July 1877, was every bit as warm as most other summer afternoons in this part of America's Rocky Mountain West. It made good sense, in these circumstances, to keep out of the sun. It made equally good sense to take advantage of anything to be obtained by way of what, if an optimist by nature, you might call a cooling breeze. This, no doubt, was why Benjamin Franklin Potts, Governor of Montana Territory, could be seen seated that Saturday on the shaded veranda of the hotel which had been his headquarters since the latest of his country's Indian wars had brought the governor hurrying here two days before.

From the governor's point of view, perhaps, there was some slight political risk in his being so conspicuously at ease when ostensibly dealing with a first-rate crisis – especially since the crisis in question looked to be about to end in an Indian raid on Missoula. But Potts, if asked why he was so visibly idling when so much danger threatened, could readily have replied – for this was certainly the case – that events had, earlier in the day, assumed an altogether uncontrollable momentum. He might have added – for this, too, was surely true – that he was simply very tired. The governor's week had been an extraordinarily busy one, after all. It had involved him, for example, in much hard riding on the dusty trail between Missoula and a mountain gorge called Lolo Canyon.

Much has altered in Montana since Governor Potts's time. Missoula, its population grown a hundredfold or more, has spread itself – in the way that cities do in a country where the supply of land has mostly been thought inexhaustible – across large tracts of what, in 1877, was open, unfenced grassland. It consequently takes a fair amount of driving on Highway 93 – which has replaced the trail Potts followed – to get clear of all the malls, motels and fast-food eateries on modern Missoula's outer rim. But eventually the city falls behind. And as Montana's underlying shape starts to show through the thinning urban sprawl, it begins to be a little easier to visualise this area as it would have looked to Benjamin F. Potts.

Ahead is the Bitterroot Valley, its flat and several-mile-wide floor stretching away to a haze-obscured horizon. On the left, picked out by sun and shadow, are the smoothly rounded ridges of the Sapphire Range. But it is neither to the valley nor to the Sapphires that one's eye is drawn when heading southwards from Missoula. What tugs at a traveller's vision are the views which open to the right – where the dark and roughly finished summits of the Bitterroot Mountains, a subset of the Rockies, reach 8,000 or 9,000 feet into the sky.

To the first whites who, nearly 200 years ago, came probing into this rugged, western end of present-day Montana from the Great Plains to the east, the Bitterroots appeared initially to be a practically impenetrable barrier. From the region's Indians, however, these whites learned of a narrow pass which, some twelve miles from Missoula, makes a right-angle junction with the much broader Bitterroot Valley. In time, the route this pass provides through the Bitterroot Mountains became known as the Lolo Trail. The cleft-like gash by which the trail is accessed from the east was named, in its turn, Lolo Canyon. Today the canyon carries Highway 12 to Lewiston in Idaho. And four miles along this highway – its location marked by one of the noticeboards Montana uses to indicate historic sites – is the spot where, on 26 July 1877, Benjamin F. Potts reined in the sweating horse that had brought him from Missoula.

The governor, despite his having journeyed to Missoula overnight from further east, had not paused there to rest. Instead he had hurried on here to inspect the makeshift fortifications then occupying this spot. Consisting of nothing more substantial than a long line of hastily felled trees and some hurriedly dug entrenchments, these fortifications were intended, for all their evident inadequacy, to stop any further advance on the part of an Indian, or Native American, people who had just completed a long and difficult journey across the Lolo Trail and who were known, when Montana's territorial governor got here, to be camped not very far away.[1]

This people were the Nez Perce. Some six weeks previously, on the far side of the Bitterroots in Idaho, a handful of their young men, reacting violently to the U.S. government's insistence that the Nez

Perce should remove themselves to a reservation, had gone on the rampage and killed a number of Idaho's white settlers — settlers whom the Nez Perce blamed for the loss of lands their families had occupied for countless generations. These killings having been interpreted by the U.S. authorities as an act of war, the Nez Perce, in the jargon of the time, were designated 'hostile'. They became liable, in other words, to be attacked by the United States army. That — given the huge disparity between the two or three hundred fighting men available to the Nez Perce and the altogether more substantial military apparatus at the disposal of the American government — should have been the end of the matter. But the Nez Perce, although they had never engaged in any such campaign before, easily defeated or eluded the various detachments sent against them, inflicting significant casualties on the U.S. army in the process.[2]

By the end of June 1877, therefore, all the white communities within striking distance of the Nez Perce country were beginning to be seriously alarmed. Just twelve months before, as everyone in the West remembered very well, another set of Indians, consisting principally of the Sioux bands led by Sitting Bull and Crazy Horse, had engulfed General George A. Custer and his Seventh Cavalry in the vicinity of Montana's Little Bighorn River, killing Custer and more than 200 of his soldiers. Those events had naturally made many whites more than usually apprehensive about Indian intentions. Could it be that the Nez Perce troubles, such whites began to wonder, signalled the start of the general Indian rising which was one of the nineteenth-century West's regular nightmares? Crazy Horse, admittedly, had been in U.S. army custody since April. But Sitting Bull, despite his having fled across Montana's border with Canada in the early part of 1877, continued to command a following and was consequently capable, or so it seemed to most observers, of raising a substantial armed force. Nor were Sitting Bull and the Sioux the only folk to whom the Nez Perce could — at least conceivably — turn for assistance. Others of Montana's native peoples, not least the Salish or Flathead bands then living in the general vicinity of Missoula, possessed both weapons and good reasons — in the shape of their own grievances arising from the loss of tribal lands — to turn these weapons against whites. Suppose, then, that the Nez Perce, capitalising on their initial victories, were to move eastwards into Montana in order both to win Flathead support and to effect a junction with Sitting Bull. Would this not be to threaten the entire white position in the region?

Among the Westerners who harboured such fears was Montana's Governor Potts. As early as 28 June, when the Nez Perce War was barely two weeks old, the governor sent his territorial secretary, Captain James H. Mills, to Missoula with a view to having this senior official report formally on what was happening in the part of Montana closest to the various scenes of fighting in neighbouring Idaho. Next Potts attempted to persuade the U.S. federal government to supply him with additional military assistance by sending a deliberately alarmist telegram – a telegram despatched before the governor had even heard from Captain Mills – to President Rutherford B. Hayes in Washington, D.C.: 'Settlements in western Montana seriously threatened by Nez Perce Indians . . . Settlers are fleeing their homes in Bitterroot Valley to Missoula for safety. More troops are needed for Missoula. We are organising and arming the people for defence. Flathead and other Indians are seriously disaffected.'[3]

At the point when Governor Potts chose thus to pressurise President Hayes, his various urgings and anxieties may have seemed more than a little overdone. But when, some three weeks into July, it became known that the Nez Perce were indeed leaving Idaho by way of the Lolo Trail and heading for Montana, the governor's warnings of imminent catastrophe – warnings which had not, at the outset, been taken very seriously in Washington – began to seem astonishingly prescient. They seemed particularly prescient, perhaps, to those who understood, as Potts himself certainly did, just how little could immediately be done to defend Missoula's ever more alarmed residents from any attack the steadily approaching 'hostiles' might launch on their town.

In all of Montana – which is roughly one-and-a-half times the size of Britain – there were, in the summer of 1877, rather less than 500 American troops. That, from the Missoula citizenry's point of view, was bad enough. What made things even worse, however, was the fact that only a very small proportion of the territory's theoretically available soldiers could be readily deployed against the Nez Perce. Because Montana's earlier Indian wars had mostly involved the Sioux, and because the Sioux were a Great Plains people, such army units as were then stationed in the territory were mostly located several hundred miles to the east of Missoula. These troop dispositions could, of course, have been changed in the weeks following the Nez Perce outbreak. But the military authorities, despite the increasingly frantic appeals made to them by Governor Potts, were by no means willing to alter their arrangements. The continuing risk that Sitting Bull might pull out of his Canadian sanctuary and embark on a new round of campaigning meant, as far as the army at least was concerned, that no worthwhile force could be sent westwards to deal with what the military considered – prior to the Nez Perce actually setting out

14

across the Bitterroots – a wholly hypothetical contingency.[4]

This meant that when, on Monday, 23 July, Governor Potts learned that the Nez Perce were definitely moving into Montana, the U.S. army's dispositions in the territory remained much as they had been a month earlier. Missoula, as a result, was garrisoned by fewer than fifty soldiers. And there was not the slightest chance of getting reinforcements to the town before the Nez Perce reached the Montana end of the Lolo Trail.

It was only by the sheerest of sheer luck, moreover, that Missoula possessed any troops at all. For most of its brief existence, the town had been entirely undefended. During 1876, however, the army – in response to local complaints that the town and its surrounding settlements were 'the least protected' places 'in the territory' – had ordered one of its officers to assess the overall military situation in western Montana. The officer in question had recommended the creation of a permanent military post in the vicinity of Missoula. This was eventually agreed. And in June 1877, at about the time the Nez Perce War was breaking out in Idaho, Captain Charles C. Rawn and 44 men of the Seventh Infantry duly arrived in the Missoula area to begin construction work on what the army – with considerable overstatement – immediately christened Fort Missoula.[5]

It was from Fort Missoula, still consisting of little more than one or two half-erected sheds, that Rawn now set out, on the morning of Wednesday, 25 July, with the aim of preventing the Nez Perce exiting from the Lolo Trail into the Bitterroot Valley and with the further, even more ambitious, objective of bringing about a Nez Perce surrender. With him Rawn had some two dozen soldiers and a rather larger number of the civilian volunteers who had been recruited as a result of Governor Potts having already authorised the 'organising and arming' of the local settler population. Few professional soldiers liked to be in any way dependent on volunteer militias of this type – such militias being commonly regarded by the army, almost always with good reason, as undisciplined, inefficient and hopelessly unreliable in combat. Captain Rawn, however, had little choice but to accept all the assistance he could get. Having reached Lolo Canyon and quickly identified the spot – nowadays occupied by a tourist carpark – where the canyon is at its narrowest, Rawn set both his troops and their civilian comrades to work on the log barricade which was soon to stretch from one side of the valley to the other. 'Am entrenching 25 regulars and about 50 volunteers in Lolo Canyon,' he reported.[6]

The people whom Rawn was preparing to confront had been more than a week on the Lolo Trail at this point. Their chosen route – which was shortly afterwards described by the U.S. army's General William T. Sherman as 'one of the worst trails for man and beast on this continent' – had proved anything but straightforward. Although familiar enough to the Nez Perce, whose hunters had long been in the habit of crossing Montana's mountain ranges in order to gain access to the buffalo herds then to be found on the Great Plains beyond, the Lolo Trail – not replaced by Highway 12 until the 1960s – was twisting, cramped and frequently obstructed by fallen trees and other debris of that kind. The Nez Perce, encumbered as they were by their having to transport all their household goods and by their having to keep under strict control a 2,000-strong herd of horses, had found the going extremely hard. Now, just when they were practically in sight of the Bitterroot Valley and at a moment when they must have thought most of their troubles behind them, the Nez Perce came up against Rawn and his men. The Nez Perce could have swept the captain's little force aside. They had dealt with much more formidable opposition back in Idaho, after all. But the Nez Perce, as will shortly be repeated, considered themselves through with fighting. They wished instead to talk.[7]

Over the next couple of days, therefore, Charles C. Rawn found himself drawn into repeated parleys with the Nez Perce who had made camp, meanwhile, at a point some three or four miles to the west of the captain's laboriously prepared defences. Precisely what was said by Rawn to the Nez Perce in the course of these negotiations is as much a matter for conjecture as what was said to him by the Nez Perce. It is obvious, however, that neither Rawn nor his political superiors were eager to do battle. To attack the 'hostiles' with such 'an inadequate force' would be 'madness', Governor Potts concluded when, on the Thursday morning of that most hectic week, he rode out from Missoula in an attempt to establish exactly what was happening in Lolo Canyon. 'The only thing that could be done,' Potts continued, 'was to hold the Indians in check until such a force arrived as to compel a surrender.' This, of course, was to assume that it was impossible simply to outflank Rawn's now quarter-mile-long barrier. But the terrain, from the perspective of the barrier's defenders at all events, seemed to justify exactly that assumption. At the point being held against the Nez Perce, one of Rawn's civilian volunteers observed, the westward-inclining Lolo Canyon's southern side was both precipitous and 'densely covered with standing and fallen timber'. To the north, admittedly, the ground was more open. But it was also so steep, the same volunteer asserted, that 'a goat could not pass, much less an entire tribe of Indians with all their impedimenta'.[8]

Lolo Canyon's surroundings, as can readily be seen from today's Highway 12, are exactly as the volunteer of 1877 described them. On looking around here, therefore, it is easy to understand why Charles C. Rawn — just like that volunteer soldier — became convinced he had succeeded, at the minimum, in preventing the Nez Perce from moving any further east.

In reaching this conclusion, however, Captain Rawn made a mistake that had been made several times already about the Nez Perce and was to be made several times again in the months ahead. He underestimated both this people's quite remarkable tenacity and the sheer quality of the leadership at their disposal.

In the early morning of Saturday, 28 July, the entire Nez Perce contingent — whose surrender Captain Rawn had so recently been hoping to obtain — was observed high on the supposedly impassable hillsides which constituted the Lolo Canyon's northern wall. 'I could see the soldiers from the mountainside where we travelled,' one Nez Perce fighter, a young man named Yellow Wolf, would subsequently say of that morning's events. 'It was no trouble, not dangerous, to pass those soldiers.'[9]

Realising that there was nothing more to be done by way of preventing the Nez Perce gaining access to the Bitterroot Valley, Rawn — with his handful of troops and with those civilian volunteers who had not already slipped back to their homes — promptly withdrew to Missoula which, as noted earlier, Benjamin F. Potts had already made his base. Not having anything else to do other than await developments, Potts, as also mentioned previously, settled himself comfortably on his hotel's veranda where, it so happened, the governor fell under the far from friendly gaze of a tall, dark-haired young man who was similarly seeking refuge from the sun. What transpired next is best told in the young man's words. A cloud of dust, he reported, was seen to be approaching the town and this dust cloud — quite understandably in view of what had occurred that morning — was immediately thought to denote an imminent Nez Perce attack. 'I was standing in the [hotel] doorway,' the nearby watcher afterwards recalled, 'and at the cry, "Nez Perce outriders!", the governor nearly upset me in his hurry to get inside.'[10]

❁

Both the dust cloud and the warning shouts accompanying it turned out to have a more innocent explanation than the one which Governor Potts had feared. This explanation was provided, long after the event, by a Missoula resident called Will Cave, then no more than a boy. His stepfather, Will said, possessed 'a train of pack mules'. Captain Rawn had hired twelve of these mules to assist with the transport of supplies from Missoula to the army's temporary camp in Lolo Canyon. On the Saturday which saw the camp's abandonment, Will's story continued, the dozen mules – their usefulness to the military now at an end – were being returned to their owner when the dust kicked up in the course of their progress was glimpsed by a Bitterroot Valley settler, one John Pickens. Events then took a turn towards the farcical.[11]

Pickens, or so Will Cave claimed, 'was not a young man and his eyesight was not of the best'. Having 'jumped at the conclusion' that the Nez Perce were making for Missoula, Cave went on, Pickens 'did not tarry to ascertain to the contrary'. Instead he mounted a horse and, riding 'as fast as his horse could travel', got himself quickly into town where he was heard 'excitedly announcing that the Indians were right upon us'. Soon 'every old shotgun and pistol' that could be found was being pressed into service as Missoula's increasingly panicky residents prepared to turn their town's more substantial buildings into improvised strongpoints.

It was at this point, it seems, that a number of Missoula families decided to remove themselves, for a time at least, to the comparative safety of more easterly Montana towns like Helena and Deer Lodge. Governor Potts, however, showed no sign of following their example. And it may well be, of course, that he had anyway behaved with just a little bit more dignity than was attributed to him by the young man whom the governor apparently came close to 'upsetting' in the course of his alleged dash for cover. Potts, after all, had seen plenty of action during America's civil war – joining the Union army as a volunteer captain and returning to his Ohio home, at the war's end, with the rank of brigadier-general. His subsequent political involvements, which led to his being appointed Governor of Montana Territory by President Ulysses S. Grant in 1870, were such as to have made Potts the target of a good deal of virulent abuse – one Montana newspaper going so far as to call the governor, who was a big and burly man, 'the two hundred and fifty pounds avoirdupois of bone and muscle and the thimble-full of brains that runs our government'. But not even his bitterest enemies thought to say Potts was a coward. This fact, together with the jaundiced tone adopted by the bystander who claimed to have seen the governor in flight, might be thought to raise the possibility that the bystander in question had his own reasons to do down the governor's reputation.[12]

And so he did. This man was Duncan McDonald. As his name suggests, Duncan's father was Scottish or, as Duncan would have put it, Scotch. His mother, however, was partly Nez Perce and his mother's mother wholly so. Duncan, as a result, had his own links with the native people who, that Saturday, had once more outsmarted the American military. Prominent among the planners of the skilfully conducted manoeuvre which got the Nez Perce safely into the Bitterroot Valley were Chief White Bird and Chief Looking Glass. Both were Duncan McDonald's close relatives.[13]

'I am in the same box,' Duncan McDonald was one day to write, 'as the Kaiser of Germany.' Wilhelm II, Duncan went on, was distrusted by the Germans 'because his mother was British'. The Kaiser, Duncan added, was equally distrusted by the British 'because his father was a German'. This may have been to oversimplify the German emperor's many problems, but in commenting, 'This is my predicament', Duncan McDonald made his own position clear. Because it was impossible to categorise such individuals as Indian or white, the 'half-breed', the term applied then to a man of Duncan's status, could all too easily find it very hard to be accepted by either of the two – often warring – groups with which he was connected.[14]

At a time when – by legally preventing whites from marrying anyone considered more than 50 per cent Indian by descent – Western legislatures were attempting to prohibit sexual relations between settlers and Native Americans, the person of mixed-blood was living proof to the West's numerous racists that, despite their best endeavours, men and women of different races were continuing to be involved with one another. This made the half-breed or the 'breed' – the latter expression being even more dismissive than the former – a favoured target for racially inspired abuse. To be of mixed-blood, ran a 'common saying' in the West, was to be 'half Indian, half white man and half devil' – a judgement which, it is a good deal more than probable, was unhesitatingly applied to Duncan McDonald by a fair proportion of the whites with whom he regularly came in contact.[15]

Duncan was certainly considered unreliable by some at least of the various army officers and territorial officials whose task it was to cope with Montana's steadily developing Nez Perce crisis. When a military man heard, on 20 July 1877, that McDonald, who earned his living as a trader, had taken delivery of 'four thousand rounds of ammunition', one of this officer's civilian colleagues was brusquely instructed to ensure 'that none of it gets into the possession of any Indian whatsoever'. There were, as it happened, all sorts of legitimate reasons as to why Duncan – whose Indian customers depended heavily on hunting – should have been dealing in such goods. And he himself was quick to protest that he knew better 'than to let hostile Indians have

19

cartridges'. But the episode was revealing all the same. It demonstrated that, by important elements in what was then an obviously endangered white community, Duncan McDonald was by no means wholly trusted.[16]

This, from a white perspective, was maybe justifiable; for Duncan, on the Saturday the Nez Perce seemed about to take Missoula, was clearly subject to conflicting loyalties.

That morning, according to his own account, Duncan McDonald had been riding hard in the direction of Lolo Canyon and 'calculating to go right into' the Nez Perce camp when, 'about four miles west of Missoula', he encountered several of the volunteers who had been rendered surplus to Captain Charles C. Rawn's requirements by the Nez Perce having so triumphantly bypassed the captain's barricade. On enquiring what had transpired and on learning that the Nez Perce were no longer where he had expected to find them, Duncan 'changed [his] notion,' as he put it, 'and returned to Missoula'. There he found the approaches to the town deserted except for a lone sentry who was standing guard on the bridge which gave access to Missoula's main – and then more or less only – street. Slung across the bridge's decking was a chain. And when Duncan, reining in his horse, enquired as to the chain's purpose he was told it was intended to hold back the Nez Perce who were expected to approach at any moment. On hearing this, Duncan's badly stretched nerves clearly snapped. Pointing at the easily fordable river upstream and downstream from the bridge, he shouted: 'There! There! See the Indians' bridges. They can cross anywhere. But if they choose to pass on this bridge, your chain will hold them about thirty seconds. You better show a spirit of hospitality by taking it down.'[17]

While it is possible – as will shortly be seen – to hazard a guess as to the original aim of Duncan McDonald's failed expedition to the Nez Perce camp, it is much more difficult to be certain as to how exactly Duncan might have responded had the Nez Perce actually come in strength into Missoula. But the whole tenor of his conduct, both on 28 July and later, was such as to make one suspect that, if Duncan McDonald had found himself drawn into a shooting war between Indians and whites, he would not necessarily have been on the same side as Benjamin F. Potts.

As it was, neither Duncan nor the governor were put to this particular test. On reaching the Bitterroot Valley, Looking Glass, White Bird and the rest of the Nez Perce, instead of turning north in the direction of Missoula, headed south towards Stevensville and the several other small communities strung out along the valley's floor.

❁

Described just prior to its settlement by whites as a place of 'perpetual spring' and as 'the most beautiful and productive' piece of land in all Montana, the Bitterroot Valley continues to do its best to live up to the many such claims which have been made on its behalf. Although neither its winter nor its summer temperatures seem particularly spring-like, the Bitterroot country is certainly spared both the bone-chilling cold and the shrivelling heat of the Great Plains. That helps make the Bitterroot, as its modern realtors so insistently point out, a most liveable locality. And now that Montana – which is larger than most European countries but which is inhabited by only 800,000 people – has started to be regarded by many Americans as their nation's 'last best place', the loggers and agriculturalists who have long earned a living hereabouts are beginning to be outnumbered by newcomers of one kind or another.[18]

Modern Stevensville, because of these developments, is a busy little town. The Stevensville of July 1877 – despite one of its early visitors having discovered several 'good, industrious, enterprising families' in this general vicinity – was, in contrast, no more than a hamlet. Stevensville's permanently resident population of around 150, however, had been swollen by farming folk who, fearful of what might follow the arrival of the Nez Perce, had abandoned their homesteads in the surrounding countryside with a view to gaining the somewhat spurious protection offered by the nearby Fort Owen – a former trading post where, with the onset of the Nez Perce crisis, some effort had been made to repair and reinforce a perimeter wall of crumbling, sun-dried brick.[19]

What especially worried the men and women who came crowding into Stevensville was the possibility that the Nez Perce invasion of the Bitterroot Valley might trigger a new and much more local Indian rebellion. Their farms, as the Stevensville refugees were all too uncomfortably aware, had been created at the expense of the Salish, or Flathead, bands who had occupied the Bitterroot country for many centuries before the first whites got here. These bands had long been under pressure to take themselves off to the Flathead Reservation which had been established well to the north of Missoula and which, incidentally, was the place where Duncan McDonald both lived and carried on his trading business. But many of the Bitterroot Valley Flatheads had simply refused to leave their ancestral territories. And all such Flatheads, in July 1877, inevitably found themselves the focus of increasingly fevered speculation as to their intentions. 'As happens on such occasions,' commented one of the Jesuit priests who had come to the Bitterroot with a view to ministering to the valley's Indian inhabitants, 'timid people began to frighten the others by their conversation and suggestions of dangers. The idea that the Flatheads, who had been so much abused, might avail themselves of the chance to revenge themselves . . . greatly excited the settlers.'[20]

As far back as the weeks following the Seventh Cavalry's annihilation at the Battle of the Little Bighorn, the *Weekly Missoulian* – the local newspaper – had been reporting 'rumours of Indian movements' in the Bitterroot country. Now many more such rumours were put quickly into circulation. The *Weekly Missoulian*, along with other Western news-papers, began to carry stories which dealt, often in gory detail, with the horrors which different Indian groups were supposedly planning to inflict on whites. There was talk, as mentioned earlier, about the risk of the Nez Perce War turning into a much more general Indian uprising. There was also talk of 'a coalition' allegedly involving both the Flathead and the Nez Perce peoples – a coalition which, it was said, had been formed in order to 'precipitate a destructive war upon western Montana'.[21]

Much was made, in this connection, of the undoubted fact that the Nez Perce and Flathead nations, as a missionary had commented almost half a century before, were 'allies and friends from time immemorial'. The two peoples were known to be in the habit of travelling together to the Great Plains each year in order to hunt buffalo. Nez Perce and Flathead intermarriage was common. And so generally cordial were relations between the two groups that, some years prior to the 1877 troubles, the dozen or so families constituting one Nez Perce band had begun to live permanently among the Bitterroot Valley Flatheads.[22]

This band was led by Eagle-from-the-Light, another of Duncan McDonald's Nez Perce relatives and, according to the *Weekly Missoulian*, 'a noble savage who declares he never accepted a present from the white man'. A once formidable buffalo hunter who was now getting on in years, Eagle-from-the-Light, despite much white gossip to the contrary, was by no means anxious to become embroiled in armed conflict. 'Partly on account of old age,' Duncan McDonald reported of his Indian kinsman, 'and partly due to a conviction . . . that his people had no chance of redressing their wrongs by fighting, he declined to take part in the . . . war'.[23]

Just prior to the Nez Perce reaching the Bitterroot Valley, Duncan himself is known to have added – perhaps mischievously – to settler anxiety by making a comment to the effect that 'preparations had long been progressing for an alliance of all the Indians to fight the whites'. As Duncan would have known very well, however, the truth was that almost all the Native Americans then residing in western Montana were inclined to share the opinions which Duncan had heard articulated by

Eagle-from-the-Light. For reasons which will be explored in one of this book's later chapters, those Nez Perce bands who were already at war with the United States army had not had much choice in the matter. Those who did have such a choice, whether Eagle-from-the-Light or that veteran chief's Flathead neighbours, were not inclined to embark on what most of them knew or suspected to be a hopeless struggle. 'It was my father's boast that the blood of a white man never reddened the hands of a single Indian of the Flathead tribe,' Chief Charlo of the Bitterroot Valley Flatheads told a U.S. government representative in July 1877. 'My father died with that boast on his lips. I am my father's son and will leave that same boast to my children.'[24]

Charlo thus adopted a policy of strict neutrality. Should the Nez Perce come to the Bitterroot country, he made clear before the Nez Perce got here, he 'would not fight with them against the whites'. But neither, Charlo added, would he 'fight against the Nez Perce'.[25]

Nor, it transpired, did the Nez Perce themselves harbour any aggressive intents on Bitterroot Valley residents. What they wanted, it soon became apparent, was to engage in trade, not robbery. And the valley's settlers – practically none of whom proved averse to supplying and provisioning the very people they had earlier accused of planning mass-murder – were happy to oblige. 'The Indians . . . have been paying exorbitant prices for flour, coffee, sugar and tobacco,' Governor Potts was told by one of his Bitterroot Valley informants. 'So far as I am advised, they have killed no stock and molested no one, except to disarm two or three citizens, returning their guns . . . but keeping their ammunition.'[26]

In the course of the first evening the Nez Perce spent in the Bitter-root Valley, a party of civilian militiamen, returning to their homes in the wake of the Lolo Canyon fiasco, blundered into the Nez Perce camp. They were promptly sent safely on their way by Looking Glass who, like other Nez Perce commanders, was to make it his business, in the days ahead, to ensure that nothing was done to make unnecessary trouble between his people and the local population. 'Never shall I forget their formidable appearance,' one of the Bitterroot Valley's white inhabitants commented at this time of the Nez Perce, 'their stern looks, their aggressiveness and their actions which, in themselves, placed us immediately on the defensive.' But the Nez Perce paid, it was admitted, 'for everything they got' – leaving, someone calculated, the then considerable sum of $1,200 with Bitterroot Valley storekeepers.[27]

This was not at all, of course, how the Nez Perce had been expected to behave. And that may be why contemporary accounts of their Bitter-root Valley progress place so much emphasis on this Indian people's wholly unanticipated discipline.

When his men came into town to buy provisions, stressed one report from Stevensville, Chief White Bird 'sat on his horse . . . and talked to them constantly in the Nez Perce tongue', clearly ensuring that order was always maintained and going so far as to give some Nez Perce youths, who had managed to purchase whiskey, 'a whipping with his quirt'. One temporarily abandoned homestead, it must be said, was broken into and some of its contents stolen. But the thieves were quickly brought to heel, and given a tongue-lashing, by a furious Looking Glass. On the chief's instructions, as Duncan McDonald was eventually to hear from some of those involved, the ransacked homestead's much-chastened looters 'took three of their horses and left the horses . . . for the stuff they took'.[28]

Underlying Looking Glass's determination to deal firmly with any disorder was his profound conviction, held equally strongly by his fellow chiefs, that the Nez Perce, simply by removing themselves from Idaho, had somehow closed their account with the United States army. 'Looking Glass,' as Duncan McDonald subsequently attempted to explain to Montanans, 'said he did not want any trouble on this side of the Lolo . . . He did not want to fight either soldiers or citizens east of the Lolo because they were not the ones [he] had fought in Idaho. The idea among the Indians . . . was that the people of Montana had no identity with the people of Idaho, and that they were entirely separate and distinct, having nothing to do with each other.' Hence the lighthearted mood which clearly gripped the Nez Perce as they made their way steadily south from Stevensville. 'We travelled through the Bitterroot slowly,' the then 21-year-old Yellow Wolf was long afterwards to recall of the opening days of August 1877. 'The white people were friendly. We did much buying and trading with them. No more fighting! We had left . . . war in Idaho.'[29]

❀

Beyond the present-day town of Darby, the previously open and spacious Bitterroot Valley transforms itself into a thickly forested mountain pass. This pass's modern road – flanked by one of the broiling trout streams that have always been among Montana's more attractive assets – climbs steeply here, eventually attaining a height of some 7,000 feet. At the pass's summit, where winter snows invariably linger into early summer, today's tourists, like the Nez Perce back in 1877, are presented with a choice of routes. Southwards is Idaho's Salmon River country. But the Nez Perce, of course, now wanted to keep clear of Idaho. And so White Bird, Looking Glass and their people headed east, crossing the Continental Divide – the Rocky Mountain ridge which

separates rivers flowing into the Pacific from rivers flowing into the
Atlantic – and dropping down, after another fifteen or so miles, to a
valley occupied by the meandering stream that is the North Fork of the
Big Hole River.

On a meadow-like expanse of grass beside the Big Hole, the Nez
Perce set up camp. Their campsite – at a spot which, in their own
language, the Nez Perce called the Place of Ground Squirrels – was one
that had long been familiar to their people. Hunting parties heading to
or from the buffalo grounds habitually broke their journeys here. And
strolling along the river's banks it is easy to see why.

The Big Hole marks the transition from densely wooded mountain-
sides to a much flatter region where, because this area gets less rain
than the high country to the west, trees are comparatively few and far
between. From the Place of Ground Squirrels, then, it was possible for
the Nez Perce to access the different resources associated both with
woodland and with grassland.

On Wednesday, 8 August 1877, their first full day here, having
waded across the shallow Big Hole to the forest's edge which lies just
beyond the river to the west, women set to felling and trimming lodge-
pole pines in order to provide their family tipis with new supports.
Elsewhere in the vicinity, meanwhile, others of the Nez Perce were
hunting elk, gathering berries and digging up camas roots, a longstanding Indian staple. And if, as would afterwards be recalled by Yellow
Wolf and others, a man by the name of Wotolen had made it known
that he had 'dreamed of soldiers', this premonition of disaster was not,
it seems, being taken very seriously.[30]

That same Wednesday, however, U.S. troops were indeed closing in
on the Nez Perce. Their commander was Colonel John Gibbon who,
on the day the Nez Perce broke out of Lolo Canyon, had left Fort
Shaw, about 150 miles east of Missoula, at the head of a hastily
assembled force which – a modicum of reinforcements having been
acquired en route – eventually consisted of some 15 or 16 officers and
around 145 men. Gibbon, known to Indians as No-Hip because of the
debilitating effect on him of a wound he had received while serving with
the Union army at Gettysburg, was a 50-year-old professional soldier
whose hard-fighting Civil War unit had been thought by his Union army
superiors to be 'equal to the best . . . in the world'.[31]

Gibbon's latest command was rather less impressive. The million-
strong army of which the colonel had been part in the early 1860s –
when the threat posed to the American union by its own southern
secessionists was countered only by mobilising the entire military
resources of the northern states – had long since been disbanded. The

entire U.S. army, by the mid-1870s, consisted of fewer than 25,000 men – the bulk of them engaged, as Colonel Gibbon was now engaged, in operations against the various Indian peoples with whom the United States had been intermittently at war ever since American politicians had decided that their nation's western border should be on the Pacific.

The American troops who actually fought their country's Indian wars ought not to be confused with the well-fed and neatly uniformed young men who have been employed to represent them in a thousand twentieth-century movies. There was little that was glamorous or appealing about the real-life frontier army. In 1871 a penny-pinching Congress had cut its soldiers' pay to levels well below those earned by their far more numerous Union army counterparts of six or seven years before. And the typical frontier soldier's day-to-day conditions were every bit as miserable as his wages. He subsisted largely on a scurvy-inducing diet of hardtack, salt pork and coffee. When fires could not be lit for fear of attracting enemies, as was frequently the case in Indian country, men ate their salt pork rations raw. Their hardtack biscuits, when conditions permitted, they took care to dunk in scalding coffee – taking equal care to skim from the coffee's surface the innumerable maggots which this process was intended to reveal.

Troops who are indifferently treated are most unlikely to feel any very great loyalty to the cause they are supposedly serving. So it was with America's frontier forces. As many as 90,000 soldiers deserted the U.S. army in the course of the quarter-century it took to subdue the West's Indian population. And the overall unattractiveness of the military existence is underlined by the fact that the army contained large numbers of recent immigrants who had become soldiers mostly, one suspects, as a result of their failure to find alternative employment rather than out of any sense of dedication to the winning of the West. Thus the infantry column that Colonel John Gibbon marched out of Fort Shaw on 28 July 1877 contained 21 men who had been born in Ireland and 20 who had been born in Germany. Also present in this one small detachment's ranks were men whose birthplaces were in France, Switzerland, Canada, England and Scotland – one of Gibbon's three Scots-born soldiers, Private Malcolm MacGregor, choosing to desert on the day his unit finally tangled with the Nez Perce.[32]

That day had been some time in arriving. It took Gibbon the better part of a week's hard marching to get from Fort Shaw to Missoula. It took his little force another four or five days to track the Nez Perce through the Bitterroot Valley where Gibbon, on learning that his Indian adversaries looked to be both well led and well armed, took the precaution of augmenting his force with some three dozen civilian volunteers – men whose role in what followed was particularly resented by the Nez Perce.[33]

There has always been dispute as to what, if anything, was agreed by the Nez Perce leadership and Captain Charles C. Rawn in the course of their negotiations in Lolo Canyon on 26 and 27 July 1877. All such discussions – not least because of their being conducted mostly through interpreters – were liable to result in mutual misunderstandings. And both sides in the Lolo Canyon talks had a retrospective interest in distorting what was actually said. But the Nez Perce seem genuinely to have believed that they had been given an undertaking that, if they did no harm to the Bitterroot settlers, the Bitterroot settlers, in turn, would do no harm to them. This 'peace pact', Duncan McDonald wrote, ended in the 'betrayal' of the Indian parties to it. 'The Nez Perce had held that pact inviolate and they justly thought that the Montanans had no right or business fighting them.'[34]

Montanans thought otherwise. A local rancher and a number of Bitterroot Valley volunteers had key roles in the reconnaissance effort which resulted in Colonel John Gibbon – now across the Continental Divide – finally being informed, on Wednesday, 8 August, as to the exact location of the Nez Perce camp on Big Hole River. The Nez Perce, still convinced their war was over, had neither sent out scouts nor posted sentries. The troop movements which Gibbon set in train that evening were consequently unobserved. And by the early hours of the following morning, the colonel's men had been deployed in attack formation on rising ground so close to the clustered tipis of the Nez Perce that, the night being still, 'the sleepy cry of a baby' every now and then reached the ears of the waiting soldiers – those soldiers whose coming Wotolen would afterwards be said to have foretold.[35]

So relaxed now were the Nez Perce that they had given over their Wednesday evening to partying and to ritual dancing. 'This,' as Duncan McDonald would observe a few months later, 'caused a deep sleep to fall on them after they went to their lodges', thus rendering them all the more vulnerable to the terrors brought by Thursday's dawn. 'The camp,' Duncan wrote, 'not apprehending danger, was sleeping soundly when, suddenly, the rifles of the soldiers belched forth their deadly fire. The camp was awakened to find their enemies plunging through it, dealing death and destruction in every direction.'[36]

Yellow Wolf – this man 'of twenty-one snows' by his own reckoning – was jerked from sleep by 'bullets . . . pattering like raindrops', as another Nez Perce put it, on the skin or canvas walls of his family's tipi. 'I grabbed my moccasins and ran out,' Yellow Wolf remembered. Somewhere he heard a woman calling, 'Why not all men get ready and

27

fight? Not run away!' But because no attack had been anticipated, as Yellow Wolf later explained, 'few warriors had rifles in their hands' and the Nez Perce were unable, therefore, to return the fire to which their whole camp was now exposed. 'I had only my war club,' Yellow Wolf went on. Soon, however, he got an unexpected chance to arm himself. 'I . . . saw a soldier crawling like a drunken man. He had a gun and a belt full of cartridges. I struck him with my war club and took his government rifle and ammunition belt . . . I now had a gun and plenty of shells.'[37]

Others of the Nez Perce were less fortunate than Yellow Wolf. A man called Wounded Head awoke to the sickening realisation, as he afterwards recalled, that 'my wife and my baby had both been shot'. A lot more such horrors would occur that morning. 'Many women and children were killed before getting out of their beds,' Duncan McDonald claimed. 'In one lodge there were five children. One soldier went into it and killed every one of them.'[38]

Some of this can be attributed to the difficulty of maintaining discipline in what was, as mentioned earlier, a highly heterogeneous unit with – in all probability – no very well developed sense either of mission or of duty. But that is not by any means to suggest that Colonel Gibbon's troops were a mere rabble. Many took no part in atrocities. Some tried to stop them occurring. An officer was heard to tell his men to desist from killing females. A soldier was seen to pick up a baby that had been left lying beside its dead mother and to hand the infant to another woman. Other soldiers, for their part, were to speak about that August Thursday's happenings in ways which make it seem unlikely that they had had any hand in the worst of what went on. Thus Corporal Charles Loyne from Pittsfield, Massachusetts, would always recall seeing a young Nez Perce woman 'lying dead with the baby on her breast crying as it swung its little arm back and forth – the lifeless hand flapping at the wrist [which had been] broken by a bullet.'[39]

But this was an Indian war and it was the misfortune of practically all the Native Americans who became caught up in such conflicts that they were not permitted the luxury of dividing their societies into distinct compartments of the kind that mostly enabled whites to prevent military conflict spilling into family life. Colonel John Gibbon brought only fighting men to this Big Hole battlefield. The Nez Perce presence here, however, was entirely different. It consisted of women as well as men, and it consisted, too, of infants, children and the elderly. It was, then, inevitable – given the extent to which any military engagement dissolves rapidly into chaos and confusion – that Nez Perce casualties would not be solely male. What was not inevitable – what remains, if it actually occurred, quite inexcusable – was the deliberate slaughter of people who were, and could be seen to be, defenceless.

Duncan McDonald, who talked to several Nez Perce survivors of Big Hole within a few months of the battle having taken place, was one of those – and there were many – who never did accept that all the killing at Big Hole was strictly necessary. 'It was shameful,' Duncan insisted, 'the way women and children were shot down in that fight . . . About forty women and children were piled up in one little ravine where they had run for shelter. Many women, with from one to three children in their arms, were found dead in that ravine. Some of the children had their mothers' breasts in their mouths.'[40]

The spot where this grim tragedy occurred is reckoned today to be among one of western Montana's more significant historic sites. The Big Hole battlefield, as a result, is kept so neat and tidy that, even when you leave its busy visitor centre in the hope of getting more privately to grips with this Place of Ground Squirrels, it is difficult to visualise the human consequences of what happened here in August 1877. But when, just two years after the battle, Andrew Garcia, a Texan trader of Mexican descent, came this way in the company of his wife, In-Who-Lise, these consequences were all too grimly apparent. 'The site was awful to see,' Garcia observed. 'Human bones were scattered through the long grass and among the willows . . . and leering skulls were scattered around us as though they had never been buried.'[41]

Garcia was no romanticiser of the Nez Perce. 'The Indian,' he remarked in the course of his comments on the events that culminated in the Battle of the Big Hole, 'is in a class of his own when it comes to low-down devilry and brutality.' But what Garcia saw at the Place of Ground Squirrels clearly got to him in a very powerful manner – all the more so, no doubt, because In-Who-Lise was herself Nez Perce and because her sister had been among the victims of the Big Hole fighting.[42]

'This ghastly display of Indian dead,' Garcia wrote, 'made me doubtful for the first time in my life if there is a Jesus or a God. And to make matters worse, my wife, since we came to this cursed place, has been crying and calling to her dead sister's spirit . . . There is nothing so weird or mournful in heaven or hell as a wild squaw wailing for her dead. You can hear it a long way and it haunts you for days. As her piercing wails came and went, far and near through this beautiful still valley of death, they would come echoing back, in a way that made me shiver, as though in answer to her sad appeals.'[43]

❦

Duncan McDonald, the events of that incident-filled Missoula Saturday now nearly two weeks behind him, was at home on the Flathead Reservation when Colonel Gibbon's infantry went into action in the valley of the Big Hole. But Duncan, some months later, was to make the journey here – discovering, on his arrival, that grizzly bears had been playing havoc with such corpses, meaning most of them, as had not been very deeply buried. Like Andrew Garcia and In-Who-Lise, Duncan was evidently much affected by his exposure to the Big Hole battle's gruesome aftermath. Unlike them, however, this mixed-blood trader was determined to take these matters further.[44]

Even prior to his seeking out the Place of Ground Squirrels, Duncan had made up his mind to do what he could to establish – and to publicise – the sequence of events which culminated in the carnage at Big Hole. Hence Duncan's decision to write an account of the Nez Perce War as that war seemed to the Nez Perce. This account, it is virtually certain, was compiled, in part at least, at the prompting of Duncan's parents, Angus and Catherine McDonald, who, as much as In-Who-Lise, had reason to mourn the outcome of the Battle of the Big Hole – Catherine's associations with the Nez Perce going all the way back to her birth and Angus's having lasted for most of his adult life.

The McDonald family home, at the time of the Nez Perce War, was at Post Creek on the Flathead Reservation. The creek's name commemorated the location's close association with the fur trading post which Angus, then serving with the British-owned Hudson's Bay Company, had helped set up nearby some thirty years before. Duncan, as it happened, was born there in 1849 and, although his father's fur trading activities resulted in the family moving elsewhere for a time, the McDonalds – from the 1840s onwards – had maintained links with Post Creek. Around 1871, following his retirement from the Bay Company which was then closing down its operations in the United States, Angus McDonald acquired the company's Post Creek property and, on he and Catherine settling down there with a number of their younger children, the place began to be managed by the McDonalds as an increasingly successful ranch.[45]

This McDonald ranch eventually carried many hundred head of cattle. Angus, it thus seems likely, would have been one of the several cattle-rearers who helped get together the thousand-strong herd which a 20-year-old cowboy by the name of Billy Irvine – like Duncan McDonald the product of a Scots-born fur trader's marriage to an Indian – drove from the Flathead country to Cheyenne, Wyoming, in the summer of 1876. These Flathead cattle were bound ultimately for Chicago slaughterhouses and it seems, at first glance, just a little odd that Irvine, whose drive was one of the first such enterprises to be organised in western Montana, should have headed for so southerly a railhead. But the Sioux rising then being masterminded by Sitting Bull and Crazy Horse made it much too risky to drive cattle across the eastern Montana plains in 1876. Hence young Billy Irvine's choice of a route which, in May that year, took him through Missoula – in the company of eleven other cowhands, an oxen-drawn chuck wagon and relay after roaring relay of half-wild Flathead steers – at the start of a southbound journey which would last for several months.[46]

Although paved roads are a twentieth-century innovation in most of this part of Montana, to take the modern highway from Missoula to the Flathead Reservation is simply to reverse the earliest section of Billy Irvine's pioneering trip. Today's highway, like the nineteenth-century trail which was its predecessor, heads north by way of Arlee to Ravalli – where, for a time, Duncan McDonald ran a trading post or store. Duncan's store has long gone, but Ravalli still consists of no more than a handful of buildings. And since a hefty slab of country hereabouts has been designated a National Bison Range, a good deal of the surrounding terrain – grazed by one of North America's few surviving herds of buffalo – remains much as Duncan would have known it.

Past Ravalli, the highway, having headed a bit east of north up a steep gradient, without any advance warning tops a ridge and unveils one of this scenically spectacular area's more especially impressive vistas.

'It seems to me,' the novelist John Steinbeck once wrote, 'that Montana is a great splash of grandeur. The scale is huge but not overpowering. The land is rich with grass and colour, and the mountains are the kind I would create if mountains were ever put on my agenda.'[47]

From the roadside rest area which has been installed on this crest some three or four miles from Ravalli, the view is one of the sort that Steinbeck evidently had in mind. Below is the little town of St Ignatius which owes both its name and its location to the mission which Jesuit priests established here in 1854. What dominates the scene, however, is not St Ignatius but the 'mountain labyrinth' – to borrow words used by one of the Jesuit mission's nineteenth-century visitors – which commences just a mile or two beyond. This is the Mission Mountain Wilderness. McDonald Peak, named after Angus, is – at 9,868 feet – both the wilderness's highest point and its best-known feature. Its sharply angled and iced-over summit, seen projecting into a clear blue sky from a lower-level springtime haze, is the sort of sight that stays a long time in the mind.[48]

Below McDonald Peak, fed by streams which emanate from a glacier on the mountain's northern flank, is Mission Valley which, more than a hundred years ago, Angus McDonald reckoned 'one of the most beautiful valleys of America'.[49] Then Mission Valley was unpartitioned cattle country. Now it is occupied by fenced-in farms and ranches which are approached by way of dirt roads branching off the highway leading northwards from St Ignatius to Pablo, the modern Flathead Reservation's principal administrative centre. Eight miles along that road, and a little to the right, you glimpse what looks to be – and is – a tumble-down log cabin standing in the middle of a field. This cabin – the other buildings which once surrounded it having long since disappeared – is all that remains of Fort Connah, the fur trading post which Angus McDonald had the job of operating on his first coming here in 1847 and which he was eventually to make his permanent residence.

In the nineteenth-century watercolour which provides this book's cover illustration, Fort Connah – then a substantial complex – is flanked by Indian tipis. That Indians were indeed in the habit of camping here is confirmed by the numerous tipi 'rings', or foundation markings, which show up in infra-red aerial photographs of the Fort Connah site. A number of the Indian bands with whom Angus McDonald had dealings during his fur trading phase, it thus appears, spent a lot of time in this vicinity; socialising, one suspects, as well as doing business; providing Angus, as his surviving writings demonstrate, with a good deal in the way of Indian legend and tradition.[50]

Among Angus McDonald's more frequent Indian visitors at Fort Connah, during the 1870s at any rate, was Eagle-from-the-Light, the Nez Perce chief – 'a close relative of my children', Angus called him – who had earlier settled in the Flathead country and who, as a result of his familiarity with the geography of the area, was convinced, even prior to the Battle of the Big Hole, that his Nez Perce kin had made a serious error in turning south when they moved into the Bitterroot Valley from Lolo Canyon on 28 July 1877. Looking Glass, White Bird and their followers, in Eagle-from-the-Light's opinion, would have done much better at this stage in their trek to have turned north. Then, by way of the Flathead Reservation, the Nez Perce could have made straight for the comparative safety of Canada, which White Bird, Looking Glass and their people could certainly have reached in a matter of just a few days.[51]

The McDonald family, for their part, appear to have been divided on this issue. Duncan's Nez Perce grandmother, who was also Looking Glass's great-aunt and who was then living with Duncan's parents in Mission Valley, was reported by Angus McDonald to have sent a message to Looking Glass, advising the chief to move south 'instead of northwards . . . as he first proposed'.[52]

Angus himself, meanwhile, considered riding out to Lolo Canyon and offering his services as a mediator between the Nez Perce and the U.S. government. But the Nez Perce, he remarked, 'dreaded . . . treachery'. And Angus consequently hesitated to put himself in a position where he might feel obliged to make promises to the Indians that the American authorities might subsequently refuse to honour. 'I thought of going up to see . . . Governor Potts,' Angus wrote to a friend in October 1877, 'to see if a solid peace could not be effected with that fine tribe of Indians, but as I could not . . . conceive what might be done to them afterwards, I remained at home.'[53]

An inactive neutrality of this kind held no appeal for Duncan McDonald who clearly felt impelled – very probably because of his awareness that he was himself part-Nez Perce – to intervene directly in the developing crisis. Like Eagle-from-the-Light – who was either Duncan's cousin or, as was certainly the case with Looking Glass, his second-cousin – Duncan McDonald took the view that the Nez Perce should immediately seek sanctuary in Canada. And according to one account of what took place that day, Duncan's abortive mission of 28 July to the Nez Perce camp in the Lolo Canyon – a mission cut short, as mentioned earlier, when Duncan heard that the Nez Perce were already moving into the Bitterroot Valley – had its origins in Duncan's intention of making it known to the Nez Perce that he was prepared to show them the best way to the Canadian border.[54]

This offer, it should be said, would not necessarily have been accepted. The Nez Perce were themselves at odds on the question of which route to take. This became apparent on the evening of the Saturday which Duncan had spent kicking his heels in Missoula when a number of Nez Perce chiefs, including both White Bird and Looking Glass, met in council to debate the different options open to them. The gathering in question took place in the presence of Left Hand, a member of Eagle-from-the-Light's band, and Left Hand, a little later, was to provide Duncan McDonald with details of the 'arguments' in which the council's various participants had engaged. Counting against the northern route, it seems, were growing Nez Perce suspicions as to the intentions of the Flathead Indians whose reservation the Nez Perce were being invited to traverse. Why should the Nez Perce, it was asked, place any trust in a people whose chief had already made clear that he would not take the Nez Perce side in any fighting? Would it not make more sense to strike south through the Bitterroot Valley and then follow the traditional Nez Perce path across the Continental Divide to the buffalo grounds where badly needed food could be obtained and where the Nez Perce, it was hoped, would be made welcome by those other Indian peoples with whom they had hunted regularly in the past?[55]

Although it seems unlikely that Looking Glass – 'a famed old blood of the tribe,' according to Angus McDonald – was greatly swayed one way or the other by his great-aunt's intervention, he certainly came down in favour of the southern route which she had recommended. White Bird – thought by Angus to be by far the most skilled military tactician among the Nez Perce – held out for the Flathead Reservation and for Canada, but was outvoted. A majority of the chiefs who attended this key council opted to head for the Continental Divide and for the buffalo grounds on the Great Plains. The Nez Perce consequently found themselves committed to the course of action that would leave them so vulnerable, in the end, to attack by Colonel John Gibbon.[56]

At this point, of course, the Nez Perce knew nothing either of Gibbon or of his plans for them. Had they done so, both their council and their story would no doubt have turned out very differently. As it was, the Nez Perce – an 'honourable and fearless' tribe, Angus called them – were to find themselves drawn inexorably into the anguish that was the Battle of the Big Hole. And the McDonald family were left to contemplate what might have been.

'It is the old drift,' Angus McDonald wrote of the fighting at Big Hole and of that fighting's outcome. 'The strong oppresses the weak and power is always power, right or wrong.' This was a verdict, as it happens, which could equally have been applied to the experiences of the faraway people among whom this Mission Valley rancher had been born more than sixty years before.[57]

SCOTLAND

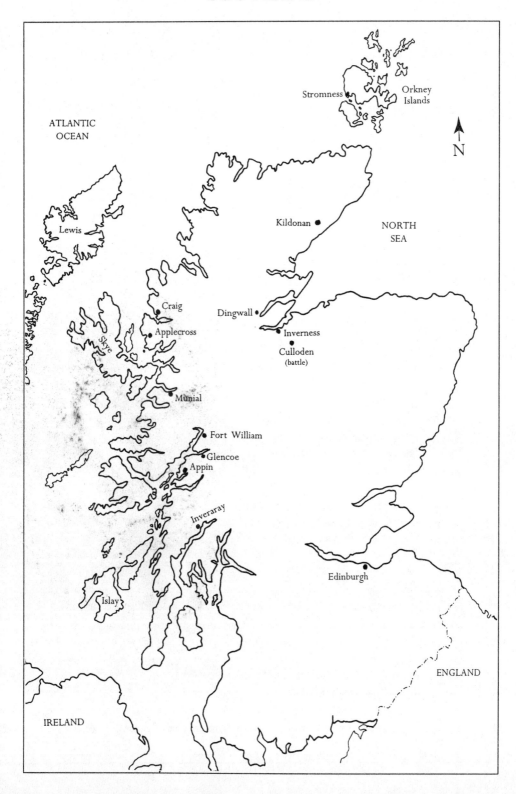

ATLANTIC
OCEAN

Stromness

Orkney
Islands

N

NORTH
SEA

Lewis

Kildonan

Craig

Dingwall

Applecross

Inverness

Skye

Culloden
(battle)

Munial

Fort William

Glencoe
Appin

Inveraray

Edinburgh

Islay

ENGLAND

IRELAND

CHAPTER TWO

Put all to the sword under seventy

Rather like one of those Rocky Mountain trails which get tougher
and more tortuous as you go on, the story which this book tells
was easier to start than to complete. The book originated in its Scottish
author's interest in discovering how a man called Duncan McDonald —
a name as redolent of Scotland as it is possible for any name to be —
came to be so powerfully identified with the Nez Perce. And at first
the explanation seemed straightforward. Duncan's mother — although
her own background will eventually be shown to be more complex than
this statement might suggest — was born and raised among the Nez
Perce. But if that fact accounts for the link between Duncan McDonald
and this Indian people, it also serves to raise — and here the trail gets
noticeably steeper — a whole set of new questions. By what means
exactly did Catherine, Duncan's mother, get involved with Angus,
Duncan's father? Just who was Angus anyway? And what had brought
him to the Rocky Mountain West?

The search for answers to these questions began on the Flathead
Reservation. From the late Charlie McDonald, one of the reservation's
tribal elders and a grandson of Catherine and Angus, it was possible to
learn something of why Angus had left Scotland and to learn something,
too, of Angus's relationship with Catherine. Eileen Decker, a great-
granddaughter of Angus and Catherine, provided additional information,
some of it in the form of family correspondence dating from the nineteenth century. And there were further insights to be gleaned from
Wyman and Joe McDonald, both great-grandsons of Catherine and
Angus — Wyman being a retired Bureau of Indian Affairs man and Joe
being president of the Flathead Reservation's Salish Kootenai College.

In Joe McDonald's Mission Valley home are genealogical charts which establish the connections between some 170 members of this now enormously extended family. To talk with Joe about the contents of these charts is immediately to be aware that his ancestral link with Scotland is of some importance to him. But to talk with this Salish, or Flathead, tribal member is equally to appreciate that a person's ethnic make-up and identity cannot be deduced simply from that person's surname. Joe is part-Scottish, certainly. But he is also – for reasons which have already been touched on and which will subsequently be explored in greater detail – descended from several Indian peoples.

'Folk ought to take pride in all of their ethnicity,' Joe McDonald remarks. 'It isn't good to reject any part of who you are. That's what I learned when, as a kid, I heard about Angus McDonald as well as hearing about my Indian ancestors.'[1]

Joe is making this comment while negotiating his four-wheel-drive truck expertly through the thick mud he has encountered on the track leading to the private graveyard – not far from the remnants of Fort Connah – where Angus and Catherine McDonald, together with several members of their family, are buried. It is early spring. The sun is warm. But snow still lies deep on McDonald Peak. And the birches and the cottonwoods around Post Creek, which flows by the McDonald graveyard, are a good month short of coming into leaf.

Joe indicates the site of the house – it was burned out some fifty years ago – where his McDonald great-grandparents lived at the time of the Nez Perce War. Not far beyond this point, the muddy track gives out completely, making it necessary to walk. Joe's wife, Cheri, helps her granddaughter, Jessica, to get down from the now dirt-spattered truck. And Jessica, who is six, immediately runs towards the post-and-rail fence which Joe has had put up around the tombstones standing in what – since he chose the graveyard's site – must surely have been one of Angus McDonald's favourite spots.

Jessica is enjoying her excursion. And if there was any chance of this trip to the last resting-place of Catherine and Angus McDonald turning into an over-solemn occasion, their great-great-great-granddaughter has successfully kept solemnity at bay. But standing in the McDonald graveyard, listening to Jessica's chatter and reading the wording on the century-old monuments to this little girl's ancestors, Angus and Catherine begin to be all the more intriguing. How could two lives which began so far apart, and in such different circumstances, have become so inextricably intertwined as those of the man and woman who are buried here? And what further discoveries, if any, can be made about this nineteenth-century couple's origins?

37

❁

The inscription on Angus's Post Creek tombstone describes him as a 'native of Scotland', states that Angus was born in that country in 1816 and adds that he died in 1889. These, however, are the barest of bare facts. It is just as well for this enquiry into Angus McDonald's antecedents, therefore, that an early-twentieth-century Missoula author, Alfred J. Partoll, should have been sufficiently interested in Angus's career as to obtain – almost certainly from Angus's son, Duncan, who was well known to Partoll – some further items of information about this rancher and former fur trader.

Angus McDonald, according to Partoll, was born at Craig, in the Scottish Highlands, on 15 October 1816. That was nearly forty years before births in Scotland were recorded by public officials. Fortunately, however, the place where Angus's life began was one of those where registers of births, baptisms and the like were maintained – well in advance of the state bureaucracy taking a hand in such matters – by local clergymen. The registers in question show that Angus was indeed born at Craig on 15 October 1816 and christened the following day – this being the common Scottish custom at a time when, as a result of high infant mortality, parents who delayed their children's christening ran no small risk of these children dying unbaptised.[2]

Craig is located on the north shore of Loch Torridon, one of many Atlantic inlets reaching deep into the Highland hills. The place today is uninhabited and the nearest road – a narrow, twisting thoroughfare redeemed only by its constantly changing views of the Torridon mountains – gives out finally at Diabeg, some four miles east of Craig.

From Diabeg, a typically scattered Highland village consisting of a handful of stone-built and white-painted homes, a footpath leads westwards across a series of steeply sloping hillsides. The terrain hereabouts is of the sort which it has recently become fashionable, in Scotland at all events, to call wild land. Most land of this type is, by definition, scenically impressive. And despite the fact that Torridon's summits are only one third as high as McDonald Peak, those Highland mountains are every bit as magnificent, in their way, as the Rockies – partly because the Torridon hills rise directly from the Atlantic rather than from a valley floor which is itself three or four thousand feet above sea level.

The ocean's proximity, however, makes the Highland climate far wetter than that of Montana. The path to Craig is boggy and broken as a result, its surface badly eroded by the storm-driven rains which are one of the Scottish climate's less attractive features. To pick one's way along this path, especially on the sort of day when downpour after downpour comes hurtling inland on a south-westerly gale, is immediately to appreciate why the people who once occupied this area tended automatically to gravitate towards such little shelter as their surroundings provided.

By Torridon standards, Angus McDonald's birthplace is certainly a sheltered spot. Craig is enclosed by hills. These hills fence out the wind sufficiently to allow trees – of which there is not one to be seen along the entire length of the path from Diabeg – to grow in several lower-lying corners. And the consequent sense of Craig being the Torridon equivalent of a desert oasis is heightened by the presence here of a piece of land which is both flatter and more fertile than any other to be found for several miles around.

This piece of land was clearly cultivated in former times. It equally clearly contains the ruins of several buildings. And any one of these could conceivably have been the home in which Angus McDonald was born. Angus, however, was apparently in the habit of referring to this home as 'Craig House'. That suggests – in a Scottish context anyway – a building rather more substantial than the average. And the one such building to have existed at Craig, as it happens, is still standing. Formerly it was a farmhouse. Now it is a hostel which offers basic, but undoubtedly welcome, accommodation to the growing number of trekkers and backpackers who come each summer to the Scottish Highlands from – as is demonstrated by this Craig Hostel's visitor book – practically every corner of the world.

In winter the hostel is normally deserted. But its front door is permanently – and trustingly – unlocked. It is irresistibly tempting, therefore, to enter by this door; to climb the wooden staircase leading to the bunk-filled dormitories which must, in the building's earlier incarnation, have been family bedrooms; to wonder, while standing quietly there, if one of those bedrooms once resounded to the infant Angus McDonald's earliest cries.

From the former farmhouse's narrow upstairs windows – which are just high enough to provide a clear line of sight across an intervening ridge – it is possible to see Loch Torridon, its waters scuffed and ruffled by the wind. Beyond is Applecross, where Angus McDonald's father, a farmer by profession, went in October 1816 to register his son's birth. Beyond Applecross, like Torridon a mainland district, is the Isle of Skye. Beyond Skye is the more distant, and only intermittently visible, Isle of Lewis. Beyond Lewis is the open Atlantic. And beyond the Atlantic, some thousands of miles to the west, is North America.

Almost always at Craig there are to be heard the sounds of wind and rushing water – the latter sound emanating from the fast-flowing River Craig which passes close to Craig House just prior to emptying itself into Loch Torridon. And so attractive is this locality's overall setting that it seems surprising that Angus McDonald's various writings – of which substantial quantities survive in the United States – make so little mention of Craig. A boyhood spent here would surely have occasioned at least something in the way of reminiscence.

The consequent possibility that the McDonald family lived here only briefly is made more likely by one of two still-existing letters to Angus from his younger sister, Margaret. This letter – preserved now in the Flathead Reservation home of one of Angus McDonald's descendants, Eileen Decker – dates from 1845. Margaret, the letter shows, was then living in or close to Dingwall, a small town on the eastern, or North Sea, coast of the Highlands. Since Dingwall is a long way from Craig, and since Margaret wrote of her mother and father in such a way as to make clear she was in regular contact with them, it follows that Angus's and Margaret's parents had left Craig by the 1840s. Indeed, they may have gone from Torridon a good deal earlier.[3]

That would explain why Angus made so little of Craig when asked about his background. It was his birthplace clearly, but his family's roots, so Angus evidently felt, were elsewhere. He was 'of the clans of Glengarry and Glencoe and MacRaes of Kintail', Angus commented, near the end of his life, to the United States federal marshall, William Wheeler, a leading member of the then recently established Montana Historical Society and a man who made it his business, at this time, to interview a number of Montana Territory's veteran settlers.[4]

To make sense of Angus's remark to William Wheeler – a remark made in Mission Valley in 1885 – it is necessary to return to the Applecross registers which note the fact of Angus's birth. The relevant register entries reveal that Angus's father was Donald MacDonald. They show, too, that his mother – who, in accordance with the then standard Scottish practice, retained her own name in such contexts – was Christian, or Christina, MacRae.[5]

This disposes at once of Angus McDonald's Kintail connection. His mother was a MacRae. And Kintail – which lies due south of Torridon and which is separated from that more northerly locality by a tangled set of mountain ranges interspersed with further fiord-like inlets of the Loch Torridon type – was long the home of the MacRae clan.

Highland clans, about which more will be said in a moment, were very similar both in origin and in function to Native American tribes like the Nez Perce. Just as the Nez Perce were traditionally linked with the lands which they left at the start of their trek across the Bitterroots in the summer of 1877, so each Highland clan had its own longstanding territorial affiliations. Kintail, to reiterate, was identified strongly with the MacRaes. Glengarry and Glencoe, the other Highland districts which Angus mentioned in the course of his 1885 conversation with William Wheeler, were every bit as firmly associated with distinct, but inter-related, branches of Clan Donald – the collective designation habitually applied to Scotland's various MacDonald groupings.

Since Angus was born neither in Glengarry nor Glencoe, his family's links with both these places, or so it seems reasonable to deduce, must have stemmed from an earlier generation than his own. So what clues can be uncovered that might result in the identification of some at least of Angus's remoter ancestors?

Most such clues derive from articles published, half a century ago or more, by Alfred J. Partoll and by those other Western writers who, as a result of their contacts with a number of Angus's children, were able to access McDonald family tradition much more comprehensively than can now be attempted.

Angus McDonald is stated in these articles to have been the nephew of Archibald McDonald who preceded Angus into the Hudson's Bay Company and who, by the 1830s, had become one of this fur trading corporation's leading representatives in the part of North America which lies west of the Rocky Mountains. Archibald, as will be seen a little later, made a substantial contribution to the development of this region – where some of his several sons also made something of an impact. Since one of those sons survived into the twentieth century, he was available to be interviewed by people of the sort who, in the century's early decades, made it their business to collect frontier reminiscences. Much the most interesting aspect of the reminiscences in question, from this book's standpoint at any rate, is the way in which they show that Archibald McDonald's children were in the habit of referring to Angus McDonald as their cousin.[6]

This appears to confirm that Angus was Archibald's nephew. Further evidence to the same effect can be found in one more of the nineteenth-century letters which survive on the Flathead Reservation. Sent by Archibald to Angus in 1852, this letter deals largely in family news and contains a sentence in which Archibald refers explicitly to himself as Angus's 'uncle'.[7]

Since Archibald is known to have been born in 1790 in Glencoe and to have been the thirteenth child of Angus MacDonald, tenant of the Glencoe farm of Inverigan, it began to look at this stage in these enquiries as if Angus of Mission Valley – some such terminology being necessary to distinguish the later Angus McDonald from Angus of Inverigan – must have been the son of one or other of Archibald's elder brothers. This was made all the more probable, or so it seemed, by notes which Archibald compiled on his family history. These show that one of Archibald's brothers, born at Inverigan in 1780, was named Donald. It thus became almost irresistibly tempting to assume that the Donald MacDonald who is known to have been the father of Angus of Mission Valley was also the Donald MacDonald whose birthplace is known to have been Inverigan.[8]

This, if it had actually been the case, would have had the effect of tying Angus of Mission Valley very neatly to Glencoe – a mountainous locality which lies a good way south of Angus's Torridon birthplace. Unfortunately for what would otherwise have been a reasonably convincing theory, however, the Glencoe-born Donald MacDonald at this theory's centre is known to have been resident in 1816 – when Angus of Mission Valley first saw the light of day at Craig – in the vicinity of Glenstrathfarrar. Glenstrathfarrar is nowhere near Torridon. And there is the further awkward fact – awkward, that is, if one is anxious to stick with the longstanding notion of Angus of Mission Valley having been the nephew of the Hudson's Bay Company trader, Archibald McDonald – that the Donald MacDonald who was certainly Archibald of the Bay Company's elder brother is stated, in Archibald's own notes, to have married, in 1830, a 'Miss Fraser'. Since the Donald MacDonald who was Angus of Mission Valley's father is known, from comments made in letters to Angus from his sister, to have still been married in the 1840s to Christian MacRae, Angus of Mission Valley's father – despite the confusing identity of name – cannot have been the same person as the Donald MacDonald who was Archibald of the Bay Company's brother. And Angus of Mission Valley – irrespective of the lavish use of terms like 'uncle' and 'cousin' by the various parties to this particular kinship link – cannot, therefore, have been Archibald's nephew.[9]

This, on reflection, was perhaps implicit in Angus's 1885 listing of his clan affiliations. For if his father was a Glencoe MacDonald, why should Angus – whose interest in his Highland origins is revealed by his own writings to have been more than merely casual – have given Glengarry precedence over Glencoe in the course of his remarks to Marshall Wheeler?

The consequent possibility that Angus of Mission Valley's father was, after all, a Glengarry – not a Glencoe – MacDonald is strengthened by a reference which Angus himself once made to an early fur trader by the name of Finan McDonald. Finan, an especially colourful member of an always colourful profession, was one of the first whites to make fur-gathering expeditions into what is now western Montana. Finan's travels, as luck would have it, took him into the Flathead country. And Angus, having had occasion to mention these travels, claimed kinship with Finan by referring to that pioneer fur trader as 'a bough of the same tree as my own'.[10]

Finan, for his part, was certainly a Glengarry MacDonald. He was born in the mid-1770s when his father, one more of this book's numerous Angus MacDonalds, occupied a farm at Munial on the north shore of the Knoydart peninsula. Although separated from Glengarry proper by a roadless tract of hill terrain known as 'the rough bounds', Knoydart — to the south both of Torridon and Kintail but to the north of Glencoe — was very much a part of the extensive, if not always terribly productive, lands which had been occupied since the Middle Ages by the Glengarry clan. Nowadays as inaccessible and deserted as Craig, Munial, when Finan was growing up here, was home to four 'servants', or hired hands, as well as to the family who were its farming tenants. But Angus MacDonald of Munial — for all that the size of his workforce suggests, in relation to that time and place, a modestly comfortable standard of living — was one of many Highlanders who came to feel, as the eighteenth century advanced, that North America offered better prospects than were available then in Scotland.[11]

Many Glengarry MacDonalds emigrated in 1774 to the Mohawk Valley in what is now upstate New York. There, for a variety of reasons which need not be examined here, these newly arrived settlers were drawn into America's Revolutionary War on the loyalist, or pro-British, side. On the war ending with the enforced termination of Britain's colonial rule in what had now become the United States, the Mohawk Valley Highlanders — whose harrying of American forces had been so persistent as to make such a course all but inevitable — chose to migrate to the Canadian territories which, following U.S. independence, were all that remained of British North America. There the Mohawk Valley loyalists were installed, just a little to the west of Montreal and on the north bank of the St Lawrence River, in a district which its much-travelled settlers, by way of commemorating their Highland origins, were to name Glengarry County. It was to this new Glengarry — very probably at the invitation of relatives already among its inhabitants — that Angus MacDonald of Munial, together with the young Finan and other members of their family, emigrated in 1786.

That explains how Finan McDonald got into the North American fur trade. What it does not explain is how the Munial MacDonalds were related to Angus of Mission Valley. But this puzzle, too, is capable of resolution — in principle at any rate.

Archibald McDonald, the Glencoe-born Hudson's Bay Company man who was supposedly Angus of Mission Valley's uncle, had a sister, Margaret, 27 years Archibald's senior, whose husband's surname – by way of further complicating what is already complex – was the same as her own. This man is known, from Archibald's notes on these matters, to have had a connection with a place called Abertarf. Since Abertarf, although well to the east of Munial, was another of the areas with which the Glengarry MacDonalds were identified, it is, at the minimum, possible that the MacDonald whom Margaret married was a member of the Munial family. Might he have been, for instance, a brother or, failing that, a cousin of the future fur trader, Finan MacDonald? And might Margaret and her MacDonald husband have been the parents of Donald MacDonald who, at Craig in 1816, became the father of the man who was eventually to be laid to rest in that Mission Valley grave-yard beside Post Creek and below McDonald Peak?[12]

This hypothesis, for what it is worth, accommodates all the known facts. If Angus of Mission Valley's father, Donald, was, as here suggested, related to Angus of Munial, then Angus of Mission Valley would have been a Glengarry MacDonald by paternal descent – which is why the then elderly Angus would have given Glengarry precedence over Glencoe when telling William Wheeler something of his Scottish origins. The same set of relationships would result in Finan MacDonald – that 'bough of the same tree as my own', in Angus of Mission Valley's neatly turned phrase – being descended either from the Mission Valley rancher's paternal great-grandfather or, and this is a little more likely in view of what is known about the Munial family, from his paternal great-great-grandfather. As to Archibald McDonald of the Hudson's Bay Company, he would have been not Angus of Mission Valley's uncle, as generally stated, but Angus's great-uncle – Archibald's sister, Margaret, if these various connections were as postulated here, having been the mother of Angus's father.

❀

Those suppositions looked to be, for long enough, unprovable. Then, towards the end of the researches on which this book is based, one of them at least was suddenly confirmed by a letter which is nowadays in the possession of the Oregon Historical Society. Written by Angus McDonald at his Mission Valley home in January 1877 and sent by Angus to Matthew P. Deady, an Oregon judge, the letter first refers to its writer's Glencoe 'forefathers' and then goes on to mention Archibald McDonald. 'He was my grandmother's youngest brother,' Angus commented of Archibald.[13]

This, of course, does not quite demonstrate that Angus's paternal grandmother was, as suggested two or three paragraphs back, Margaret MacDonald. She could – though this is most unlikely – have been one of Archibald's several other sisters. Even if that were the case, however, it would not break the chain of descent which that 1877 letter establishes between Angus of Mission Valley and Angus of Inverigan – the latter having been both Archibald's father and, as the 1877 letter makes clear, Angus of Mission Valley's great-grandfather.

This is important. For the chain of descent in question is an altogether lengthier one than has so far been indicated. Just how lengthy will become apparent in a moment. But first it is necessary to return to Archibald McDonald and to the notes – already mentioned more than once – which Archibald compiled with a view to making a permanent record of what he had learned, while growing up in Glencoe, of his ancestry and background.

Those notes date from December 1830. They were written at Fort Langley, a Hudson's Bay Company post on the Fraser River in present-day British Columbia. And they start with Archibald's statement that he was 'Gillespie, Moach Aonish, Ic Iain, Ic Alan Dhu, Glenocoan'. This is a phonetical rendering of a genealogical formulation originally passed on to Archibald in the Gaelic that was, until fairly recently, the common speech both of Glencoe and of the rest of the Scottish Highlands. Although relatively well schooled in English, Archibald, like many Highlanders of his and later generations, could neither read nor write his own first language. But he could, and did, reproduce the sound of his Gaelic *sloinneadh*, or lineage, as he would have heard that lineage voiced often by his father.[14]

Such lineages were – and, to an extent, still are – the common currency of the Gaelic-speaking Highlands. All that is unusual about Archibald McDonald's is that its possessor took the trouble to set it down in writing.

The 'Gillespie' with whom the Fort Langley fur trader began his sloinneadh was himself – Gilleasbuig being a Gaelic name which is commonly rendered into English as Archibald. 'Moach Aonish', proper-ly Mac Aonghais, means simply 'son of Angus'. This Angus, the sloinneadh continues, was the son of Iain, or John, who was in turn the son of Ailean Dubh, or Black Allan – this Allan, in his turn, being related, or so it can arguably be inferred from that final 'Glenocoan', to the family of the Glencoe clan's MacDonald chiefs.

Having thus outlined his descent, Archibald – who can readily be imagined as having taken up this task in order to give purpose to a Fraser Valley winter's evening – goes on to relate what he had been told of the ancestors he has listed. Angus, Archibald's father and Angus of Mission Valley's great-grandfather, is described as the principal farming tenant of Inverigan, one of several small communities in Glencoe. His father, Archibald adds, was born in 1730. While still 'but a stripling', or so his son asserts, Angus served with the largely Highland army which was defeated by British government forces at the Battle of Culloden in 1746. Having escaped unscathed from that débâcle, Angus MacDonald returned to Glencoe where, in due course, he married a local woman called Mary Rankin – a surname still to be encountered in the Glencoe area. When this marriage took place is not mentioned. Since the first of the couple's children is stated by Archibald to have been born in 1761 and since his father was 60 at the time of Archibald's own birth in 1790, however, it can be fairly confidently deduced both that Angus married Mary around 1760 and that Mary was a good deal younger than her husband.

Archibald's grandfather, John MacDonald, is said by his grandson to have been born in 1680. This means that grandfather and grandson were separated by no less than 110 years – something which is rendered less implausible than might otherwise be the case by Archibald's father having been fairly elderly when his fur trader son was born and by Archibald's grandfather also having become a parent at a relatively advanced age. His grandfather, Archibald continues, 'with difficulty escaped with his mother and brother, Donald, from the slaughter committed by William's troops at Inverigan . . . [in] February 1692'. Here Archibald refers to the notorious massacre of the Glencoe MacDonalds by a military detachment acting on the authority, as Archibald observes, of the then recently enthroned King William. More will be made of these events a little later. More will be made, too, of the career of Archibald's great-grandfather who, his great-grandson comments, 'at the age of 20 was in the field . . . in 1645 at Inverlochy, Auldearn, Alford and Kilsyth'. For the present, however, it suffices to emphasise that the youthful Archibald had heard, no doubt repeatedly, how his grandfather had been lucky to evade death at the hands of government soldiers and how his great-grandfather, the man whom Archibald calls 'Alan Dhu', had played a key part in ensuring that other government soldiers went down to defeat at the different seventeenth-century battles which Archibald so carefully enumerates.

Although Archibald's notes succeed in conveying the wholly accurate impression that the Glencoe MacDonalds were regularly embroiled in conflict with Scotland's rulers, the Fort Langley fur trader, it has to be said, went slightly astray in naming 'Alan Dhu' as his great-grandfather. A Glencoe soldier certainly features in records dealing with the 1645 campaign which Archibald mentions. But that soldier appears in those records as 'Angus MacAllan Dubh', meaning Angus, son of Ailean Dubh. Archibald – not surprisingly in view of his being separated from Glencoe, at the point when he jotted down his family history, by many years and by several thousand miles – seems simply to have omitted a generation. The man who, 'at the age of 20', went to war in 1645 was clearly Ailean Dubh's son, Angus, rather than, as Archibald believed, Ailean Dubh himself.[15]

What the Fort Langley trader did not get wrong, however, was his family's claim to kinship with the Glencoe chiefs – men who were as important to their clan as White Bird, Looking Glass and other such chiefs were important to the Nez Perce. Ailean Dubh, who is known from quite independent historical sources both to have existed and to have held lands at Laroch, a little to the south of Glencoe proper, was the son of Iain Dubh – which translates literally as Black John. And this Black John was the second son of Iain Og, Young John, a sixteenth-century chief of the Glencoe MacDonalds.[16]

Archibald McDonald's detailed knowledge of his family tree seems to have extended little further back than the time of Ailean Dubh. That is far enough, however, to enable Archibald's ancestry to be connected with the fairly well-known genealogy of Glencoe's MacDonald chiefs. And this connection, once established, has the effect of pushing Archibald's lineage into a much more distant past than he himself could access.*

The sixteenth-century chief of the Glencoe MacDonalds, Iain Og, whose second son was Archibald's great-great-great-grandfather, is generally thought to have been himself descended, through some eight generations, from the similarly named Iain Og an Fhraoich, Young John of the Heather. This John, the first MacDonald to occupy lands in the vicinity of Glencoe, was both the founder of a long line of Glencoe chiefs and the man through whom these chiefs were to claim kinship with still more remote figures. Young John's father was Angus of Islay who, by means of the military assistance which he rendered to King Robert Bruce in the course of Scotland's early-fourteenth-century War of Independence, helped decisively to curtail the medieval English monarchy's attempts to bring the more northerly kingdom under England's jurisdiction. And Angus of Islay's forebears, too, were men of substance. His father – the first known holder of the name which Angus of Mission Valley also bore – was Angus MacDonald. This Angus's father was Donald, founder – in principle anyway – of Clan

---

* These family connections are summarised in this book's Appendix.

Donald and son of Ranald who, in turn, was son of Somerled.[17]

Somerled, born some 400 years before Christopher Columbus sailed from Spain to America, was a warrior-aristocrat who made himself overlord of an extensive realm which, at its greatest extent, included much of the south-western Highland mainland as well as most of Scotland's many west coast islands. To be able to anchor one's genealogy to so prestigious an individual might be thought to have been sufficient for even the most ancestor-obsessed member of what was certainly – because a man's standing in his clan depended on his having suitably high-ranking forebears – an ancestor-obsessed society. But Clan Donald poets and tradition-bearers, not content with tracing their people's beginnings to Somerled and his grandson, Donald, claimed customarily that Somerled, who died in 1164, was himself descended from an infinitely more shadowy figure – an Irish hero-king, called Conn of the Hundred Battles by Highland storytellers, who was said to have lived as much as a thousand years earlier.

Here history, admittedly, becomes confused with legend. But this account of Angus of Mission Valley's remote origins need not, for all that, stop with Somerled. The earlier part of Somerled's own genealogy, as regularly recited in the Scottish Highlands of some centuries ago, is undoubtedly incomplete and possibly fictitious. But the seven or eight names which precede Somerled's in that particular formulation are a very different matter – 'the genealogy of Somerled's ancestors,' according to authoritative researchers in this area, being 'almost certainly authentic back to Gofraid, son of Fergus, who . . . came over to Scotland from Ireland . . . in 835'.[18]

❋

While it would be hazardous to insist on the absolute dependability of the extraordinarily long lines of descent which have been traced across preceding pages, these lines of descent, because of the comparatively detailed nature of the evidence on which they depend, are by no means implausible. There is clearly a possibility, then, perhaps even a probability, of Gofraid, son of Fergus, having been the ancestor – across a thousand years and thirty generations – of Duncan McDonald, that 'half-breed Indian trader' whom this book first encountered in Missoula on the day the Nez Perce looked to be about to take the town. But even if his Scottish pedigree was not quite as here suggested, Duncan's roots clearly ran deep in Clan Donald. As a prelude to the story of how it came about that Duncan was of Indian as well as Highland ancestry, it consequently makes sense to investigate just what it meant to have been part of the society on

48

which Clan Donald, for a long time, exercised so great an influence.

It is symbolically appropriate, in this context, that Gofraid, son of Fergus, should have come to Scotland from Ireland; for it was in Ireland that there originated the highly distinctive culture with which Highland clanship was to become inextricably bound up.

Some four centuries into the Christian era, and at about the time the Roman Empire was withdrawing the last of its legions from more southerly parts of Britain, Gaelic-speaking migrants from Ulster began to move across the narrow seas which separate that most northerly segment of Ireland from the Highlands. Settling first in the comparatively fertile Kintyre peninsula and on equally attractive islands like Islay, these migrants pushed steadily northwards – one of their small kingdoms, it seems likely, eventually including the mountain ranges which surround Glencoe. There or thereabouts, this people, who called themselves Gaels but who were known to the Romans as Scoti, established a frontier between themselves and the Picts whose territories the Gaels had partly seized. That frontier was not destined to become permanent, however. In the ninth century's opening decades – and it is by no means inconceivable that Gofraid, son of Fergus, was personally involved in these developments – the Gaels became masters of the entire country to which there was attached, about this time, a version of the Latin name which the Gaels themselves had earlier been given by the Romans.[19]

Although largely Gaelic-speaking in the centuries immediately follow-ing its creation, the kingdom of Scotland was not destined to remain in the control of Gaels. During the lifetime of Gofraid, son of Fergus, Viking raiders from Norway established themselves on many of the Scottish islands which the Gaels had previously colonised. And within two or three centuries of Gofraid's death, at a point when Scotland's northern and western fringes were still under Norwegian control, the Scottish monarchy – looking increasingly now to England and to continental Europe for its political and cultural inspiration – began gradually to abandon its Irish heritage. Both by Scotland's kings and by those of Scotland's people who lived to the south and east of the Highlands, therefore, Gaelic was steadily given up in favour of the originally Germanic language which is today known as Broad Scots.

Deprived now of the organisational focus which had formerly been provided for them by the Scottish monarchy, Scotland's Gaels looked elsewhere for an institution capable both of embodying their strong sense of identity and of offering some overall political leadership. This institution Gaels found in the Lordship of the Isles – the semi-autonomous principality created by Somerled and his Clan Donald successors. Its extent varied over time. In general terms, however, the Lordship included all the west coast archipelago from which it derived its name. It came to include a large part of the Highland mainland also.

As is demonstrated most graphically by the sea-going galleys which were central to its power and which were so clearly the lineal successors of Viking longships, the Lordship of the Isles was, in part, the product of Norse influences. But for all that Somerled and many of its other leading men undoubtedly numbered Norwegians as well as Gaels among their ancestors, the Lordship was wholly Gaelic in language and culture. Its bards, or poets, looked invariably to Ireland – then largely Gaelic-speaking also – both for their training and for many of their themes. These themes were usually of a kind which stressed the continuity of the society to which the Lordship's poets belonged. This was deliberate. In everything from their music to their ceremonies, the Lordship's ruling orders consciously strove to perpetuate a way of life which, in its essentials, had not changed greatly in the five centuries separating Gofraid, son of Fergus, from Young John of the Heather, first of Glencoe's MacDonald chiefs.[20]

As one of his rewards for having rallied to the cause of Robert Bruce at the point when that most renowned of Scotland's kings most needed help to win his battles with the English, Angus MacDonald of Islay, Somerled's great-great-grandson, had been granted lands in and around Glencoe. These lands Angus afterwards made over to Iain Og an Fhraoich, Young John of the Heather, who, as was subsequently observed by a seventeenth-century chronicler of Clan Donald's history, was Angus of Islay's 'natural son . . . by Dougal MacHenry's daughter'. Who Dougal MacHenry and his daughter were exactly, the chronicler does not say. Since MacHenries or Hendersons were long to be common in the area, however, it is probable that Iain Og's mother was herself connected with the territories which her son was to inherit – something which, if indeed the case, would doubtless have helped Young John overcome any local opposition there might have been to him setting himself up as the Glencoe people's chief.[21]

'O children of Conn, remember hardihood,' the men of the Lordship were urged by one of their bards in a Gaelic battle-incitement which contains repeated references to the long-dead soldier-king from whom Clan Donald's leaders claimed descent. 'O children of Conn, remember hardihood . . . Be watchful, be daring, be dexterous, winning renown; be vigorous, pre-eminent; be strong . . . O children of Conn of the Hundred Battles, now is the time for you to win recognition, O raging whelps, O sturdy bears, O most sprightly lions, O battle-loving warriors, O brave, heroic firebrands, the children of Conn of the Hundred Battles.'[22]

Whether in John of the Heather's time or later, sentiments of this sort would have been warmly appreciated in Gaelic-speaking Glencoe where the traditions of Clan Donald were always carefully nurtured. Such sentiments would have been appreciated, too, in much of the rest of the Gaelic-speaking Highlands. From the perspective of non-Gaelic-speaking Scotland, however, the Lordship of the Isles and all it stood for seemed increasingly alien, even threatening. Lowlanders, a Scottish churchman observed as early as the 1380s, were 'domesticated and cultured'. Highlanders, in contrast, were 'untamed people'. And during the fifteenth century, as this type of distinction between a 'civilised' south and a 'wild' north began to be made routinely by Scotland's Lowland rulers, it was inevitable that these rulers should have begun to behave as if their increasingly acrimonious dealings with successive Lords of the Isles had something of the character of a conflict between good and evil — with Lowlanders, needless to say, representing the forces of enlightenment and with Highlanders, just as predictably, cast in the role of agents of the devil.[23]

Thinking themselves secure in their Highland fastnesses, meanwhile, the Lords of the Isles seriously underestimated the hostility with which they were more and more regarded by Scotland's kings. Continuing to conduct themselves in the casually self-reliant manner of all their predecessors since Somerled, fifteenth-century Lords of the Isles made their own treaties with the English, waged their own wars and generally behaved as if they owed no real allegiance to the Scottish monarchs whose subjects they nominally were. In so doing, however, Somerled's Clan Donald heirs at last over-reached themselves. Royal power was mobilised increasingly against the Lordship. And in 1493, by James IV, one of Scotland's lengthy line of Stuart kings, the Lordship of the Isles was finally destroyed.

In spite of their having managed to overthrow the Lords of the Isles, Scotland's royal authorities — based in the distant national capital of Edinburgh — lacked the power to impose their own rule on the Highlands which, in consequence, were left without any very effective source of social and political cohesion. Highlanders attempted to make good this deficiency by trying repeatedly to restore the Lordship of the Isles. In 1501, for instance, the MacDonalds of Glencoe, always to the fore on such occasions, managed to rescue from the castle in which he had been imprisoned the leading claimant both to the title of Lord of the Isles and to the headship of Clan Donald. The anti-government rising which ensued was eventually crushed, however, as were the several other risings which followed. Clan Donald, as a result, began to break apart with the Glencoe MacDonalds, the Glengarry MacDonalds and all the other groupings who had previously considered themselves to be components of a wider entity now going their own ways under their own local chiefs.[24]

With MacDonald power thus fragmenting, and with other smaller clans taking the opportunity to assert their separate identities in a wholly new manner, the Highlands, for much of the sixteenth century, experienced unrest bordering occasionally on anarchy. In the absence of the Lordship's overarching authority, and in the equal absence of anything other than occasional military interventions from the south, clans went to war increasingly with one another. There was a growing tendency, too, for bands of Highlanders – the Glencoe MacDonalds prominent among them – to descend on various Lowland localities with a view to seizing cattle and other booty. This served both to provide an outlet for clansmen's martial energies and to stave off the food shortages to which the Highlands, a far from fertile region, were occasionally prone. But cattle-raids, clan feuds and other violent episodes of that kind did absolutely nothing to make Lowlanders feel more positive about their Highland neighbours – the overall tendency, in these increasingly chaotic circumstances, being for the Lowland-Highland relationship to deteriorate still faster than before.

The results are plain to see in the opinions held about Highlanders by James VI, the Stuart monarch who, following the union of the two countries' crowns in 1603, became England's king as well as Scotland's. James was typical of Lowland Scots in thinking Highlanders 'utterly barbarous' – not least in their conspicuous lack of enthusiasm for the Protestant faith which had been firmly established in southern Scotland in the course of the sixteenth century. Because Highlanders lacked 'religion and humanity', King James commented, they were 'void of all fear . . . of God'. Some were 'cannibals'. Others were collectively responsible, or so it was alleged by the king and his ministers, for the 'most detestable, damnable and odious murders, fires, ravishing of women, witchcraft and depredations'.[25]

These sentiments have a great deal in common with the views which a number of King James's English subjects were just then beginning to express about the Native Americans they had encountered in the course of England's early colonising ventures in places like Virginia and Massachusetts. It is not at all surprising, therefore, that there are striking similarities between what was done to Highlanders and what was done to American Indians on the orders of the Scottish and English politicians who, from this point forward, were looking to gain more and more control over both these sets of 'savages'.

When King James commented that certain parts of the Highlands should ideally be taken over by Lowlanders and that this should be accomplished 'not by agreement with' Highlanders 'but by extirpation of them', he was advocating a course of action which – in the seventeenth century and later – would have been enthusiastically endorsed by the numerous whites to whom North America's indigenous peoples were simply so many obstacles in the way of their own settler society's expansion. And when James's Scottish ministers decreed in 1616 that the Gaelic language, being 'one of the principal causes of the continuance of barbarity' in the Highlands, should be 'abolished and removed', they were espousing attitudes of a kind that would influence white thinking about Indian culture well into the twentieth century.[26]

Neither Highlanders nor Indians, of course, were tamely to accept their own subordination. And both groups, had they been able to mobilise effectively against the growing threats to their autonomy, might well have been able to ensure that such autonomy lasted a good deal longer than it did. Ever since the era of the Roman Empire, however, tribal civilisations of the North American or Highland type have been hopelessly susceptible to the tactic of divide and rule. Just as Indian peoples were repeatedly to be set against one another in order to facilitate the advance of white settlement across the North American continent, so the Scottish government was deliberately to foment clan rivalries as a means of furthering its own objectives in the region. Hence the extent to which the Campbells – whose original homelands were in the vicinity of Loch Awe in the south-western corner of the Highlands – were encouraged, from the early sixteenth century onwards, to enlarge their territories at the expense of the previously dominant Clan Donald and its allies. When the MacDonalds were eventually presented with the opportunity to launch something of a counter-attack, therefore, it was inevitable that this counter-attack was directed against the Campbells rather more than it was directed against the southern governments whose Highland agents the Campbells had become.

It is a somewhat paradoxical element in this story that the several Highland rebellions which occurred between the 1640s and the 1740s were, to a greater or lesser degree, a consequence of disaffected Highlanders increasingly aligning themselves with the kingly dynasty which – in the persons of James IV and James VI especially – had earlier been so aggressively anti-Highland in its outlook. By the middle years of the seventeenth century, however, the Stuarts were embroiled in serious disagreements with their southern subjects. The outcome was a civil war in the course of which the latest Stuart monarch became sufficiently desperate as to turn to the previously despised Highlanders for help. Thus it came about that a Hudson's Bay Company fur trader by the name of Archibald McDonald was able one day to tell of how his great-grandfather had been 'in the field with Montrose'.[27]

The Marquis of Montrose to whom Archibald thus referred was the Scottish aristocrat who, during 1644 and 1645, led a predominantly Highland, indeed largely Clan Donald, army to victory after victory over a Scottish government which – along with its English counterpart – had fallen out spectacularly with one of the Stuart dynasty's least fortunate representatives, King Charles I. Montrose was Charles's man in Scotland. But that probably mattered a good deal less to Montrose's MacDonald followers than the fact that the marquis, by virtue of his being the enemy of Scotland's government, was also the enemy of the Campbells who, as usual, were acting as the government's proxies in the Highlands.[28]

Among the Glencoe men who rallied to Montrose were Ranald and Angus MacDonald. Being sons of Ailean Dubh who was himself the grandson of the sixteenth-century Glencoe chief, Iain Og, Ranald and Angus belonged to one of their clan's leading families. Ranald was to add to that family's standing by becoming a modestly successful Gaelic bard. None of his poems, however, brought this Glencoe man anything like the fame which came his way as a result of his fighting, and winning, an epic duel with an English officer who had rashly sought to cast aspersions on the fighting skills of Highlanders. This much-celebrated triumph had the inevitable effect of slightly overshadowing the military accomplishments of Ranald's brother, Angus. But Angus's own services to Clan Donald, Montrose and Charles I – the order in which Angus would probably have listed his different loyalties – were also to feature in the repertoire of Glencoe's Gaelic storytellers for as long as such storytellers existed.[29]

When, in November 1644, the Marquis of Montrose and his commanders met in council at Blair Atholl in the south-central Highlands to debate their next move in a campaign which had already made them masters of much of the northern half of Scotland, Montrose, for all his soon-to-be-proverbial daring, was taken aback by the fervour with which the MacDonalds among his senior officers canvassed an immediate invasion of the Campbell heartland of Argyll. Most armies of that time neither marched nor fought during winter. And even if he was to break this particular rule, as Montrose knew very well, there was no guarantee of his getting so much as a toehold on Campbell territory. Access to Argyll could only be gained, the marquis pointed out, by way of mountain passes of the sort which 'might be easily kept by five hundred against twenty thousand'. The MacDonalds, however, were adamant. Its sheer unexpectedness, they said, would make a winter attack on the Campbell country much less risky than such an enterprise might at first appear. And there was available to Montrose, they added, a young man named Angus MacDonald or Angus, son of Ailean Dubh, who, most likely because of his experience of cattle-raiding in that quarter, could readily act as the army's guide should the marquis agree to march into Argyll.[30]

At this point, according to one centuries-old account of these events, 'Angus, son of Allan Dubh, was invited before the council'. Montrose, this account continues, at once began to question Angus who is described as 'a gentleman of the men of Glencoe'. Was Angus indeed acquainted with Argyll? And did he think badly needed supplies could readily be got there? There was not a township in Argyll 'but was known to him', Angus is said to have replied. 'If . . . fat cows as victuals to feed upon . . . would answer their purpose,' this Glencoe MacDonald is reported to have added, 'he would procure them.' With that, it appears, Montrose's mind was made up. Argyll was both attacked and overrun. Soon Montrose's troops were in Inveraray, the little town that served the Campbells as their capital, forcing the pro-government Earl of Argyll, who was also Clan Campbell's chief, to flee for his life and destroying such property as could not be carried away. 'Throughout all Argyll,' one of Montrose's commanders reported, 'we left neither house nor hold unburned, nor corn nor cattle, that belonged to the whole name of Campbell.'[31]

Withdrawing eventually from Inveraray, Montrose and his force of some 3,000 men headed north by way of the eastern shore of Loch Linnhe, passing close to the western end of Glencoe and halting, some days later, about halfway up the Great Glen – the natural thoroughfare which runs north-eastwards from Loch Linnhe, an arm of the Atlantic, to Inverness, a town which stands near the North Sea. Knowing that one government army awaited him at the Inverness end of the Great Glen and knowing also that the Earl of Argyll had managed both to raise an additional government army and to move that army to Inverlochy Castle, at the Great Glen's other outlet, Montrose – having first conducted a daring march through snow-covered hills – unleashed against the Earl of Argyll one of the furious charges which were always a clan army's favoured tactic.

When directed against a more orthodox troop formation, a Highland charge was invariably met by a musket volley. No single volley, however, was capable of stopping such a charge. And a second volley was seldom forthcoming. Although some clansmen inevitably fell victim to the initial volley, their comrades simply kept running forward at full speed, sometimes throwing aside their tartan plaids to gain extra velocity, aiming to deprive their opponents of the time needed to recharge muzzle-loading firearms, screaming the Gaelic battlecries which were meant both to boost a clan's own courage and to terrify its enemies. These enemies, for their part, were – not unnaturally – inclined to panic as soon as the still-yelling Highlanders came hurtling and hacking into their closely compressed ranks. 'Do not let the sound of gunpowder put the slightest anxiety into your bodies,' his fellow-clansmen were accordingly advised by a seventeenth-century Glencoe bard who had himself participated in one such onslaught. 'Whenever that sound dies away, distress and hurt are at an end and you will be tackling [the enemy] at close quarters according to your immemorial practice.'[32]

That is exactly what happened in the vicinity of Inverlochy Castle on Sunday, 2 February 1645, when Montrose's Highlanders swept down on the Earl of Argyll and his combined force of Lowland and Campbell infantry. 'I climbed early on Sunday morning the brae [slope] of the Castle of Inverlochy,' a MacDonald bard exulted. 'I saw the army get into order and victory was with Clan Donald . . . Yet more pleasing news kept coming concerning the fate of the . . . Campbells. As each of their bands made its appearance their heads were battered in by sword-blows.'[33]

❁

Heading north from Argyll, following much the same route as was taken by the Marquis of Montrose's army in the opening weeks of 1645, a modern traveller comes eventually to the well-wooded district of Appin. In Montrose's time this was the country of the Stewarts, a clan whose lands marched with those of the Glencoe MacDonalds. There had been occasional hostilities between the Glencoe men and their Stewart neighbours. There had been occasional hostilities, too, between the MacDonalds and the Camerons whose territories lay beyond Glencoe – from which the Cameron country was separated by an eastward-tending inlet called Loch Leven. By the seventeenth century, however, the Glencoe MacDonalds, the Camerons and the Stewarts lived mostly at peace with one another, their relative amity a consequence of their need to co-operate in the face of the common threat posed, to Appin and Glencoe in particular, by Campbell expansionism.

If, as is virtually certain, Angus MacDonald, the Glencoe man who had played such a key part in Montrose's decision to invade Argyll, was still with the army as it moved north towards the Great Glen, then Angus, on reaching Appin, would have felt increasingly at home. His mother, Janet Stewart, belonged to one of the area's leading families and it is likely that, when returning to Glencoe with her at the end of visits to the family's Appin kin, Angus would regularly have made the journey which he and the rest of Montrose's troops now made through Duror and on to the point, at Ballachulish, where the narrow waters of Loch Leven branch off from the much more extensive Loch Linnhe.[34]

In Loch Leven – a mile or two to the east of the Ballachulish narrows which are nowadays spanned by a bridge but which, for centuries prior to the bridge's construction, were the site of one of the many ferries made necessary by Scotland's endlessly indented coastline – is Eilean Munda, the little island where both the Glencoe MacDonalds and the Camerons habitually buried their dead. 'Put a sword in my fist and my face to the Camerons,' one Glencoe man was said by MacDonald story-tellers to have instructed the friend whom he made responsible for his Eilean Munda funeral arrangements. And for all that the Camerons were, by the mid-seventeenth century, the frequent allies of the Glencoe people in the cattle-raids in which both clans commonly engaged, this was a saying which Angus MacDonald had no doubt heard repeated often at his family's Glencoe fireside.[35]

Glencoe itself runs eastwards into the hills from a point more or less opposite Eilean Munda. Noting that 'it pertaineth to certaine of the Clandonald', the author of a seventeenth-century description of the glen continued: 'This countrie is verie profitable, fertill and plenteous of corne, milk, butter, cheese and abundance of fish.' While it was certainly the case that Loch Leven contained 'herrings and other kynd of fishes', and while it was equally the case that it was possible at some seasons 'to take abundance of salmond' from the 'little river' which flows through Glencoe itself, this was very much to indulge in exaggeration of the kind that frontier America would one day call 'boosterism'. Neither in the seventeenth century nor at any other period could Glencoe legitimately be labelled a land of plenty. But it was home to its people all the same. And they undoubtedly felt for it the almost irrational affection which Gaelic-speaking Highlanders – in this, as in much else, very like the American Indians with whom the seventeenth-century Angus MacDonald's nineteenth-century descendants were to have so many dealings – always felt for those places which had been inhabited by successive generations of their families.[36]

Writing of the way in which an intense love of locality pervades the work of twentieth-century Scotland's leading Gaelic poet, Sorley MacLean, a literary critic has commented: 'This sense of landscape and attachment to place is closely bound up with human relations, not merely with personal memories of friends and their company . . . but with a profound awareness of . . . community extended not only in place but also in time; an awareness of all those who lived and strove and were buried in the earth, not as remote figures in a history-book but as part of one's own flesh and blood.'[37]

What is true of twentieth-century Gaels was no doubt truer still of their seventeenth-century predecessors. Glencoe tradition-bearers, as well as endlessly rehearsing the tale of how their glen was made over by Angus of Islay to Young John of the Heather, told story after story to make the point that here was a place which had been occupied by Gaelic-speakers since well before the departure from Ireland of Gofraid, son of Fergus and forebear of Young John of the Heather's celebrated great-great-great-grandfather, Somerled. It was in Glencoe, so MacDonald storytellers insisted, that the Fenians – who loom large in Gaelic myth and whose warlike exploits both antedated and surpassed even those of Conn of the Hundred Battles – kept the riches they had looted from their foes. Nor was this Glencoe's only Fenian connotation. Even their country's natural features, so Glencoe storytellers said, had been re-arranged by these bygone warriors. That was why, the storytellers pointed out, so many of Glencoe's mountains bore the names of the Fenian heroes who had given these mountains their distinctive shapes.[38]

Whether or not their homeland had been designed in such a way as to provide the Fenians with an easily defended hide-out, Glencoe's MacDonald occupants certainly took every advantage of the fortress-like character which their narrow valley derived from its encircling hills – secreting among these hills the numerous cattle driven here at the end of raids which the Glencoe men's Lowland victims were seldom able to fend off successfully.

If, as one eighteenth-century commentator wrote of Glencoe, 'this small country was famous for murder, theft and rapine', then that was largely owing to the cattle-raiding activities of a clan whose chief was described by the Scottish government in 1610 as a 'common and notorious thief'. The MacDonalds, of course, would have taken issue with any such description of Young John of the Heather's latest heir. Lowlanders might have considered them the merest bandits, brigands and cut-throats, but the Glencoe men would doubtless have argued that their cattle-raiding was firmly in accord with their people's Fenian traditions. They might have added, in their more prosaic moments, that their lands – irrespective of that seventeenth-century account in which these lands are portrayed as overflowing, if not with milk and honey, then at least with grain and fish – were such as to make it necessary for Glencoe's meagre crops to be supplemented by one means or another.[39]

Understandably enough, there never was agreement between Highlanders and Lowlanders about these matters. One thing is clear about Glencoe's reputation, however. That reputation – deserved or undeserved – contributed significantly to the creation, in the Lowlands and beyond, of a climate of opinion which made it possible for the Scottish government to treat the Glencoe MacDonalds in much the same way as Native American peoples like the Nez Perce were one day to be treated by the government of the United States. The outcome, in the Glencoe case, was the officially inspired 'slaughter' which, as Archibald McDonald of the Hudson's Bay Company long afterwards observed, brought so much misery to Glencoe in the early hours of what Archibald called the 'tragical' morning of 13 February 1692.[40]

The celebrated victory which the Glencoe men had helped the Marquis of Montrose secure at Inverlochy in 1645 had proved, by the seventeenth century's closing decade, to be of no more enduring significance than the several other engagements in which Archibald of the Bay Company's great-grandfather had participated. Montrose's rebellion, for all its initial success, had ended in defeat. So, too, had the more recent Highland rising of 1689. Like Montrose's campaign, that venture had been undertaken on behalf of a Stuart king – this king's throne having been occupied by William of Orange whom both the Scottish and English parliaments, for a whole complex of political and religious reasons, had invited to take the now-exiled Stuart monarch's place. Although yet another Highland charge had broken yet another government army at the Battle of Killiecrankie in July 1689, King William's forces had promptly foiled a Highland lunge into the Lowlands and the Glencoe MacDonalds, who had inevitably joined the rebels, were consequently left to salvage what they could from their defeat by taking time, while on their way back north, to raid some handily located Campbell lands around Glenlyon.

One inevitable consequence of these events was a growing conviction in the south, not least on the part of King William and his ministers, that the Highland clans should have their still-considerable autonomy curtailed. At the head of Loch Linnhe, and within a mile or two of the place where the Battle of Inverlochy had been fought, the government thus established a military outpost of the kind that would soon be common on the western frontiers of Britain's North American colonies. Intended both to intimidate and to impress the Glencoe MacDonalds, the Camerons, the Appin Stewarts and all the other clans in its general vicinity, this permanently garrisoned strongpoint was named Fort

William in honour of the new king. That same new king, in August 1691, put his name to a decree which obliged the chiefs of all those clans which had taken part in the 1689 rebellion to swear an oath of allegiance to him. This oath, King William and his ministers made clear, would have to be sworn by the start of 1692.

If it was nobody's fault but his own that Alexander MacDonald, the Glencoe people's chief, should have defiantly refused to register his oath until the last possible moment, it was arguably no more than a catastrophic misunderstanding which resulted in the Glencoe chief thinking that the oath could be sworn before Fort William's military commander. When, on travelling to the fort at the end of December 1691 and learning that he should actually have made his pledge of loyalty to King William before the sheriff of Argyll whose base was in the Campbell stronghold of Inveraray, Alexander MacDonald, then well into his sixties, was left with no alternative but to make the long journey to Inveraray in the teeth of a New Year snowstorm. The Glencoe chief's oath, though certainly sworn, was not sworn in advance of the king's clearly stated deadline. And in government circles – where there had developed a fervent desire to teach Highlanders an unforgettable lesson – this news was greeted with quite evident delight. 'It would be a proper vindication of the public justice,' one of William's ministers observed on hearing of the Glencoe clan's failure to comply with the king's terms, 'to extirpate that sept of thieves.'[41]

Soon just such an extirpation was being planned. The fact that its agents were to be a military detachment raised two years previously by the Earl of Argyll and commanded by Captain Robert Campbell of Glenlyon – whose lands the Glencoe MacDonalds had happily ravaged in 1689 – might make it seem that the killings which were shortly to take place in Glencoe were simply one more instalment in an inter-clan feud which had already lasted for some 200 years. But to reach such a conclusion is to be too kind to Scotland's government. MacDonald-Campbell rivalries, rivalries which dated back to the demise of the Lordship of the Isles, undoubtedly played a part in the events of early 1692. Government ministers played a more important role, however. Those ministers sent Robert Campbell and his soldiers to Glencoe. They expressed the wish, in correspondence, that Campbell's troops would 'not trouble the government with prisoners'. And they were ultimately responsible for orders which instructed Campbell's men 'to fall upon . . . the MacDonalds of Glencoe and to put all to the sword under seventy'.[42]

This was to embark on an explicitly genocidal policy. It was to do so in the absence of the excuse or justification that might have been provided by the Glencoe MacDonalds being engaged in an active attempt to end King William's rule. Unlike the Nez Perce, who were considered to be at war with the U.S. government when Colonel John Gibbon's troops descended on their camp beside Montana's Big Hole River in August 1877, Glencoe's population could not very plausibly be said to be endangering the national security of the state which ordered their destruction. The MacDonalds, to be sure, were no angels. They were habitual cattle-raiders. They were habitual rebels also. But their chief – even if belatedly and reluctantly – had formally declared his loyalty to King William. His clan consequently thought themselves at peace. That was why Captain Robert Campbell and his 120 men, on their getting to Glencoe on 1 February 1692, were made comparatively welcome. 'They were billeted in the country,' as a commission of inquiry was afterwards to comment of the reception accorded to Campbell's troops, 'and had free quarters, and kind entertainment, living familiarly with the people.'[43]

The people in question numbered several hundred. All of them lived in the western, lower, part of Glencoe where the valley's northern and southern walls are set sufficiently far apart as to make space, one might say, for just a little in the way of cultivable land. This land, as it had been for centuries, was divided between several different townships. In charge of each township – and accommodated, therefore, in a house that was of a slightly higher standard than the low-walled, earthen-floored and thatch-roofed cottages which were home to most of Glencoe's inhabitants – was that township's principal tenant. This tenant or 'tacksman', a tack being the Scottish equivalent of an English lease, headed one of the district's more important families – Glencoe's tacksmen, like their equivalents elsewhere in the Highlands, constituting a local gentry. To be a tacksman was to be a man of standing. It was, for instance, automatically to have command rank in time of war. And in seventeenth-century Glencoe, all such status in a clan depending ultimately on ancestry, tacksmen were tacksmen by virtue of their connections with the family of their chief. Thus it mattered greatly to one set of Glencoe MacDonalds that Iain Dubh, or Black John, a sixteenth-century Glencoe chief's second son, had himself fathered a third son, Ailean Dubh, who, in his turn, had gone on to marry Janet Stewart from Appin and become father of those MacDonald brothers, Ranald and Angus, who had served the Marquis of Montrose with such distinction.[44]

Little was recorded in the Highlands about the later career of the second of these brothers. 'Of Angus and his descendants,' commented the authors of the early-twentieth-century volumes which still constitute the fullest history of Clan Donald, 'we know nothing.' This deficiency, however, is made good by the notes compiled in 1830 by the Hudson's Bay Company fur trader, Archibald McDonald, who claimed descent from Ailean Dubh in such a way as to make it practically certain that the Glencoe man who guided Montrose into Argyll was the Bay Company trader's great-grandfather. Since Archibald of the Bay Company's father was tacksman of Inverigan in the eighteenth century, and since Archibald explicitly places both his grandfather and his great-grand-mother in that same Glencoe township in 1692, it is more than likely that the Angus MacDonald who served with Montrose and who, in 1692, would have been in his late sixties by Archibald's reckoning, was tacksman of Inverigan at the point when Robert Campbell marched his troops into Glencoe. If so, this Angus would have been Campbell's host. For as Archibald McDonald noted in 1830, and as is confirmed by contemporary documentation, Captain Campbell – having installed most of his officers and men in the homes of other Glencoe families – made his own headquarters in the house of the tacksman of Inverigan.[45]

Being a mile or so to the east of the lower Glencoe townships of Invercoe and Carnoch, and being a similar distance to the west of upper townships such as Achnacone and Achtriochtan, Inverigan probably became Robert Campbell's headquarters because of its central location. Today the fields in which the Inverigan people grew their crops have been transformed into a caravan, or trailer, park. And the immediately adjacent hillside has been planted over with conifer trees of a sort which certainly did not exist in seventeenth-century Glencoe. But the mountain landscape which the caravan park's many visitors come here to see has not, in its essentials, altered. When you stand at Inverigan and – first facing north, then turning slightly to the east – allow your gaze to run from Sgorr na Ciche's rounded summit, by way of the long ridge of Sgorr nam Fiannaidh, to Bidean nam Bian's high rock walls, you are taking in scenes known from childhood to every one of Inverigan's numerous MacDonald generations.

Although it was by no means unusual, in these often troubled times, for troops to be quartered suddenly on a civilian population, the Glencoe MacDonalds – who were no friends either of the government which Captain Robert Campbell served or of the clan to which the captain belonged – began by being highly suspicious as to the intentions of the soldiers who, by 12 February 1692, had been stationed in their glen for nearly a fortnight. Campbell, however, had issued assurances – assurances which, at the outset, were probaly given in good faith – to the effect that he and his men would shortly be leaving for another part of the Highlands. And for all that the MacDonalds – just like the Nez

Perce in the months and years following Colonel Gibbon's attack on them – were to tell of various forewarnings of catastrophe, nobody in Glencoe seems to have sought safety as a result of such premonitions. The notion that men might rise in the night and start killing their hosts was, in any event, so totally at odds with Highland custom as to have made it unlikely that the Glencoe people would have believed anyone in a position to apprise them of their fate. It was also the case, to be fair, that it was only on the evening of Friday, 12 February, on his receiving written orders from Major Robert Duncanson, then recently arrived at nearby Ballachulish with additional government troops, that Robert Campbell became fully aware of what his superiors expected of him.

Duncanson's letter to Campbell, the text of which survives, is clarity itself. Campbell, as previously mentioned, was 'to fall upon the MacDonalds . . . and to put all to the sword under seventy'. Campbell was 'to have a special care that the old fox and his sons', by which Duncanson meant Glencoe's chief and his immediate heirs, 'do upon no account escape'. Campbell was 'to secure all the avenues' leading out of Glencoe with a view to ensuring that the MacDonalds were utterly annihilated. And all these things Campbell was to do 'by the king's special command', it being 'for the good and safety of the country that these miscreants be cut off root and branch'.[46]

The 'slaughter committed by William's troops', to borrow the phrase which Archibald McDonald would long afterwards apply to this government-sanctioned massacre of his people, began several hours before dawn on Saturday, 13 February 1692, a day of snow and bitter cold. Because the Glencoe MacDonalds were asleep when the killing started and because they had earlier hidden away their weapons for fear that these weapons would be confiscated by the troops who were their guests, Robert Campbell's soldiers encountered practically no resistance. Alexander MacDonald, chief of Glencoe, died as he struggled into his clothes. One bullet had entered his body. Another had passed through his head, from the back to the front, blowing his face apart in the process. And as the sound and smell of musketfire spread inexorably across Glencoe, from one township to the next, plenty of other men, women and children of the dead chief's clan were to suffer a similar fate.[47]

At Inverigan, where Robert Campbell was personally in charge, nine men who had earlier been bound hand and foot were brought into the open, one by one, and shot or bayoneted. Among those to die in this fashion was the township's tacksman – who received no designation other than 'MacDonald of Inverigan' in contemporary documents but whose first name, so this book postulates on the basis of Archibald McDonald's account of his family's history, was very probably Angus. Also killed at Inverigan was an unidentified 'young man of about 20 years of age'. Captain Campbell, or so it was subseqently reported, was initially 'inclined to save' this young man. But he was promptly seized by another officer who 'shot him dead'. And when a 'boy of about 13 years of age' ran to Campbell in the hope of gaining protection, 'he was likewise shot dead'. Elsewhere in the township, where houses were now being set ablaze by soldiers, 'a woman and a boy [of] about four or five years of age' were killed in an equally casual fashion.[48]

Others of the Glencoe people, however, managed to avoid death – not least because the troops who had been sent to kill them, just like their Big Hole counterparts of nearly 200 years later, were not unanimously enthusiastic about the blood-letting which was going on around them.

Among the survivors was John MacDonald, Archibald of the Bay Company's grandfather, then barely twelve years old. John, in his grandson's words, 'with difficulty escaped with his mother and brother' from their Inverigan home. Where the little party then headed, Archibald does not say. But this MacDonald family, as noted earlier, had relatives in the Stewart country where a number of the Glencoe people are known to have found refuge. It is probable, therefore, that little John MacDonald, his brother – whose name, according to Archibald, was Donald – and their mother struck out across the hills to the south of Glencoe and, by way of Glen Duror or Glen Creran, came down eventually into Appin. That is no mean journey to undertake in summer. On the February day in question, a day which had already brought so much terror, it is little short of astonishing that women and children were physically able to walk so far across this rough terrain in the most appalling weather. 'The mountains,' as was remarked by the author of one early account of what now confronted the Glencoe massacre's survivors, 'were covered with a deep snow, the rivers impassable, storm and tempest filled the air . . . and there were no houses to shelter them within many miles.'[49]

❁

Because the Massacre of Glencoe was a lot less total than its perpetrators had intended, Inverigan and its neighbouring townships were eventually reclaimed by surviving members of the families who had lived for so long in these places. Nor were these families noticeably cowed by their 1692 experiences – experiences which, if anything, served to make the Glencoe MacDonalds even more contemptuous of

Duncan McDonald, then in his eighties, attending the opening of the Going-to-the-Sun Highway, Glacier National Park, Montana, 1932

Angus McDonald, the Hudson's Bay Company fur trader who left Scotland for the American West in 1838

Catherine McDonald, Angus's wife. Catherine's mother was Nez Perce,
her father part-Mohawk
UNIVERSITY OF MONTANA ARCHIVES

Previous Pages: Duncan McDonald, Angus McDonald's son (in head-dress),
with Louisa, Duncan's wife (on horseback)

The town of Missoula, Montana, as it was about the time of the
Nez Perce War of 1877

Charlie McDonald, Salish tribal elder and grandson of Angus and Catherine McDonald
SALISH KOOTENAI COLLEGE

authority than they had been before. This was demonstrated in July 1745 when Prince Charles Edward Stuart landed on Scotland's Atlantic coast and launched what turned out to be the last of his dynasty's attempts to regain its former power. Around 120 Glencoe men quickly joined the prince's army – their recruitment to the rebel cause being celebrated by a MacDonald bard in Gaelic verses which portrayed Glencoe's 'heroes' as sweeping aside their enemies with all the ferocity of 'forest fires on the mountainside'.[50]

With the help of the Glencoe MacDonalds and several thousand other Highlanders, Charles Edward Stuart managed first to conquer Scotland and then to advance deep into England. But this very success was to prove the undoing of the clans which had provided the rebel prince with so many followers. Since 1707, when Scotland and England merged politically, Glencoe and the rest of the Highlands had been part of a United Kingdom which, from America in the west to India in the east, was carving out a global empire. It was never very likely that the rulers of this empire, which was enormously stronger than the independent kingdom of Scotland had ever been, would allow themselves to be deposed by Gaelic-speaking clansmen of the sort that English propagandists described in 1745 as 'uncouth savages', 'robbers', 'hungry wolves', 'bare-arsed banditti', 'wild and barbarous beyond expression'. Much the more probable outcome of Prince Charles Edward Stuart's rising was the one that actually occurred. A badly frightened but unbeaten government in London, now the capital of a unified British state, resolved, as one government minister put it, that Highlanders should be 'absolutely reduced'. Not only were the rebel prince's forces to be defeated militarily, in other words. The clans which had provided the bulk of these forces were also to be made incapable of ever again endangering the country which, in 1745, they had tried, and failed, to conquer.[51]

At Culloden, to the south of Inverness, on the cold and miserable morning of Wednesday, 16 April 1746, with an east wind blowing rain into their faces and with the British army's field artillery tearing great gaps in their ranks, the Highland clans made what was, in effect, their last stand. Their cause, perhaps, was less that of Charles Edward Stuart than that of a way of life which, as Gaelic bards at least understood, was fighting now for its existence. It is not without significance, then, that when he sat down in his Mission Valley home to write about this battle, Angus McDonald – whose Glencoe great-grandfather fought at Culloden – was contemptuous of Prince Charles Edward Stuart's claims to leadership. Observing that 'evil luck and evil judgement are inseparable twins', Angus thought the prince the victim of his own stupidity as much as of ill-fortune. At Culloden especially, or so Angus maintained, Charles 'showed little capacity'. On the prince's orders, Angus went on, the many MacDonalds who were at Culloden – and who included the MacDonalds of Glengarry as well as the MacDonalds of Glencoe – were obliged to position themselves on the Highland army's left. This was at variance with a tradition which dated from the time, more than 400 years before, when Angus of Islay had thrown the weight of Clan Donald behind King Robert Bruce, thus making a major contribution to the king's decisive victory over the English at Bannock-burn. Throughout the intervening period, as Angus commented correctly, the MacDonalds had always been stationed on the right of any army to which they had attached themselves – 'the position,' Angus explained, 'being that of our clan given by Bruce at the Battle of Bannockburn'. But Charles Edward Stuart, for no very good reason, had upset that age-old arrangement. His clan's consequent feeling that disaster was bound to ensue, was, as Angus McDonald reflected sadly, soon borne out by events.[52]

'*Air thus an latha dol sios,*' Angus now wrote, drawing in Montana on a Gaelic song which he would have learned in the course of his Scottish youth. '*Bha gaoth a' cathadh nan sian, As an athar bha trian ar leiridh.*' Composed by a Culloden veteran, the song tells of the wind-driven rain which was so terrible a 'torment' to Charles Edward Stuart's Highlanders on their going into battle on that icy April morning in 1746. It tells, too, of the hopeless charge made by these same High-landers; of the terrible casualties caused by 'the fire of the foe'; of how this fire was so heavy that the Highlanders were not able satisfactorily to engage their enemies in the hand-to-hand combat in which Gaels had always excelled. His people, Angus McDonald declared, 'never fought better'. But they were 'out-generalled' and 'out-numbered'. Their defeat was consequently as unavoidable as it was absolute.[53]

The Glencoe teenager who was among the broken Highland army's soldiers and whose name – like his Mission Valley great-grandson's – was Angus MacDonald had been born, as already mentioned, in 1730. And prior to his involvement in the Battle of Culloden, neither he nor any of his contemporaries had any very pressing reason to suspect that the traditional pattern of life in Glencoe – a pattern which had been maintained for so long in the face of so many external pressures – was about to be destroyed. But by 1815, when Angus MacDonald was buried on Eilean Munda, where his tombstone describes him as 'late tacksman of Inverigan', both Glencoe and the rest of the Highlands had witnessed the complete disintegration of the clans which had for so long been central to the lives of Scotland's Gaelic-speaking communities.[54]

This disintegration was as inevitable – and had much the same causes – as the collapse, a hundred or so years later, of tribes like the Nez Perce. The civilisation which was coming into existence in eighteenth-century Britain – and which, in the course of the next century, was to become dominant in most other parts of the world also – was utterly intolerant of older forms of social organisation. This civilisation was founded on trade and, increasingly, on industry. This civilisation was predominantly urban in character. This civilisation consequently looked to the land primarily as a source of the commodities – whether food-stuffs or other raw materials – which its burgeoning cities required in ever larger quantities. It followed, this new civilisation being universal in its impact, that land had everywhere to be reorganised; that it was no longer sufficient for the Scottish Highlands to be given over to subsistence agriculture of the sort which had been practised by the clans; that it was no longer sufficient either for the American West, a region which possessed many more natural resources than the High-lands, to remain the exclusive preserve of its indigenous peoples. Thus it came about that the Highlands, during the lifetime of Angus MacDonald of Inverigan, were made wholly subordinate to the economic and other requirements of Britain's urban centres. Thus it came about that even the Nez Perce, for all their comparative remote-ness from such centres, were, by the time of the Inverigan tacksman's death, beginning to be affected also by forces of the kind which had already transformed Glencoe. And it was, of course, indicative of the global nature of these events that Highlanders who were set adrift, so to speak, by what happened to their homeland should have become the means, very often, by which the lives of the Nez Perce and their neighbours were, in their turn, to be altered irrevocably.

As far as Scottish Highlanders were concerned, then, the Battle of Culloden was an event of much greater magnitude than earlier catastrophes of the kind which had occurred in 1692. Initially, perhaps, it did not seem so. There was, for instance, much that was familiar about what occurred when, a fortnight or so after Culloden, British army units came to Glencoe in search of its people's chief, Alexander MacDonald. This man, whose grandfather had been the most prominent victim of the 1692 killings, was known to have got back to Glencoe from Culloden towards the end of April 1746. And since he had been a leading participant in Charles Edward Stuart's now-collapsed rebellion, the authorities badly wanted him in custody. 'I ordered two detachments of 80 men each to march by different routes so as to meet at his house at the same time,' an army commander reported of his attempt to make a prisoner of Glencoe's chief. 'But . . . violent rains made a delay of one day, by which my design was discovered, and when the parties met, which was in the night, the bird was flown . . . man, woman and child having retired to the mountains which are inaccessible.'[55]

Such defiance was not long to be maintained, however. In mid-May, by which point it had become clear that government forces had no intention of ever again permitting Highlanders to revert to their old ways, Alexander MacDonald was putting his signature to a letter containing what amounted to an offer of unconditional surrender. He was 'very sensible' of his 'folly and great error' in 'taking up arms' against the British government, MacDonald wrote. Throwing himself on the 'clemency' of the officer to whom his letter was addressed, he added: 'I have ordered such of my people as live in Glencoe to meet you and to deliver all their arms to you as an evidence of my submission.'[56]

Although it did not keep him out of prison, his submission, as he called it, undoubtedly helped Alexander MacDonald escape execution at the hands of a government which showed no compunction about hanging Highland rebels. But this is not to say that the Glencoe chief acted solely on the basis of self-interest. By surrendering himself when he did, Alexander MacDonald may have helped save his own life. But he equally may have helped preserve his clansfolk's lives and livelihoods – in that Glencoe, during the summer of 1746, seems to have been spared the indiscriminate burnings and plunderings which British troops were then inflicting on so many other parts of the Scottish Highlands.

To the extent that Alexander MacDonald acted as he did out of concern for his clan, his motives would not have been readily recognised by the next generation of Highland chiefs – men who adopted the manners, attitudes, outlook and language of the southern society whose encroachments their predecessors had so strenuously resisted.[57]

By choosing thus to integrate themselves into a social order which would otherwise have cast them aside, the leading families of the Highlands avoided the fate which overtook the leading families of the Nez Perce and of other Native American peoples. Highland chiefs survived, indeed prospered, by turning their backs on the men and women to whom – as is indicated by the relationship implicit in the fact that 'clan' derives from a Gaelic word meaning 'children' – these chiefs had once offered leadership of a very special kind. An Indian chief, even if he had wanted to, would have found it virtually impossible to embark on a similar course. The traditional society of the Highlands, despite its having differed enormously from the society which its leading men now joined, had existed side by side with that society for so long as to enable clan chiefs to be familiar with – even, as time went on, attracted by – the way that life was lived in Lowland Scotland and in England. The links between native America and settler America, in contrast, were always very tenuous. And though Highlanders were, from time to time, subjected to discrimination and persecution of a quasi-racial type, Highlanders were white. Highland chiefs, by virtue of that fact alone, had many more options open to them than were available to men like Sitting Bull, Looking Glass or White Bird.

Because there was no insurmountable racial obstacle in the way of their being assimilated into the upper echelons of British society, and because it suited the British government to hasten the destruction of clanship by thus subverting clanship's ruling élite, clan chiefs, in the post-Culloden period, found it surprisingly easy to take on what amounted to entirely new identities. They abandoned Gaelic for English. They married into the southern aristocracy. They swapped their Highland castles for homes in Edinburgh or London. And with a view to financing these increasingly lavish lifestyles, they began to treat clan lands as revenue-generating assets rather than – as had been standard practice in the past – sources of military manpower.

Among the earliest victims of this last development were tacksmen such as Angus MacDonald of Inverigan. Although men like Angus rented their farms from their chiefs, the relationship between chief and tacksman had traditionally been anything but strictly commercial. A tacksman, as had certainly been the case in Glencoe, was usually his chief's kinsman. And such money rent as changed hands in respect of any particular tack was usually nominal – the tacksman's role, prior to Culloden and its aftermath, having more to do with helping to turn out the clan in time of war than with furnishing his chief with a cash income.

By the 1760s and 1770s, however, tacksmen's rents were being raised sharply by chiefs who, as one visitor to the Highlands concluded at this time, were ceasing to be 'patriarchal rulers' and becoming instead 'rapacious landlords'. Soon more and more tacksmen – among them Angus MacDonald of Munial who, as mentioned earlier, emigrated with his family from Knoydart in 1786 – were responding to such exactions by surrendering their tenancies and taking themselves off to North America. There, as these emigrants were quick to report from North Carolina's Cape Fear River country, from New York's Mohawk Valley, from Glengarry County and from the various other localities where numerous Highlanders settled in the course of the three or four decades following the Battle of Culloden, land was to be had virtually for the asking. There, as is commented by one of the many Gaelic songs which Highlanders composed in North America, people were 'free . . . from the landlord's arrogance'.[58]

Although large parties of emigrants left the Appin and Glencoe area for North Carolina in 1775 and 1789, Angus MacDonald of Inverigan, having married Mary Rankin and having started what was to be a large family, clearly decided to stay at home and to make some small attempt of his own to profit from the further round of social and economic upheavals which now began in the Highlands. These upheavals were associated with the introduction of large-scale sheep farming to the region towards the close of the eighteenth century. Sheep farming was much encouraged both by Britain's rulers, who wanted to gain new sources of wool for the country's expanding textile industry, and by Highland landlords, who were anxious to enhance the income-producing potential of their estates. Sheep farming had its opponents too – most notably among the thousands of Highlanders who, in order to make way for this new activity, were forcibly deprived of their land and their homes. These people's feelings, however, counted for very little in the United Kingdom of the time. In the ten or twenty years on either side of 1800, therefore, sheep farming spread to practically every part of the Highlands. Prominent among its backers was Alexander MacDonald of Glencoe. His grandfather had led the Glencoe men to war in 1745, but this latest successor to Young John of the Heather was by no means a clan chief of the traditional variety. He was, in fact, a businessman and speculator whose financial adventures were to turn the lives of the MacDonalds of Inverigan, among others, in wholly unforeseen directions.[59]

Like their counterparts elsewhere in the Highlands, the generality of Glencoe people were to fall victim to the land-use revolution caused by sheep farming. As late as the 1770s, when its inhabitants were reported to be growing oats and raising cattle much as they had always done, there were few signs that Glencoe was about to be depopulated. But the next half-century was to witness the virtual eradication of a people who had earlier contrived to survive their planned extinction. 'The sheep-farming system has done the work of extirpation more effectively than the . . . massacre,' one early-nineteenth-century visitor to Glencoe commented. 'But slight traces now remain of the warlike tribes of this . . . valley.'[60]

Glencoe's chief – if such a term has any meaning in the context of what was being done now to his clan – had meanwhile made himself, as one contemporary put it, 'perhaps the greatest and most extensive sheep farmer in the Highlands'. This was not something which could be accomplished within the comparatively narrow confines of Glencoe. It resulted from Alexander MacDonald having rented a remarkably large number of the sheep farms which were then being created right across the Highlands. The Glencoe chief, however, was to prove a good deal more reckless than shrewd. Eventually, and somewhat predictably in view of the extent of his reliance on borrowed money, Alexander badly overreached himself. Among the consequent casualties were the family of Angus MacDonald – the Glencoe man who, when 'but a stripling', had fought at Culloden prior to becoming, probably in succession to his father, tacksman of Inverigan.[61]

Because its size was such as to rule out its day-to-day management by a single individual, Alexander MacDonald's sheep-farming empire depended very largely on the men who were placed in charge of its component units. These men may have included Angus MacDonald of Inverigan. They certainly included several of Angus's sons – at least three of whom had some connection, for example, with the sheep farm which the Glencoe chief, Alexander MacDonald, rented at Monar in Glenstrathfarrar. This particular glen, which runs into the hills above Beauly, itself a village to the west of Inverness, had been given over to sheep production in 1803. Alexander MacDonald was thus provided with the opportunity of taking on another farming lease. But the Inverigan brothers, John, Ranald and Donald, all of whom appear to have served at one time or another as Alexander's on-the-spot subordinates at Monar, were to have cause to regret their move from the western to the eastern Highlands. From their Glenstrathfarrar base, admittedly, the Inverigan family were able to diversify into other sheep-farming enterprises in adjacent localities such as Strathconon. But the family were also drawn so deeply into their chief's various wheelings and dealings as to be, by the start of the nineteenth century's second decade, fairly heavily in debt. It must have been with some relief, therefore, that the now elderly Angus MacDonald of Inverigan found himself presented, at just this point, with the chance of despatching his youngest son, Archibald, to North America.[62]

❋

Archibald McDonald's eventual career as a fur trader had its origins in a letter written on 14 August 1811 by Thomas Douglas, Earl of Selkirk, a Scots nobleman who was anxious to establish a Highland colony in the North American interior and who, as a means to this end, had been involving himself for some years in the affairs of the London-based Hudson's Bay Company. The Bay Company, as it happened, was then losing out rather badly to a rival corporation operating out of Montreal. This corporation, by sending its traders much further west than Bay

Company representatives ever ventured, had managed to secure an increasingly dominant position in the international fur market. But the Bay men, for all their difficulties, possessed one unmatchable asset. Since its formation in 1670, their company had held rights of ownership over all the enormous territories drained by watercourses flowing into Hudson Bay. Hence the Earl of Selkirk's interest in an organisation which he eventually persuaded to transfer to him a 116,000-square-mile slice of real estate in the vicinity of Red River – a northward-flowing stream which meanders sluggishly into Lake Winnipeg from present-day Minnesota.

The earl was a most untypical aristocrat. Much more radical in his political views than most members of his class, he sympathised greatly with the many Highlanders who were being evicted as a result of their landlords turning over so much land to sheep farmers. While recognising that little could be done to prevent evictions or 'clearances', as these removals of population came to be called, Selkirk became increasingly committed to the notion that dispossessed Highlanders could, and should, be helped to make new homes for themselves in North America – where, the earl argued, Highlanders could reconstitute something at least of the communities which Scotland's former chiefs were so comprehensively destroying. It was with a view to putting this thinking into practice that the Earl of Selkirk set out to acquire his Red River landholdings. It was with a view to transforming these landhold-ings into a well-peopled colony that the earl began to recruit prospec-tive settlers in the Highlands. And it was with a view to providing these Gaelic-speaking settlers with Gaelic-speaking leadership that Selkirk, on 14 August 1811, wrote to one of his Highland friends and asked this friend to recommend a young Highlander 'of respectable character and, at the same time, of talents' who might be hired 'to go out' with an emigrant party to Red River.[63]

A man of the type Selkirk had in mind was almost certain to be of tacksman stock – Highland tacksmen, in their longstanding role as the former clan society's officer class, being accustomed to exercise com-mand functions of the kind the earl clearly thought necessary in the Red River country. And since Selkirk's Highland contact was a MacDonald, it is no great surprise, given kinship's enduring significance in the High-lands, that another MacDonald, in the person of the 21-year-old son of the tacksman of Inverigan, was brought to the earl's attention.

Selkirk seems to have had no cause to regret the choice thus made for him. 'I am greatly pleased with young Archibald,' the earl observed in 1812. 'He seems indeed a very fine young man.' It had been his intention, Selkirk continued, to send Archibald to Red River that year.

But he had decided to keep his new employee a little longer in London where, Selkirk wrote, 'I may give him an opportunity of acquiring some branches of knowledge that will be useful'. This meant that when, in the spring of 1813, the Earl of Selkirk undertook to ship a party of emigrants from the Highlands to Red River by way of Hudson Bay, Archibald McDonald was available to assume control of what was to prove an almost unimaginably demanding expedition.[64]

The emigrants in Archibald's charge came from the Strath of Kildonan in Sutherland. There, by means identical to those already employed in Glencoe, Glenstrathfarrar and scores of other Highland localities, family after family was evicted in early 1813. Kildonan's hundreds of homes were destroyed, its land rented out to sheep farmers and its former inhabitants directed towards the pitifully inadequate smallholdings, or crofts, which served as convenient receptacles for the victims of all such clearances. These crofts, being remote, tiny and infertile, seemed no more attractive to the Kildonan people than the typical reservation seemed to the Native Americans who were forced to move in ever larger numbers to such places as the nineteenth century advanced. But the feelings of nineteenth-century Highlanders, as far as those in authority were concerned, counted for little more than the feelings of nineteenth-century Indians. Indeed to Patrick Sellar, the man who organised the clearance of the Strath of Kildonan on behalf of its owner, the Duke of Sutherland, the one group was every bit as undeserving of consideration as the other. Kildonan's inhabitants, Sellar wrote, were 'a parcel of beggars with no stock but cunning and laziness'. Like Highlanders generally, they were 'barbarous hordes' and 'aborigines' whose position 'in relation to the enlightened nations of Europe' was 'not very different from that betwixt the American colonists and the aborigines of that country'. Just as the Indian was fated to give way to the white settler, men like Patrick Sellar thought, so the Highlander was destined to yield to the sheep farmer.[65]

It is readily understandable, then, that the overwhelming majority of the Kildonan people, on hearing of the Earl of Selkirk's offer of free passages to Red River, expressed a lot more interest in that distant destination than in the wholly unenticing prospect of life on one of Patrick Sellar's proffered crofts. Selkirk, as things turned out, could find places for no more than about 100 men, women and children on the regular Hudson's Bay Company summer convoy from London to Hudson Bay. But in view of what was shortly to transpire, this was maybe just as well.*

---

* This episode is recounted in greater detail in the same author's book, *A Dance Called America.*

Archibald McDonald's emigrant party joined their Bay Company ship, the *Prince of Wales*, at the end of June 1813. The Atlantic crossing was both protracted and stormy. 'Seasickness prostrated so many to so great a degree that they could not think of anything but their own suffering,' one Bay man wrote of the Kildonan folk. And as was then commonplace among emigrants, seasickness was quickly followed by typhus. 'This day have 19 passengers and eight seamen ill,' the captain of the *Prince of Wales* recorded in his log on 15 August. 'The groans and cries of the sick on one side and the delirious on the other is dreadful beyond description.' Deaths inevitably ensued. And so badly delayed was the *Prince of Wales*, both by unusually bad weather in the Atlantic and by exceptionally dense pack ice in Hudson Bay itself, that Archibald McDonald and the surviving members of his party – not having time to head south before the freezing of the rivers on which they were to travel – found themselves forced to overwinter on the blizzard-raked coast of an iced-over sea where temperatures fell so low that fahrenheit thermometers often recorded more than eighty degrees of frost.[66]

But somehow the Hudson Bay winter was survived. And in the opening week of April 1814, wearing snowshoes and travelling at night in the hope of avoiding snowblindness, the Kildonan folk, accompanied by a Hudson's Bay Company guide, set out on the last stage of what had turned into one of the most daunting journeys ever undertaken by any of North America's millions of European immigrants. 'They took their departure by single files,' Archibald McDonald wrote of the people he had brought safely through so many months of bitter cold. 'The guide . . . took the lead, followed by the men and sleds, and they succeeded by the women . . . Single files would tend to make the track more firm and smooth that the women were enabled to walk in the snowshoes with greater facility, as they were by no means calculated for that arduous task.'[67]

In view of what he had accomplished in the course of his year-long travels, it is little wonder that Archibald McDonald should eventually have been offered a job by the Hudson's Bay Company. This was in 1820. Archibald for some time had been adding to his reputation by helping to consolidate, at Red River, the North American continent's westernmost white settlement outside the then Mexican territory of California. Now he was presented with a new challenge. The Bay Company, having managed at last to see off its Montreal-based competitors, was anxious to extend its domains into the Columbia River country on the far side of the Rocky Mountains. And its latest recruit featured largely in the company's expansion plans. 'We possess little information about the Columbia,' one of the Bay Company's senior representatives noted in 1821. That was why, this man added, he had 'sent Archibald McDonald thither . . . to give a full and accurate report of it'.[68]

Archibald was to remain in the West for much of the next quarter-century. He rose steadily in the Hudson's Bay Company hierarchy. He took charge of a succession of fur trading posts in widely separated parts of the vast area which is today occupied by Oregon, Washington State and British Columbia. He married twice. He raised a large family. And among these North American grandchildren of the Culloden veteran, Angus of Inverigan, was a man whose life-story — which outdid even his father's in the sheer unlikeliness of its escapades — would have done credit to a Fenian saga of the kind that Archibald must have heard recited often in Glencoe.

This man, whose late-nineteenth-century photograph has been carefully preserved by McDonald family members on Montana's Flathead Reservation, was Ranald MacDonald. His mother, who died soon after Ranald was born in 1824 and who was Archibald McDonald's first wife, was the daughter of a Chinook chief whose people occupied lands adjacent to the point where the Columbia River exits into the Pacific Ocean. His varied ancestry, Ranald believed, accounted for his character — with his 'wild strain for wandering freedom' being traceable both to his 'Indian mother' and to his 'Highland father of Glencoe'.[69]

It was Ranald's conviction — and in this he anticipated, in some ways, modern anthropological theorists — that the remote origins of North America's native peoples were to be found in Asia. Japan, in particular, fascinated Ranald and he was determined to go there. Having run away from the Ontario bank where he had been apprenticed by his father, Ranald became a seaman on American ships trading in the Pacific and, Japan then being firmly closed to westerners, he finally gained entrance to the country which he so much wanted to visit by having himself cast adrift in a dinghy off the coast of Hokkaido. Initially imprisoned by Japan's rulers, Ranald was then given the task of teaching English to a number of the Japanese officials who were afterwards to be involved in the commencement of their country's westernisation. But neither his Japanese involvements nor his subsequent career as a gold prospector in Australia and Canada were to make Ranald's fortune. Eventually he returned to the Columbia country where he had lived as a boy with his father and where Ranald now became a good friend of a man who had come to the Columbia from Scotland in 1839 — a man whom Ranald always called his cousin.[70]

This was Angus McDonald who, since it is still in the possession of his Flathead Reservation descendants, must have kept Ranald's photograph by him in his Mission Valley homestead. Nor was that out of character. His many kinship links – those links which this chapter has outlined – were obviously important to Angus McDonald. He was, after all, a Highlander. And to Highlanders these things mattered a great deal.

CHAPTER THREE

A parcel of upstart Scotchmen

Angus McDonald was born at Craig in 1816 and entered the service of the Hudson's Bay Company in 1838. Little more can be said with certainty about the early life of this man whose fifty-year career in the American West was to become so inextricably bound up with what was then happening to the West's native peoples. From Angus's Indian descendants on the Flathead Reservation, however, it is possible, even more than a century after Angus's death, to obtain one or two additional insights into his youth, education and upbringing.

A good starting point is provided by the box of McDonald family papers kept nowadays by Angus McDonald's great-granddaughter, Eileen Decker, of St Ignatius, Mission Valley. Among these papers are the two surviving letters – mentioned at the start of the preceding chapter – to Angus from his younger sister, Margaret. One dates from 1845, the other from 1884.

'My dear Angus,' the first of these letters begins, 'There are not many things on earth that can afford us greater pleasure than to hear of you living well.' By 'us', Margaret makes clear, she means all Angus's close relatives. 'And we have great cause for thankfulness,' she tells her brother, 'that each member of our family are still preserved . . . with the exception of your excellent mother who is failing . . . She has been often thought at the gates of death, but the Lord has been merciful.'[1]

Any such letter, of course, contains its share of conventional sentiment. But there is sufficient emotional force in Margaret McDonald's sentences to create an impression of Margaret and her brother having belonged to a close family – an impression strengthened by remarks occasioned by Angus having evidently asked Margaret to send him some items of clothing. His mother, Margaret informs him, 'is busy for some time back knitting a few stockings for you'. And Angus 'cannot think,' Margaret adds, how his 'poor mother rejoiced at the very sight' of a suit prepared for Angus by a local tailor. 'She thought almost that she was seeing yourself.'

Margaret, it appears, was by no means Angus McDonald's only source of family news. 'Duncan [presumably Angus's brother] and father,' she remarks, 'are writing to you.' But these letters, if they ever got to their intended recipient, have long since been lost. And while it may be the merest of coincidences, one is left with the thought that Margaret's 1845 letter – which would have taken many months to reach its destination and which Angus clearly carried with him from trading post to trading post over several decades – must surely have been preserved because of some particular bond between Angus and his sister. 'I shall be looking and looking for a letter from you,' she writes towards the end of her own note.

Margaret McDonald, as previously noted, posted her 1845 letter to Angus from Dingwall, a smallish country town some fifteen miles to the north-west of Inverness. That is one of several circumstances which point to Angus's parents, Donald and Christina, having moved from Craig to this more easterly part of the Scottish Highlands when Angus was still fairly young. In 1857, to cite one more such instance, Angus McDonald gave Dingwall as his parish of origin in a Hudson's Bay Company document. Additional pointers of the same sort include the fact that Angus, in a number of the poems to which he turned his hand from time to time, mentions Ben Wyvis, the mountain which rises above Dingwall, as well as several other local landmarks of that sort. Then there is Albert J. Partoll's account – which this Missoula author derived, no doubt, from Angus's son, Duncan – of how Angus McDonald's Mission Valley trading post, Fort Connah, got its name: 'The name Connah was a variation of Connen, which Angus had applied to the stream in the vicinity, after a waterway in Scotland.'[2]

The River Conon, with which Angus McDonald explicitly associated himself in a letter written in 1877, flows into the Cromarty Firth a mile or two from Dingwall. What may be more to the point, however, is the same river's association with Strathconon – a valley just a little further to the west and one of the places where the MacDonalds of Inverigan became involved in sheep farming. From statements made in Archibald McDonald's Fort Langley note of December 1830, and from legal and other records of the time, it can be shown that a number of Archibald's brothers, together with one of his sisters, were resident, in the years around 1810 and 1820, in various places which are fairly close to Dingwall – in Beauly and in Glenstrathfarrar, for example, as well as in Strathconon. Since, as demonstrated previously, Angus's father, Donald, was the nephew of these particular MacDonalds, it may be that he moved east with a view to becoming involved in one or other of their different agricultural enterprises. These enterprises, it is relevant to note again at this stage, were not always successful. More than one member of the Inverigan family encountered some degree of financial difficulty in this general period. And it is by no means impossible that Donald MacDonald, Angus's father, got into money troubles of his own.[3]

The MacDonalds, it needs to be re-emphasised, were of tacksman stock. They were not at all the sort of people who were cleared from Glenstrathfarrar in 1803 or from the Strath of Kildonan in 1813. Almost all such victims of eviction were descended from the commons of the clans. They were folk of few possessions and − whether in relation to the kinship-orientated society of former centuries or in relation to the money-based society which took the older order's place − of very lowly social status. Angus McDonald, Archibald McDonald and all their numerous relatives, in contrast, were of comparatively high standing. When Archibald noted carefully that he was 'Gillespie, Moach Aonish, Ic Iain, Ic Alan Dhu, Glenocoan', or when Angus told Marshall William Wheeler that he was 'of the clans of Glengarry and Glencoe', these McDonalds were, and knew themselves to be, staking their claim to a prestigious ancestry. This ancestry, with all its manifold connotations of distinction, meant that, even when clans and clanship had ceased to count for very much, men of Archibald's or Angus's sort made every effort to adjust to change in ways that enabled them to retain something of their families' former eminence. Thus tacksmen and their sons became army officers, entered the professions, took to landholding in overseas colonies or, as appears to have happened in the case of the Inverigan MacDonalds, attempted to join the ranks of those sheep farmers who, at the start of the nineteenth century, were taking over the Highlands in much the same exploitative spirit as gold-miners, lumbermen and cattle ranchers were later to take over the American West.

Angus McDonald's parents almost certainly began by thinking of themselves as belonging to this socially elevated group. And for a period at least, they must have actually done quite well financially. This follows from the youthful Angus having clearly received an education of a sort that was then most unlikely to be obtained by anyone whose parents were not at least modestly affluent. The Mission Valley rancher's writings, though sometimes overly ornate for modern tastes, are replete with classical and other allusions of a kind which testify to their author having had much more than a rudimentary schooling. Angus McDonald, it thus seems probable, was being prepared for a professional career in Scotland. So why, in the early summer of 1838, when 21 years old, did Angus suddenly turn his back on such a career by joining the Hudson's Bay Company and taking himself off to North America? Why, in particular, was he so anxious to get away as to have entered the Bay Company's service at a much lower level than was normal for someone of his background and attainments?

Angus McDonald joined the Hudson's Bay Company, in June 1838, as a 'general servant'. In an organisation which made something of a fetish of grading its employees, this was one of the more subordinate ranks. Its holders were, in effect, manual labourers, and their earnings – £25 a year in Angus's case – were no more than about a third of what the company paid the so-called 'clerks' who were its junior administrators. The latter were typically young men whose families were of some slight social standing and who had received a reasonable education. Angus, then, was very much a potential clerk. Indeed he was eventually to become one. But he was prepared in 1838 to join the Hudson's Bay Company as a general servant and to sign a contract stipulating that he would remain in this comparatively menial position for at least five years. Why?[4]

On the Flathead Reservation there is a persistent family tradition that the explanation for Angus's apparently precipitate departure from Scotland is to be found in his having broken the law. Angus's grandson, Charlie McDonald, who died in 1995 at the age of 97 and whose father, Joe McDonald, would have had the story from Angus himself, was firmly of the view that Angus 'got into some little kinda mix-up back in Scotland' – the 'mix-up', in Charlie's recollection of what he heard in his own youth, having had to do with Angus's killing of a red deer stag on 'some hunting outfit's place'.[5]

Unless one had the permission of the landlord on whose property the stag in question chanced to be, it was certainly illegal to shoot such an animal in nineteenth-century Scotland. But if Angus's parents felt themselves to be in some disgrace in the later 1830s, that may have had as much to do with their reduced circumstances as with any crime which Angus had committed. Nothing of this, admittedly, can be proved. In Margaret McDonald's 1845 letter to her brother, however, there are several possible pointers to the McDonald family having fallen on hard times. Margaret writes, for instance, of a close female relative who appears to have taken a job as domestic servant – not at all the sort of post which anyone in anything like half-reasonable circumstances would have been likely to accept. Equally suggestive is the awkwardness, even embarrassment, which is apparent in the way Margaret deals with the arrangements she has made to secure the various garments – some of them, incidentally, to be made from 'Glengarry tartan' – which Angus has apparently requested. 'Most gentlemen,' Margaret observes, 'get their clothes made in Edinburgh'. But presumably because this was much the cheaper option, she has entrusted the making of Angus's 'clothes' to a Dingwall tailor who 'is not his own master very often' – who is, in other words, a drunkard. 'It will be a great concern on my mind,' Margaret adds of the garments in question, 'till I hear from you how you shall be pleased with them.' Paying the tailor will also be far from easy, it seems. 'The suit costs £3,' Margaret writes anxiously. As for the accompanying shoes, which she hopes 'may be to your liking', they 'cost 18 shillings'.[6]

Margaret McDonald's circumstances were not to improve greatly in the years ahead. The United Kingdom census returns of 1881 describe her as a widow of 60 years of age, residing at 5 Lorne Place, Dingwall, and earning what must have been a very meagre living by letting out rooms to two male lodgers. 'Please accept my best thanks for your kindness to me,' Margaret writes to her brother at his Mission Valley home in 1884. The kindness in question very probably involved cash. Some small proportion of the profits made by Angus McDonald from his cattle-rearing and other activities, it thus seems likely, found its way to the sister whom Angus, by the mid-1880s, had not seen for nearly half a century.[7]

❦

If Angus's family were indeed slipping into relative poverty at around the time of his leaving Scotland, their predicament, though obviously distressing to them, was as nothing when compared with the desperate hardships then being suffered by the many Highlanders who would have given a great deal to lay hands on the £3 (about £150 or $240 at today's prices) which Margaret McDonald spent on her brother's suit. Something of the all-pervading grimness of the time emerges from a story carried by a Highland newspaper not long before Angus McDonald's departure for North America. Highlighting the fact that incessant rain had made it impossible for the population of a west coast island to harvest the peat, or turf, on which all such localities depended traditionally for domestic fuel, the paper commented: 'In this extremity the poor people have lately in some places been driven to consume their . . . huts and cottages for fire. They meet and draw lots whose house is to be taken down . . . and afterwards, in the same manner, determine which of their number is to maintain the poor family deprived of their home.'[8]

The crofts to which the mass of Highlanders had been driven as a result of earlier clearances had long since proved incapable of providing adequately for their occupants. Crofting families survived, if they survived at all, on a diet consisting largely of potatoes. When that crop failed – as it did regularly and as it was soon to do quite catastrophically – hunger became endemic. Landlords, practically none of whom now felt any very pressing responsibility for the Highland people's fate, mostly responded to this steadily unfolding disaster by organising still more evictions in order to create still more sheep farms. People thus deprived of their crofts were left with little alternative but to go elsewhere. Hundreds, even thousands, of evicted families consequently left each year for Canada and the United States – generally settling, because they could afford nothing better, for passages in the congested, stinking, disease-ridden holds of the run-down cargo vessels which carried North American timber to Europe and which, had the emigrant traffic not been available, would have had to make the return voyage in ballast. 'We had not been at sea one week,' an American sailor reported of one such emigrant ship, 'when to hold your head down the hatchway was like holding it down a suddenly opened cesspool.'[9]

Emigrant ships, being little more than hulks to begin with, went to the bottom of the ocean by the score. The Hudson's Bay Company, in contrast, lost only three of its many craft in the whole of the nineteenth century. This, it should be said, did not denote a marked concern for its workforce's safety on the part of what was a notoriously grasping and cheese-paring corporation. It resulted rather from the fact that the Bay Company's fleet was designed to carry North American furs from Hudson Bay to London. Since furs were extremely valuable and had to be kept dry if they were to fetch good prices, it followed that the typical Bay Company vessel was infinitely more seaworthy than those rickety ships which had 'come down', in the jargon of the time, to the altogether less lucrative trades in timber and in emigrants.

Angus McDonald, on heading north in June 1838 to Orkney where he joined the Bay Company ship *Prince Rupert* that was to take him across the Atlantic, did not have to worry greatly, then, about the possibility of shipwreck. Being only 21 and at the start of a new life, the probability is that Angus – on leaving Scotland, as it turned out, forever – was more exhilarated than anxious. The standard twelve-week voyage to Hudson Bay from the Orkney port of Stromness – where Bay-bound ships traditionally took on water, stores and new recruits – was not without its hazards, of course. Archibald McDonald and his Kildonan charges had discovered as much in 1813. But any such voyage – especially from the perspective of anyone who, like Angus, was venturing into Arctic waters for the first time – tended also to involve excitements of the sort arising from each Bay Company convoy having to thread its way through the ice-filled Hudson Strait which separates Labrador from Baffin Island.[10]

'In our passage through the strait,' one enthralled traveller wrote some years previous to Angus McDonald getting there, 'our progress was impeded by vast fields of ice and icebergs . . . The scene was truly grand and impressive . . . There is a solemn and overwhelming sensation produced in the mind by these enormous masses of snow and ice, not to be conveyed in words. They floated by us from one to two hundred feet above the water . . . resembling huge mountains, with deep valleys between lofty clifts, passing in silent grandeur, except at intervals when . . . the crashing of the ice struck the ear like distant thunder.'[11]

Angus McDonald and the other thirty or so passengers aboard the *Prince Rupert*, which had left Stromness on 23 June, glimpsed their first icebergs on 21 July. Just over a week later, with the *Prince Rupert* now well into Hudson Strait and painstakingly negotiating heavy pack-ice, Angus saw his first Native Americans – 'numbers of Esquimaux', or Inuit, having come alongside the *Prince Rupert* in their kayaks. But these were the highpoints of a voyage which was to be rendered increasingly tedious by the sheer density of that summer's ice – the *Prince Rupert*, at one stage, making little or no headway for a whole fortnight.[12]

Hudson Bay itself, when finally reached towards the end of August, must have been a welcome sight to men who had been cooped up together in their cramped shipboard quarters for the better part of two months. But if the prospect of getting ashore was a cheering one, there was little that was immediately enticing about Hudson Bay's surroundings. 'We beheld the low and uninteresting shore of Hudson Bay stretching before us,' one of the Bay Company's many Highland recruits recalled of his earliest glimpse of this cold, grey and almost landlocked sea, 'presenting its narrow border of yellow sand and dark blue swamp in the front, with its dark and dismal-looking line of tamarack in the background. The scenery appeared bleak and desolate beyond the power of description.'[13]

Here, because of the way the bay gave relatively ready access to some of the world's main fur-producing regions, the Hudson's Bay Company had long maintained its principal base and trading centre. York Factory this base was called, its name deriving from James, Duke of York, who, in 1683, was appointed the company's second governor and who, on his becoming king a few years afterwards, so mismanaged matters as to rapidly become one of those exiled Stuart monarchs on whose behalf the MacDonalds of Glencoe were to fight so many battles. James, it goes without saying, never set eyes on Hudson Bay. And plenty Bay Company men were fervently to wish that they had never seen it either. 'A monstrous blot on a swampy spot with a partial view of the frozen sea,' one of the company's more disenchanted employees called this set of barrack-like accommodation blocks, stores and warehouses. 'The head of my bed-place,' another York Factory resident wrote of a Hudson Bay winter, 'went against one of the outside walls of the house; and notwithstanding they were of stone, near three feet thick, and lined with inch boards, supported at least three inches from the walls, my bedding was frozen to the boards every morning; and, before the end of February, these boards were covered with ice almost half as thick as themselves. Towards the latter end of January, when the cold was very intense, I carried a half-pint of brandy, perfectly fluid, into the open air, and in less than two minutes it was as thick as treacle; in about five it had a very strong ice on the top; and I verily believe that in an hour's time it would have been nearly solid.'[14]

The early months of 1838, as luck would have it, had brought exceptionally severe weather to Scotland. Lochs had frozen over and the Highlands had been paralysed by blizzards. But nothing that Angus McDonald had ever experienced at home, whether in 1838 or at any other time, could have prepared him for Hudson Bay. It must have been with some relief, therefore, that Angus heard, in due course, that his stay here was to last through just a single winter. As soon as the 1839 spring thaw made river travel possible, he learned at York Factory, he was to head west, cross the Rocky Mountains and join his McDonald great-uncle, Archibald, at Fort Colville in the Columbia country.[15]

Angus McDonald's long journey from York Factory to Fort Colville began with an ascent of the rivers which connect Hudson Bay with the northern tip of Lake Winnipeg. This was the route taken by Archibald and the Kildonan people some 25 years earlier. But Angus, though one account of his transcontinental trip has him visiting that predominantly Highland settlement in the summer of 1839, was not bound for Red River. His itinerary took him instead up the North Saskatchewan River to Fort Edmonton and on across the Rockies to the upper reaches of the Columbia. During one or other of his many later wanderings in this 'labyrinth of mountains, forests, lakes and rivers', as another nineteenth-century traveller described the scenically spectacular region which the fur trade's latest recruit now saw for the first time, Angus would take the trouble to seek out the spot where, as he put it in a letter to a friend, the Columbia 'starts from its mother earth not bigger than your lady's nipple'. But there were to be no such diversions on this occasion. The birchbark canoes in which Angus and his companions ascended the North Saskatchewan had been hastily exchanged for horses prior to their party commencing its assault on the Rocky Mountains and on the Continental Divide. With navigable water – this time flowing towards the Pacific rather than towards Hudson Bay – again available, the horses, in their turn, were quickly set aside in favour of the locally built boats which the Bay Company always used on the Columbia River.[16]

Columbia River boats, as Angus noted, were constructed at Fort Colville from 'native yellow pine'. Although far larger and roomier than the canoes on which the Hudson's Bay Company relied on the eastern side of the Rockies, they were also much heavier and less manoeuvrable. This defect was offset to some extent by the Bay Company's Columbia boats being crewed, like its canoes, by some of the most skilled rivermen on earth. Called *voyageurs* in the French which they invariably spoke, and justly renowned both for their strength and for their stamina, these men had been central to the North American fur trade ever since Quebec's French settlers had begun to develop this particular branch of commerce at about the time that the Glencoe MacDonalds were following the Marquis of Montrose to war.[17]

Some voyageurs were of Québecois ancestry. Others were the mixed-blood products of a 200-year-old trade which depended as much on Indians as on whites and whose pioneer practitioners, had they lived to hear of such fatuities, would have scorned the attempts made in the late-nineteenth-century United States to ban sexual contact between different races. What counted among voyageurs was a man's prowess with a paddle, not his parentage. And when, as Angus afterwards recalled, his party 'came within an inch of being lost' in the course of their 1839 descent of the Columbia River, it certainly never occurred to the whites involved to cast any kind of racist aspersions in the direction of the mixed-blood voyageur in charge. 'Big Michel was our steersman,' Angus wrote of this man, 'a splendid, chestnut-haired, half Cree and Norman-French Canadian'.[18]

Michel's undoing, according to Angus, was the tricky problem posed to any such river navigator by a set of 'dangerous whirlpools whose huge serpentine throats were darkened . . . by grand overhanging forests and perpendicular cliffs'. Michel's task was to run these rapids in a boat containing three fur-trade wives as well as Angus McDonald, several other Bay Company employees, the boat's crew and a substantial cargo. 'Everything was prepared,' Angus commented. 'Michel wound a twisted silk kerchief round his head to keep his sweeping coils of hair from blinding him and, grasping his reserve paddle, eight feet long and fourteen inches breadth of blade, turned our little Columbian craft into the current of her native river, telling the men calmly, yet sternly, to row strong, "Ramez fort!"'

Because of their role in an earlier catastrophe, these particular Columbia 'whirlpools', as Angus called them, were known to Bay Company voyageurs as Rapides des Morts, the rapids of the dead. And as Michel steered towards their broken, tumbling waters, the roar of the rapidly accelerating river was itself sufficient, Angus writes, to unnerve several of his travelling companions. 'The sound of the messenger of death in those whirlpools . . . made the party feel that a minute more would tell their fate.'

What happened next was terrifying. 'The crew gave one quick . . . look ahead. Michel cried, "Hurrah my men, row strong!"' Then, 'plunging and glancing like a pursuing eagle down the headlong leap, we landed right in the throat of death's whirlpool and the boat filled and became helpless.'

Utterly unnerved by the imminence of drowning, the Bay Company man whose task it was to bale water from the vessel in any such emergency – and who, in Angus's recollection, was a Scot like himself – 'sat forgetting his duty and prayed and wept in the bottom of the boat'.

Others seemed every bit as helpless. 'The women screamed . . . The crew held their oars and seats, silent and passive as death. Michel looked . . . too much like marble to think he was a thing that breathed. He seemed transfixed as hewn granite.'

Angus himself, being 'young and active', as he writes, 'thought of a large kettle and seized it and poured, in a short number of seconds, a large weight of water out of the boat . . . I cried, "Michel!" He looked at me as if a thrill of lightning passed through his brain and he said again, with renewed confidence, "Row strong!"'

Soon the voyageur had extricated his craft from the swirling eddy which had threatened to drag boat, crew, passengers and cargo to the bottom of the Columbia. 'Every sinew found then . . . its use and she was rowed . . . to the beach.' There Angus was overtaken by the trauma which often follows such a crisis. 'Until this I felt no fear, but now while walking on the beach, I felt . . . a certain rising spasm as if choking me. I never felt it before. I drank a good draught of . . . water and, walking away, my nervous spasm was laid.'

❖

From the mountain-enclosed town of Trail, in present-day British Columbia, a modern highway runs parallel with the course of the

Columbia River as it crosses the U.S.-Canada border into Washington State. Sometimes this highway, on the Columbia's eastern bank, climbs well above the river valley floor. Then it is possible to look down on the Columbia's wide waters as they sweep towards the still-distant Pacific, and imagine how Hudson's Bay Company boats of the sort described by Angus McDonald would have looked as – laden with cargo and with passengers – they rounded one or other of the river's successive bends.

Not far downstream, near the point where the Kettle River joins the Columbia, is the site of Kettle Falls, submerged since the 1940s by the hundred-mile-long Franklin D. Roosevelt Lake resulting from the construction of the massive Coulee Dam, but once the most impressive feature of their type on the entire length of the Columbia. These falls, Angus McDonald noted, were 'the only ones' on the Columbia River 'never run' by the voyageurs of the Hudson's Bay Company. And if the Bay Company's voyageurs 'never ran' Kettle Falls, Angus added, 'it is certain that others did not try it'.[19]

Nearby, when Angus got here 'in the fall of 1839', stood Fort Colville which the Bay Company had established some fourteen years earlier and where Archibald McDonald – after stints at Kamloops and Fort Langley in present-day British Columbia – had been in charge since 1833. Like the now-silenced Kettle Falls, whose din was such a constant backdrop to the lives of the Bay men who were based here, the fort – its name appropriated nowadays by the town of Colville, several miles to the south-east – has vanished beneath the waters backing up behind the Coulee Dam. During the thirty or forty years following its establishment, however, this Hudson's Bay Company post – 'the prettiest spot . . . on the Columbia River', a visiting U.S. army officer called it in 1853 – was the key to much of the Columbia country's economic life.[20]

In order to provide Fort Colville with its own supplies of food, Archibald McDonald and his predecessors had brought some 200 acres of land into cultivation. To anyone reaching the post by way of the Rockies, it thus had something of the character of an oasis – there then being no worthwhile farming activity anywhere else in the thousand-mile-wide tract of territory separating the Columbia from the Mississippi. 'Colville broke upon our view like a city under a hill,' an American missionary wrote to his wife when he reached the fort at the end of a transcontinental journey in September 1838. 'After being so long without seeing anything that indicated the hand of industry, to . . . see fields well-fenced, large stacks of all kinds of grain, cattle and hogs in large droves in a country so far removed from the civilised world was a feast to my eyes . . . Mr McDonald raises great crops . . . He is well provided with farming tools, carts and sleds, a sleigh and a gig.'[21]

Fort Colville itself, the same missionary reported, was 'twice as large' as any similar establishment he had seen since crossing the Continental Divide. 'It is built of timber set up on end. In and about the fort are quite a number of dwelling houses, also three or four large stables and store houses for grain.'

Angus McDonald, who arrived here twelve months after these words were written, was equally taken both by Fort Colville and by its surroundings – the Columbia country being a veritable Garden of Eden when compared with the bleak Arctic landscapes which had served as Angus's introduction to North America. There are grounds for suspecting, however, that Angus was rather less enamoured of Fort Colville's *bourgeois* – the term applied by voyageurs and other Bay Company staff to anyone occupying a position of the sort held at Colville by Archibald McDonald. Being subordinate to a member of one's own family is never easy, of course. But that, in itself, was perfectly normal in the Hudson's Bay Company of the 1830s. 'Youngsters had been following fathers and uncles into the company for five or more generations,' a Canadian historian has observed. And the individuals involved in such arrangements seem, for the most part, to have got on reasonably well together. In the particular case of Angus and Archibald, however, the evidence suggests that there was more of animosity than of affection in their relationship.[22]

Thus the stories which Duncan McDonald, Angus's son, remembered hearing about his great-great-uncle – whom Duncan never met – were by no means flattering to the Fort Colville bourgeois. 'This gentleman was noted . . . for his Scotch thrift,' Duncan said of Archibald. So stingy was Archibald, Duncan went on, that he refused even to allow those Indians who lived around Colville 'to dig up or pick up' the few stray potatoes which remained in the fort's potato fields after the crop had been harvested each fall. Although the Indians in question were 'nearly starving', according to Duncan, Archibald insisted on 'the waste' being reserved 'for his hogs' – and was defeated on this point only by one Indian woman who, on seeing Archibald bearing down menacingly on the muddy field where she was searching for potatoes, 'nonchalantly tucked up her skirts, turned her back on him and kept on digging'.[23]

Although the Fort Colville bourgeois refrained from having this woman removed bodily from the Bay Company's property, and although there were plenty of fur traders who treated Indians much more harshly than he ever did, Archibald McDonald emerges from that anecdote as just a little bit too conscious of his own importance. Archibald's one surviving letter to Angus gives a very similar impression

of its writer's character. This letter dates from 1852. Archibald, who
had left Colville in 1844 and who had afterwards retired to Glengarry
County, was apparently responding to letters which Angus had sent him
some months previously – letters in which Angus evidently asked for
Archibald's help in discovering the whereabouts of one of his, Angus's,
brothers who is known, from much later correspondence, to have been
named John and to have emigrated at about this point to the United
States.[24]

'Respecting your brother,' Archibald McDonald writes to Angus,
'from the . . . description you give of his destination in the United
States, 'tis impossible for me to trace him out.' Angus's ignorance as
to John McDonald's whereabouts, of course, is a further pointer to his
family, back in Scotland, being in some disarray. And it may be that
Archibald simply resented his being drawn, however indirectly, into his
Scottish relatives' growing difficulties. But Archibald, one feels, could
have been slightly less curt in the circumstances – just as he could have
been warmer in his reference to Ranald McDonald, his own mixed-
blood son, who is described sarcastically by Archibald as 'the hero of
Japan'. What is most striking about Archibald's 1852 letter, however,
is the extraordinarily patronising tone which it adopts towards the
letter's recipient. 'I am pleased to hear that you are . . . well and
usefully employed,' Archibald tells Angus. 'When this is the case, one
seldom fails meeting with suitable reward.'

This was written when Angus, then fourteen years in the fur trade,
had risen to a comparatively high level in the Hudson's Bay Company.
So how would Archibald have treated Angus when the latter first got
to Fort Colville as a general servant on an annual salary of just £25?
With a good deal of arrogance and pomposity, one suspects. It may be,
therefore, that Angus – one of whose surviving letters is extremely
scathing about Archibald – was as glad to hear in the spring of 1840
that he was to leave for Fort Hall in the Snake country as he had been
to learn, twelve months earlier, that he was to be posted from York
Factory to Colville.[25]

❈

Fort Hall, in the south-eastern corner of present-day Idaho, was more
than 600 miles from Fort Colville. And to make that journey today, by
way of the four-lane highways which connect this region's many modern
towns, is to be constantly reminded of the huge transformations which
have occurred – in the space of just one and a half centuries – as a
result of the white impact on the American West.

The white presence hereabouts in 1840, when Angus McDonald left

Fort Colville for Fort Hall, was both extremely limited and relatively new. It consisted almost entirely of fur traders like Angus himself. It had so consisted since such traders first began to move across the Rocky Mountains not much more than thirty years before.

Most of these traders, to begin with, were associated with the Montreal-based organisation which caused the Hudson's Bay Company so much trouble during the nineteenth century's opening decades. This organisation was the North West Company. It had been founded by, and always remained very much under the control of, a tightly knit and heavily interrelated group of Scottish Highlanders whose background and origins were very similar to Angus's own – something that was neatly symbolised by this Canadian consortium's coat-of-arms featuring, as well as a fur-trade canoe, a galley of the type on which the Lordship of the Isles had once depended militarily.*

There was about the North West Company, then, something of the character of a recreated Highland clan. This is nowhere more evident than in the remarkable extent to which the company's principals owed their positions to their kinship links with the company's leading founder, Simon MacTavish.

MacTavish, whose father was tacksman of Garthbeg in Stratherrick, some 25 miles to the south-west of Inverness, first came to North America in the 1760s when he settled, as did so many other Highland emigrants of that period, in New York's Mohawk Valley. Like most other Mohawk Valley Highlanders, MacTavish chose to remain British at the end of the Revolutionary War, moving into Canada where, during the 1780s and 1790s, he masterminded both the emergence of the North West Company and its fostering of a formidable array of fur-trading talent. Among MacTavish's recruits – very many of whom, as already indicated, were drawn from his own extended family – was William MacGillivray, MacTavish's nephew and a man who, on his taking charge of the North West Company after his uncle's death in 1804, gave a high priority to the company's drive across the Rockies.

Territorial expansionism had been integral to North West Company strategy from the outset. Unlike their Bay Company rivals, who were content for much of the eighteenth century simply to rely on the Cree and other Indian peoples bringing furs from the North American interior to York Factory, the Nor'Westers ventured further and further from their Montreal base. Within remarkably few years, thanks to their growing mastery of Indian technology in the shape of the birchbark canoe and thanks also to their skill in exploiting the communications

---

* For an account of the North West Company, see the same author's book, *A Dance Called America*.

possibilities of the Canadian river system, North West Company traders were to be found everwhere from the Great Lakes to the Athabasca country. Nor was Athabasca, nearly 2,000 miles from Montreal, the limit of these remarkable men's reach. Well before the eighteenth century's end, one of the most enterprising of all Nor'Westers, Alexander MacKenzie, had found his way both to the Arctic Ocean and to the Pacific – the latter of which MacKenzie reached in the summer of 1793.

MacKenzie, the first white man to cross the North American continent from coast to coast, did not make his epic journeys merely to satisfy his geographical curiosity. Although certainly fascinated by exploration for its own sake, MacKenzie was motivated mainly by commercial imperatives. He wanted to turn the North West Company, already a continent-wide concern, into a truly global corporation which, as well as transporting North American furs across the Atlantic and selling them to Europeans, would ship other North American furs across the Pacific to the Chinese – who had previously bought their furs from Russian traders operating out of Siberia but who were known, at this point, to be interested in alternative sources of supply.

Their many other commitments meant that the Nor'Westers – who tended always to be overstretched – were unable immediately to follow up Alexander MacKenzie's push to the Pacific. By 1807, however, they had made up their minds to move across the Rockies in strength. That summer, therefore, a North West Company party, following much the same route as Angus McDonald was to take some thirty years later, made its way over the Continental Divide and came down into the terribly fragmented and fractured hill country which surrounds the upper reaches of the Columbia River.[26]

This party was led by David Thompson. A pious and teetotal Welshman, Thompson, at first sight, seems to have had little in common with the boozy and boisterous Highlanders who dominated the North West Company's upper echelons and who were more than capable – as Alexander MacKenzie and William MacGillivray demonstrated on a famous occasion in Montreal – of drinking themselves senseless. But Thompson was an outstanding surveyor whose talents, in this regard at any rate, were warmly appreciated by his colleagues. What the Nor'Westers needed, if they were fully to exploit Columbia country furs, was some understanding of how they might develop a worthwhile communications system both inside the Columbia country itself and between the Columbia country and the wider world. Thompson, as his North West Company associates evidently appreciated, was very much the man to undertake the necessary explorations. In the end, he spent several years mapping the myriad streams, lakes and watercourses of the Columbia basin. And so meticulous were his charts and plans that they were still being consulted many decades after the Welshman's death.[27]

Thompson's trusted lieutenant and close confidant in the Columbia country was, as it happened, Angus McDonald's Knoydart-born kinsman, Finan McDonald — that 'bough of the same tree as my own', in Angus's words. 'He belonged to a highly respectable family which emigrated . . . to Canada while he was a lad,' one of Finan's Columbia country colleagues observed of him. Much the same was true, of course, of most of the many other Highlanders in the North West Company's service. But none of these Highlanders was physically so memorable as Finan McDonald. 'His appearance was very striking,' Finan's colleague wrote. 'In height he was six feet four inches, with broad shoulders, large bushy whiskers and red hair which, for some years, had not felt the scissors and which, sometimes falling over his face and shoulders, gave to his countenance a wild and uncouth appearance.'[28]

Since one of his more talked-about feats turned on his having wrestled to the ground a buffalo bull which had tried to gore him, Finan's strength was clearly in proportion to his size. And his temper, it seems, was as fiery as his hair — there being more than one report of his having duelled with men who had allegedly insulted him. But for all that his fellow Nor'Westers were inclined to make mock of the 'ludicrous *mélange* of Gaelic, English, French and half-a-dozen Indian dialects' into which Finan tended to lapse when infuriated by some suspected slight, they were entirely appreciative of his undoubted ability — as signalled by his fluency in 'Indian dialects' — to get along with the Columbia country's native peoples. And among these peoples, it appears, Finan's particular favourites were the Flathead, or Salish, bands among whom Angus McDonald was later to live in Mission Valley.[29]

It was in the fall of 1807 that Finan, on David Thompson's instructions, pushed up the Kootenai River, one of the Columbia's many tributaries, into present-day Montana. There, at a spot near the modern town of Libby, Finan established the first fur trading post in Flathead territory. Along with another Highland-born Nor'Wester, James MacMillan, whose boyhood home had been within twelve miles of his own father's farm at Munial, Finan was to spend several years in this general area. And his dealings with the Flathead people, or so one of Finan's contemporaries commented, were by no means strictly commercial: 'McDonald frequently, for the mere love of fighting, accompanied the Flatheads in their war excursions against the Blackfeet. His eminent bravery endeared him to the whole tribe, and in all matters relating to warfare his word was law.'[30]

David Thompson, needless to say, engaged in no such escapades. But he made his own fur-gathering forays – as methodically, no doubt, as he did most things – into the region lying to the south and west of Finan's base on the Kootenai. There Thompson founded the North West Company posts known as Salish House and Kullyspell House – the latter of which, incidentally, was to have its long-forgotten site rediscovered and identified by Duncan McDonald, Angus's son, more than a hundred years later.[31]

Thompson's trading expeditions, however, were merely by way of being a preliminary to the much more momentous journey which began on the morning of 3 July 1811 when he and his voyageur team lowered their canoe into the wide waters of the Columbia River at a spot just below Kettle Falls. Having demonstrated that there were plenty of furs to be obtained in the inland area where he, Finan McDonald and other Nor'Westers had now been trading successfully for the better part of four years, Thompson's remaining task was to bring Alexander MacKenzie's 1793 vision to fruition by showing that such furs could readily be got to China by way of the Pacific. 'We set off on a voyage down the Columbia River,' Thompson duly noted in the summer of 1811, 'to explore this river in order to open out a passage for the interior trade with the Pacific Ocean.'[32]

But David Thompson and his North West Company partners were not the only people attempting to cash in on the financial gains to be got from supplying China with North American furs. John Jacob Astor, a German-born New York City businessman who had been shipping tea, silks and other luxury goods out of the Chinese port of Canton since the 1790s, had also come to the conclusion that there might be substantial profits to be made by anyone who could simultaneously obtain a measure of control over the Columbia country's fur resources and provide a means of transporting the resulting pelts to China. Astor had decided, therefore, to stake his own claim to the Columbia country. The result was that David Thompson, on reaching the mouth of the Columbia River on 15 July 1811, discovered that John Jacob Astor's Pacific Fur Company had beaten his own North West Company to that most critical of destinations. A Pacific Fur Company detachment, having sailed here from New York by way of Cape Horn, had been in possession of the Columbia's estuary since April and were well on their way to completing construction of the fortified post they called Astoria.[33]

Astor's men operated under the jurisdiction of the United States government – which, for all that it did not then exercise sovereignty to the west of the Rockies, was becoming increasingly anxious to extend its national territory right across the American continent. The North

West Company, for its part, traded under the British flag and had long been run by men who were decidedly anti-American in their politics – Simon MacTavish and others of the company's founders having both opposed American independence and done everything in their power to exclude traders who were U.S. nationals from as many as possible of the territories which the North West Company regarded as its own preserve. Several of the Astorians, as Pacific Fur Company men came to be called, were not quite what they seemed, however. 'We were called Americans,' one of them was subsequently to remark to a senior Nor'Wester. 'But there were very few Americans among us. We were all Scotchmen like yourselves.'[34]

This was because Astor, in order to obtain the expertise necessary to launch his fur-trading operation on the Pacific coast, had no alternative but to turn to Highlanders of the sort who then dominated the North American fur trade. Having first tried to persuade the Nor'Westers to enter into a partnership with him and having had his approaches rejected by Simon MacGillivray and his associates in Montreal in 1808, Astor next set about signing up those Nor'Westers – of whom there were invariably some available – who had, for one reason or another, fallen out with their colleagues. Prominent among such recruits to the Pacific Fur Company's ranks was Donald MacKenzie, a cousin of the famous Alexander MacKenzie and a man who had been raised in the vicinity of Dingwall – the part of the Highlands with which the young Angus McDonald was afterwards to be closely acquainted.[35]

MacKenzie, who had left Scotland in 1801 when he was 17 and who was said to weigh more than 300 pounds while still under 30, was a larger-than-life character in every respect. An outstanding marksman who, according to one contemporary, could 'drive a dozen balls consecutively at one hundred paces through a Spanish dollar', the former Nor'Wester was appointed by the Pacific Fur Company's boss to a leading role in the party which, in October 1811, was sent to reinforce Astoria. This group, unlike the one preceding it, travelled overland, taking more than a year to reach its destination and suffering terribly *en route*. 'At this time,' one Astorian was to write of what MacKenzie and his companions had to endure in the course of their crossing of the Rockies, 'a starving dog that could hardly crawl along was a feast to our people, and even the putrid and rotten skins of animals were resorted to in order to sustain life.'[36]

Despite these privations, Donald MacKenzie eventually won through to Astoria where yet another ex-Nor'Wester, Duncan MacDougall, was in overall command. MacDougall was not well liked by his subordinates. 'He was a man of but ordinary capacity, with an irritable, peevish temper,' one of those subordinates wrote. But such subordinates, particularly if they were American, had other, deeper-seated, reasons for their mounting criticisms of their boss. MacDougall, like practically everyone else of importance at Astoria, was – as his name suggests – a Highlander. And there were beginning to be suspicions on the part of the few Americans among Astor's senior employees that to be a Highlander was almost automatically to be less than 100 per cent committed to John Jacob Astor, the Pacific Fur Company and the United States.[37]

Right from the start of the Astoria enterprise, Nor'Wester flamboyance had grated on many American nerves. When Alexander MacKay, on abandoning the North West Company for Astor, took his birchbark canoe down the Hudson River into the heart of New York City and ordered his exotically dressed crew to entertain New Yorkers to a selection of voyageur songs, this characteristic stealing of the limelight did not go down well. Nor did the 'mysterious colloquies in Gaelic' to which MacKay, MacDougall and others were said to resort in order to exclude Astor's Americans from their discussions. And nor, for that matter, did the 'free and cordial reception' which Duncan MacDougall accorded David Thompson on the latter's arrival at Astoria in July 1811.[38]

The misgivings which Astor loyalists thus harboured as to Duncan MacDougall's long-term intentions were shown to be well founded when, in the early part of 1813, news reached the Columbia country that the United States – some months before – had gone to war with Britain. This so-called War of 1812 owed nothing to what was taking place around Astoria. It resulted, in fact, from the British Royal Navy, then engaged in a blockade of Napoleonic France, having insisted on stopping and searching American merchant ships on the high seas. But the outbreak of wider hostilities nevertheless enabled the veteran Nor'Wester, John George MacTavish, a cousin of the company's founder, to turn up at Astoria and announce to Duncan MacDougall – with whom MacTavish had worked closely in the past – that a British warship would shortly be arriving in the Columbia to demand Astoria's surrender. It was at this point, according to a pro-Astor account of these proceedings, that MacDougall's 'old sympathies with the North West Company seem to have revived'. MacDougall himself would afterwards insist: 'I did everything in my power to do the utmost justice to the trust and confidence reposed in me by John Jacob Astor.' But this hardly accords with his decision, in the fall of 1813, to sell Astoria and all its contents to the North West Company which this same Duncan MacDougall not long afterwards rejoined.[39]

By disposing of Astor's challenge to them, the Nor'Westers had made themselves the masters of the Columbia country's fur resources. But Columbia country furs were not as rapidly forthcoming from the region's native peoples as the North West Company would have liked. It was left to Donald MacKenzie – who, following Duncan MacDougall's example, had rejoined the Nor'Westers by whom, in recognition of his phenomenal energy, he was promptly dubbed 'Perpetual Motion' – to solve this problem by organising his own trapping brigades. Those brigades, which remained characteristic of the region's fur trade for as long as it endured, were composed of hard-bitten individuals known to the trade as 'freemen' in order to distinguish them from the North West Company's full-time employees. Engaged by MacKenzie and his successors on short-term contracts, the typical freeman was of mixed-blood or Indian extraction. But he was also as much of an immigrant to the Columbia country as the Highlanders who hired him – being, very often, of Iroquois descent.[40]

The Mohawk and other peoples who made up the Iroquois Confederation – an Indian civilisation which, until it was gradually overwhelmed by the French, the British and the Americans, had controlled a large tract of territory in the vicinity of the Great Lakes – were drawn into the fur trade during the eighteenth century. They had long followed the trade westwards. And now, inevitably, they were being attracted in larger and larger numbers into the Columbia country where they were described by one exasperated fur trader as 'the most unruly and troublesome gang to deal with in this, or perhaps any other, part of the world'.[41]

The North West Company's Columbia country Highlanders, however, could be every bit as rough and ready in their behaviour as any Iroquois. That much is clear from an eyewitness account of how one such Highlander treated the subordinate he had ordered to provide him with what was known in the fur trade as a 'maypole'.

Fur trade maypoles owed nothing to the ribboned posts around which people dance on English village greens. They were, in fact, the means by which the Highlanders of the North West Company – those 'hyperborean nabobs', as one of Astor's propagandists so memorably called them – commemorated their connection with some newly opened-up locality. Having arrived in such a locality and having selected the tallest and most conspicuous pine tree he could find, a Nor'Wester began the making of his maypole by having his name carved prominently on the tree's trunk. Next, by way of ensuring that his name would not be missed by subsequent travellers, the trader sent one of his men up the tree to strip off all its branches – other than those constituting 'a small tuft at the top'.[42]

Everyone involved in the creation of such a landmark was usually rewarded with a generous measure of rum. On the maypole-making occasion in question, therefore, the man ordered up the tree set happily to work. 'But he had no sooner reached the top,' runs the contemporary description of what followed, 'than his master, through love of mischief, lighting a fire at the bottom, set the tree in a blaze. The poor fellow was instantly enveloped in a cloud of smoke and called out for mercy. Water was dashed on the tree, but this only increased the danger by augmenting the smoke, for the fire ran up the bark of the gummy pine like gunpowder and was soon beyond our reach, so that all hope of saving the man's life was at an end. Descending, however, he leaped, in despair, on to a branch of another tree, which fortunately offered him a chance of safety; and there he hung between earth and heaven, like a squirrel on a twig, till another man, at no small risk, got up and rescued him from his perilous situation.'[43]

Such crazy escapades aside, the life of a North West Company man in the Columbia country towards the end of the nineteenth century's second decade was generally peaceable enough. 'Spokane House,' one such Nor'Wester recalled of the trading post in present-day Washington State which became the company's regional headquarters, 'was a retired spot . . . There the bourgeois who presided over the company's affairs resided . . . At Spokane House, too, there were handsome buildings. There was a ballroom, even, and no females in the land were so fair to look upon as the nymphs of Spokane. No damsels could dance so gracefully as they, none more attractive. But Spokane House was not celebrated for fine women only, there were fine horses also. The race-ground was admired, and the pleasures of the chase often yielded to the pleasures of the race. Altogether, Spokane House was a delightful place.'[44]

There was to be a lot less time for horseracing and for dancing with Spokane's Indian women in the 1820s, however. Having finally been outmanoeuvred – politically as well as commercially – by the self-same Hudson's Bay Company they had earlier come so close to destroying, the Nor'Westers were forced, in 1821, to come to terms with the Bay men. The ensuing amalgamation of the two organisations, with the Bay Company very much in the driving seat, brought new management to the Columbia country fur trade in the diminutive shape of George Simpson, who was to dominate Bay Company affairs for the next forty years.

As had been true of the leading men of the North West Company, Simpson was a Highlander. Like Donald MacKenzie and Angus McDonald, in fact, he had close family ties with the Dingwall area. But unlike the Nor'Westers, who tended to be happier when partying than when poring over a set of accounts, Simpson was corporate man personified. Crisscrossing the continent by canoe, accompanied often by the Highland piper who was his one gesture in the direction of anything approaching flamboyance, Simpson ceaselessly demanded that expenditure be curtailed, workforces trimmed, productivity increased. And the Columbia country, for all its remoteness from Simpson's York Factory base, in no way escaped his attentions. 'Everything appears to me in the Columbia on too extended a scale except the trade,' Simpson commented caustically in 1824.[45]

'The good people of Spokane District,' the Bay Company man continued, 'have since its first establishment shewn an extraordinary predilection for European provisions without once looking at, or considering, the enormous price they cost; if they had taken that trouble, they would have had little difficulty in discovering that all this time they may be said to have been eating gold.' The 'five and sometimes six' ships which the Nor'Westers had been in the habit of despatching to the Columbia with 'eatables and drinkables' duly became a fading memory. And with a view to promoting further economies, Spokane House, together with its ballroom and its race-course, was closed down. Henceforth, George Simpson decreed, fur-trading operations in the upper part of the Columbia basin were to be transferred to a new post situated further to the north. This post, named in honour of one of the Bay Company's London-based governors, was to be called Fort Colville. And its location, as Angus McDonald discovered on his arrival there in 1839, was determined very largely by the fact that the countryside in its vicinity had been judged capable of growing the crops needed if the Hudson's Bay Company's staff in the Columbia country were to be made more self-sufficient and, as a result, more cost-effective.[46]

❧

Thanks both to its merger with the North West Company and to George Simpson's ruthless style of management, the Hudson's Bay Company, when Angus McDonald joined the organisation in 1838, was more powerful than it had ever been. From Labrador in the east to the Pacific coast in the west – an area representing one-twelfth of the earth's entire land surface – the Bay Company was king. The British government had just reconfirmed in law the trade monopoly which the Hudson's Bay Company, over the greater part of its domain at any rate, so obviously enjoyed in practice. And from the Columbia country alone in 1840, the year when Angus travelled from Fort Colville to Fort Hall,

Bay men exported no fewer than 40,000 beaver pelts – their company's staple product ever since Europe had discovered that such pelts could be readily worked into a fine felt which, in turn, could be used to provide wealthier Europeans with an especially sophisticated, and expensive, line in hats.[47]

Prominent among the former Nor'Westers who helped consolidate the Bay Company's position to the west of the Rockies was Angus's kinsman, Finan McDonald, who, during the 1820s, had co-operated closely with another ex-Nor'Wester, Peter Skene Ogden, in the formation of the trapping force which became known as the Snake Country Brigade. Consisting of some seventy or eighty freemen, operating initially out of posts in present-day western Montana and moving south by way of the route which the Nez Perce were to follow through the Bitterroot Valley in 1877, the brigade's task was to extend the beaver-trapping frontier into the region where Fort Hall was to be built in 1834.[48]

Trapping the Snake country proved no easy task. Peter Skene Ogden complained of having been reduced to 'skin and bones' by the experience. 'A convict at Botany Bay is a gentleman at ease compared to my trappers,' he added. And Finan McDonald was of much the same opinion. 'I got safe home from the Snake cuntre,' Finan wrote once in the English in which this originally Gaelic-speaking Highlander was never fully literate, 'and when that cuntre will see me again the beaver will have gould skin.'[49]

Adding substantially to the Bay men's difficulties in the Snake country was the extent to which they there encountered competition from the first American fur traders to operate on the Pacific Slope, as the area on the western side of the Rocky Mountains was then known, since the North West Company's 1813 rout of the Astorians.

These traders were so-called 'mountain men'. Very much in the buccaneering tradition of Daniel Boone and the other free spirits who, towards the close of the eighteenth century, had crossed the Appalachians in order to open up to whites the then frontier territories of Kentucky and Tennessee, most mountain men owed very little allegiance to any large-scale organisation of the Hudson's Bay Company type. Although they tended to move across country in groups very similar in their size and composition to the Bay Company's Snake Country Brigade, and although they sometimes acknowledged the temporary supremacy of a 'bushway' or bourgeois, most mountain men operated largely on their own account. This does not mean that the mountain man was always the heroic figure which Western legend has retrospectively made of him. But his chosen lifestyle – which involved him in hunting animals for food, battling intermittently with Indians, dressing his own wounds and generally going his own way – was nothing if not totally self-reliant.[50]

'When once in pursuit of the beaver,' one nineteenth-century writer noted of such a trapper, 'he was involved in extreme privations and perils. Hand and foot, eye and ear, must be always alert. Frequently he must content himself with devouring his evening meal uncooked, lest the light of his fire should attract the eye of some wandering Indian; and sometimes, having made his crude repast, he must leave his fire still blazing, and withdraw to a distance under cover of darkness, that his disappointed enemy, drawn thither by the light, may find his victim gone . . . This is the life led by scores of men among the Rocky Mountains. I once met a trapper whose breast was marked with the scars of six bullets and arrows, one of his arms broken by a shot and one of his knees shattered; yet still . . . he continued to follow his perilous calling.'[51]

The mountain men's lifestyle, then, was not one that nurtured the gentler virtues. 'Constantly exposed to perils of all kinds,' as another contemporary commented, 'they become callous to any feeling of danger, and destroy human as well as animal life with as little scruple as they expose their own.'[52]

Angus McDonald, however, made no such judgements. He was just 23 years old and only two years out of Scotland when, in the summer of 1840, he reached Fort Hall – then visited regularly by a number of mountain men. And to Angus, one suspects, there must have been much that was appealing, indeed fascinating, about those Rocky Mountain hunters who, even at first glance, looked so very different from more ordinary folk.

'The costume of the trapper,' according to one carefully observed account of men whose dress was one more statement of their insistent individuality, 'is a hunting shirt of dressed buckskin, ornamented with long fringes; pantaloons of the same material, and decorated with porcupine quills and long fringes down the outside of the leg. A flexible felt hat and moccasins clothe the extremities. Over his left shoulder and under his right arm hang his powder-horn and bullet pouch . . . Round the waist is a belt in which is stuck a large butcher-knife in a sheath of buffalo hide, made fast to the belt by a chain or guard of steel; which also supports a little buckskin case containing a whetstone. A tomahawk is often added; and, of course, a long, heavy rifle is part and parcel of his equipment.'[53]

Among the mountain men with whom Angus McDonald became friendly at Fort Hall was the redoubtable Joe Meek – one of whose claims to fame involved his having fought a hand-to-hand fight with a grizzly bear in much the same way as Finan McDonald had wrestled with a buffalo. Although he had abandoned the American east for the frontier when still a teenager, Meek, who was six years Angus's senior, claimed to belong to 'one of the first famaleys of Virginia'. And despite his always erratic spelling, he shared Angus McDonald's life-long interest in Shakespeare and in English literature generally.[54]

But it was not so much Angus's knowledge of the classics as his skill in handling a gun which drew the newly arrived Highlander to the mountain man's attention. 'I remember my first acquaintance with him at Fort Hall in 1841,' Angus wrote of his meeting with Joe Meek. 'A party of the mountain boys were gathered to try their skill at a mark,' and he, it appears, was invited to join in firing at the small and distant target which Meek and his associates had set up in the Fort Hall grounds. When his turn came, Angus recalled with understandable pride, he put 'four successive shots' into the target. 'Whereupon Meek turned round to his friends, in a smiling . . . way, and said, "Boys, you may go to your lodges now. There is no more work for you here!"'[55]

❁

'I remember he and I having a hard, short wrestle,' Angus McDonald recalled of another of his early encounters with Joe Meek. And for all that Meek was 'much heavier', Angus insisted, 'none of us fell nor tripped'. But with others of the mountain men – many of whom had long since concluded that the Snake country was their preserve every bit as much as, if not rather more than, it was the preserve of the Hudson's Bay Company – Angus's dealings were a lot less amicable. 'In two instances,' a senior Bay man reported in 1845, 'Mr McDonald has perilled his life in support of the company's rights in squabbles with some of the Rocky Mountain men.' That was why Angus, as this Bay Company representative made clear, was about to be promoted – his promotion resulting from his evident determination to 'support the rights of his employers'.[56]

The Bay man responsible for Angus McDonald's advancement was John McLoughlin, then in charge of all company affairs in Oregon, as the Columbia country was now beginning to be called. And the promotion which was thus arranged must have been a matter of some considerable consequence to Angus who now became one of the Bay Company's clerks. 'I consider I was not only doing an act of justice to the man,' John McLoughlin commented of his decision to boost his Fort Hall subordinate's prospects, 'but promoting the company's interests by letting him see that his services were appreciated . . . What energy would that man have to exert himself if he saw people in the same line of business, [but] opposed to him, getting eight hundred, one thousand and some twelve hundred dollars per annum when he was at £30, £40 and £50? It is men who have not only . . . will but . . . physical strength . . . that are required in such cases, and besides McDonald is fully qualified as to education to act as a clerk.'[57]

Angus, then, was henceforth to have an annual salary of £100 – four times the figure on which he had started some seven years before. This meant that the Bay Company's newest clerk, as was McLoughlin's evident intention, had an income which – allowing for nineteenth-century exchange rates between the pound sterling and the American dollar – was at least in the same general area as the earnings available to freelance mountain men of the type thought by McLoughlin to be grossing $1,000 or more at the end of each fur-trading season.

'The trade in furs was quite large,' Angus subsequently recalled of his seven-year stint at Fort Hall. And it was one of his responsibilities – between 1842 and 1846 at any rate – to help convey these furs to Fort Vancouver which, since 1825, had been the Bay Company's main centre of operations in Oregon. Located on the north bank of the Columbia River, about 100 miles inland from the Pacific, Fort Vancouver was John McLoughlin's headquarters. And there this prematurely white-haired giant of a man presided over as heterogeneous a collection of human beings as could have been encountered then anywhere on earth. Representatives of a whole host of Indian peoples rubbed shoulders with Kanakas from the Sandwich Islands, with English sailors, Irish artisans, American missionaries and, of course, the many Highlanders whose influence on the Hudson's Bay Company was such as to have led one irritated trader of English extraction to complain about the Bay Company being run increasingly by 'a parcel of upstart Scotchmen'.[58]

Fort Vancouver, when Angus McDonald first came here in the early 1840s, was as close as the Oregon of that time got to having a town. As well as scores of timber-built homes, it contained jetties, a shipyard, warehouses, tradesmen's workshops, a sawmill, a gristmill and a dairy – the latter two establishments being intended to handle the growing volume of produce from the farms which the Bay Company was developing nearby. Fort Vancouver, then, comprised what one Bay man called a 'vast amount of valuable property'. And the fact that Angus, in September 1844, played a key role in preventing Fort Vancouver's destruction by fire may well have had something to do with the high regard in which he was clearly held by John McLoughlin.[59]

On 24 September, runs the relevant report to the Bay Company's

London governors by James Douglas, one of the company's senior men at Fort Vancouver, 'a dense cloud of smoke, indicating the existence of an extensive fire, was observed rising from the banks of the [Columbia] River at some distance to the eastward, in the direction of the sawmill'. Since the day was one of 'parching easterly gales', and since fields, forests and buildings were all tinder dry, a fire of any magnitude, as James Douglas wrote, posed a 'dreadful and imminent danger'. Douglas consequently 'rode out . . . in company with Mr Angus McDonald who had just arrived from the Snake country . . . in order to take such precautions as might be necessary for our premises.'[60]

The inferno which James Douglas and Angus McDonald now discovered was to rage for three full days. And something at least of its ferocity can be glimpsed in Douglas's description of how the blaze, obliterating such agricultural buildings as were in its way, approached eventually to within yards of Fort Vancouver's perimeter stockades: 'The conflagration . . . burst . . . with tremendous fury, devouring, in its course, every speck of vegetation, whether dry or green. Clouds of ashes and burning leaves, falling at an incredible distance, were scattering desolation and scattering destruction to every object around. The barn was, in consequence, almost instantly wrapped in flames, the clover field caught fire, the fence burned fiercely, the orchard was in a blaze, and, for upwards of an hour, the [entire] establishment was menaced with apparently inevitable destruction. The barn was now left to its fate and our whole attention directed to the protection of the fort. The struggle with the fearful element became terrific; everyone present toiled as if life and death depended upon the issue of the contest; and after immense exertion we prevailed in arresting its approach towards the fort within three hundred feet of the stockades.'

Angus McDonald and one or two of his colleagues were primarily responsible for catastrophe having been averted, according to James Douglas. 'Though nearly suffocated by the heat and smoke', it seems, they remained 'manfully at their posts, extinguishing the burning embers as they fell, and protecting every part of the premises at the hazard of their lives'.

Back at Fort Hall, too, there was plenty to keep Angus occupied. This Snake country outpost – which the Hudson's Bay Company had bought in 1836 from the American trader who had built it two years earlier – was located on the southern bank of the Snake River at a point due north of the Great Salt Lake and some 70 miles from the present-day border between Idaho and Utah. The fort's whitewashed buildings – which one approaching traveller described as 'gleaming in the sun' – were demolished and dismantled long ago, and even its site has now been flooded by a reservoir. But Fort Hall, in Angus's recollection of the post, was 'a four-sided establishment', built of adobe, or sun-dried mud, and with 'a large, strong horse park on the north side of it'. There were generally some 200 to 250 horses on hand at Fort Hall, Angus reckoned. And it was a measure of the general lawlessness of the time that 'the horses,' as Angus put it, 'were always attended with a horse guard of one man, who sometimes had another with him, who stayed with them day and night'.[61]

Fort Hall's horses were much needed by Angus and the other Bay men who were stationed at what was rapidly becoming, for all its apparent remoteness, a leading Western landmark and communications centre. From Fort Hall, Angus remembered, trapping parties were sent for hundreds, even thousands, of miles north, east and south: in the direction of the Flathead country; towards the upper reaches of the Missouri in present-day North and South Dakota; down the Green River and the Colorado River into present-day Utah and Arizona.[62]

Fort Hall, then, was something of a rendezvous point for all kinds and varieties of people. It was while Angus McDonald was one of the post's staff, for instance, that emigrant parties in their covered wagons began to treat Fort Hall as a useful staging post on what would soon be known as the Oregon Trail. Mountain men like Joe Meek – still calling the Bay Company 'the North West' in unconscious tribute to the Nor'Westers of twenty or more years before – came regularly to Fort Hall to buy the few pieces of equipment they could not make themselves. And Indians, as Angus commented in his occasionally old-fashioned English, 'did often stay there' – the Snake country being one of the favoured hunting grounds of the Nez Perce.[63]

Among these Indians was the woman Angus McDonald married in 1842 at a civil ceremony performed by the Fort Hall bourgeois, Richard Grant. Her name was Catherine. And her life, even more than Angus's own, was bound up with the fur trade – to which, in a sense, Catherine owed her very existence.[64]

❋

In the United States census returns of 1860, Catherine McDonald's age is given as 45. Although no such information is ever wholly reliable, this suggests that Catherine was born about 1815 and that she was, therefore, of much the same age as the man she was to marry. What is certain is that Catherine's mother was Nez Perce and belonged to one of the leading families of this Indian people. Writing much later of his mother-in-law, who was to spend her last years at his home in Mission Valley, Angus McDonald described her as 'one of the last of the old royals of the Nez Perce'. Rather like Angus's own Glencoe grand-mother, then, Catherine's mother was descended from a long line of chiefs. And her appearance seems to have been in keeping with this ancestry. 'She in her age was still fine of face and of a decidedly aristocratic style of speech and conduct,' Angus remarked of his mother-in-law.[65]

Through Catherine's mother, then, the McDonald family were connected with a number of the most prominent men of the Nez Perce − including, with consequences touched on earlier, some of the chiefs who were to lead the Nez Perce in their 1877 battles with the U.S. military. Catherine's father, on the other hand, came from a very different background. Known only as Baptiste, he was one of the mixed-blood 'freemen' who had made their way into the Columbia country in the wake of the Nor'Westers. Part-Mohawk in origin, Baptiste had evidently taken an active part in the War of 1812 − when, as had also happened during the earlier Revolutionary War, the Mohawk and other peoples making up the Iroquois Confederation tended to take the British side. 'He was full of the story of the American War,' Catherine McDonald was afterwards to recall of what her father had said about his part in the fighting which took place in the Great Lakes region at about the time that Astoria was being handed over to the North West Company, 'and used to tell me how the British ran this way and the Americans ran that way, how the British fought there and the Americans charged here, and sometimes how both ran away, leaving the Indians behind them. And he would then dance and sing Indian war songs of the east, songs of chiefs long gone to join the dead.'[66]

About a year before she married Angus McDonald at Fort Hall, Catherine accompanied her father − to whom she was clearly very close − on a trapping and trading expedition made by a hundred or more freemen and mountain men into the arid regions of the American South-west. This was 'a long trip', Angus McDonald wrote much later to a friend, 'the first from the Rocky Mountains . . . down by the deserts and ravines of the Colorado to the Gulf of California. My wife was there with her father and she it was and is who tells and told me these things.'[67]

As was the custom with Indian mothers, Catherine was to entertain her children − including, of course, the young Duncan McDonald − to long stories featuring events in which she herself had been involved. Because of this, as he indicated in the letter quoted in the preceding paragraph, Angus, too, became familiar with the frequently repeated tale of Catherine's Colorado River excursion − a tale which he duly took down in the heavy ledger he kept for such purposes and which is preserved today in the Missoula library of the University of Montana. In its surviving version, then, Catherine McDonald's story bears the imprint of Angus's literary style. But the story's narrative thrust and content — not least its wealth of detail — are indubitably Catherine's own.[68]

In the month 'when the antelope were fawning', as Catherine put it, she and Baptiste joined their travelling companions, who included women and children as well as men, at 'the place of gathering' — a predetermined spot just to the west of the modern Idaho-Wyoming border in the vicinity of today's Yellowstone Park. In charge of their party was Thomas L. Smith, a veteran mountain man who was better known as Pegleg because one of the bone-shattering accidents to which all mountain men were prone had forced him personally to amputate the limb in question just below the knee. It was now late spring, in Catherine's recollection, and 'grass of rich growth was out on every hill' while 'game . . . grazed far and near'.[69]

To begin with, all went well. 'The first river we crossed was a swift stream of about seventy paces broad. The men made rafts to carry their little baggage. The women stripped and, lightening the saddles on their best horses, plunged into the stream with them, having tied their children one by one on their backs, and, swimming along with the horses, made several trips that way across the river before they had landed safely . . . I swam . . . stripped to the cotton shirt. The water was very cold.'[70]

This comparatively tranquil moment soon gave way to the anxiety aroused by a distant 'cloud of dust . . . which made us very uneasy'. The dust cloud, it soon transpired, had been raised by an Indian band of '150 warriors' who, to everyone's obvious relief, turned out to be friendly. 'We smoked heartily with them,' Catherine remembered, 'as they met us kindly.' And soon the band had gone about their business. 'They were . . . armed as usual with quiver and bow and shield of buffalo-hide,' Catherine said, 'with guns and lance and knife, and their garniture of bits of brass and game eagles' feathers and rare shells . . . made them look pretty as they passed on in the shining sun.'[71]

As is demonstrated by a dust cloud being automatically a cause of apprehension, the Rocky Mountain West of the early 1840s was a desperately disordered region. The lives of its native peoples had been disrupted by the fur trade and by the violence and depredations which had all too often resulted from the successive arrival of Nor'Westers, freemen, Bay men and mountain men. Native societies which had evolved over an enormously long period were beginning suddenly to disintegrate. But no alternative social structure had as yet fully taken their place. Rather like the Scottish Highlands in the period following the collapse of the Lordship of the Isles, therefore, the early-nineteenth-century Rocky Mountain West was a place of practically incessant conflict: of raids and counter-raids in which different sets of Indians fought both with each other and with trapping parties of the sort which Pegleg Smith was leading deep into the Colorado country.

It is no surprise, then, that Pegleg and his people soon came on the remnants of a camp where other trappers had been surprised by Sioux raiders. 'Two men were killed and all the horses gone,' in Catherine's recollection. 'One of the men was dragged by the enemy . . . for miles,' she added. The other had been tortured by the women among his captors – these women 'tormenting him with awl and gun until he danced his life away'.[72]

The risk of suffering some such lingering death was merely one of the more spectacular hazards confronting men of the sort with whom Catherine McDonald seems to have spent much of her youth. These men's daily existence, even at the best of times, was one of almost unrelenting harshness – the taking of the beaver pelts on which they relied for a livelihood being as gruelling as it was time-consuming. Because beaver can readily detect the scent of anyone who walks along the banks of the rivers they inhabit, the trapping of these animals involved a man in wading, mile after mile, through icy mountain streams in search of signs of recent beaver activity. On discovering such signs, the trapper, with numbed fingers, set one of his cumbersome steel traps, forcing its spring-propelled jaws apart with his boots, carefully priming its release mechanism, and placing the trap some four inches below the running water's surface in order to conceal it. The chain attached to all such traps was attached, in its turn, to a log which acted as an anchor. And taking advantage of the beaver's fondness for willow, the trapper now baited his trap by extending over it from the creek's bank a long and freshly cut willow wand. Just prior to moving on, the trapper, taking out the bottle in which he carried this precious fluid, smeared the willow wand's tip with castorum – a glandular secretion taken from a dead beaver calculated to add to the bait's appeal by giving it, as far as any living member of the same species was concerned, an element of sexual attraction. This, the trapper hoped, would ensure that a passing beaver would be tempted to rear up and seize the overhanging willow, thus triggering the trap which, snapping shut on the beaver's leg, would first disable and then drown this animal whose pelt, a year or more later, would help provide some faraway aristocrat or businessman with a new hat.[73]

The daily grind of the trapper's existence, however, must have seemed positively idyllic to people caught, as Pegleg Smith's party were shortly to be caught in the Colorado country, by Indians intent on taking, in roughly this order, their horses, their equipment, their guns, their lives and their scalps.

This crisis began, Catherine remembered, with 'a trembling of the ground and yells and cries of men'. Then, pursued by the mounted raiders whose thundering approach had caused the ground to shake, 'our mules and horses, snorting and sniffing like stampeded elk, with manes and tales up, rattled by us'. Somewhere a man shouted: 'Rush, boys, rush. We must have a horse each anyhow!' And Catherine, following his lead, dashed in among the fleeing animals. Glimpsing her father's 'favourite moose-coloured horse', she 'sprang and laid hold of him' while, all around, the sound of shooting began.[74]

Having secured Baptiste's horse to a heavy pack, Catherine now threw herself to the ground beside the watercourse where the party had been camped. 'Two of our men were close to me,' she recalled, 'one standing and the other resting at his length on the ground. He was the most powerful man of our party, a large, auburn-haired Canadian. An arrow lashed into the air from the other side of the river and struck down obliquely into his backbone.' Attempts were made to remove the arrow, Catherine said. But its barbed head being embedded in its victim's body, it could not be extracted. 'The wounded man walked about forty steps, staggered as if drunk and fell forward,' Catherine remembered. 'Clots of blood, with a spasmodic effort, followed and, in a few more pulses, he was dead.'

But the raiders, too, suffered casualties. That night, Catherine went on, 'two large fires reddened the sky within a thousand paces of us. War songs, shots and yells arose from one of them, wails and screams from the other, as the foe buried his dead'. And despite Pegleg Smith's force now being short of mounts, they survived to struggle on southwards.

All this time, Catherine continued, her father had been absent on a hunting trip. And the next alarm, which occurred when a lone horseman was glimpsed in the distance, was consequently to have a happier outcome. 'Soon his motions were too well known to me to be mistaken,' Catherine said of the approaching horseman, 'and the . . . affection in my poor eyes made them flow freely as I knew and discerned the motions of my father. He was in full warpaint, with quiver and gun, and his hair all tied on the top of his head . . . as he rode dashing into camp, driving five good horses before him. His bold, defiant aspect sent a sense of courage and cheer through all our disheartened party.'

❁

Pegleg Smith's foray along the line of the Colorado River — 'a dreary, treeless stream of about 400 paces broad', Catherine McDonald called it — was to last for several months. Its fur-gathering results are unclear. But there is some evidence that Angus McDonald, in his Hudson's Bay Company capacity, had a hand both in organising and financing this Colorado country expedition. If that were so, it would go some way to explain how Catherine met her future husband. But nobody, it has to be admitted, now knows the exact circumstances of their meeting; just as nobody now knows what it was exactly that attracted Angus, who must have encountered many such young women both at Fort Hall and in the course of his regular travels between Fort Hall and Fort Vancouver, to this young woman in particular.[75]

Catherine, it should be stressed in this context, ought not to be imagined as anything other than supremely self-assured. Her mother's elevated social origins — together with the life she had led when in her father's company — would have seen to that. The chances are, therefore, that Catherine would have impressed Angus in much the same way as another young woman of the Nez Perce impressed a Philadelphia naturalist, John K. Townsend, who, in the 1830s, made a scientific expedition into the Rocky Mountains where he attended one of the periodic get-togethers — part trade fair and part carnival — at which the mountain men sold beaver pelts and other furs to the St Louis merchants who were their principal customers. Many Indians took part in these proceedings and Townsend was very much struck, as he wrote, by 'some of the women . . . of the Nez Perce nation' — the nation which, of course, included Catherine McDonald. 'I observed one young and very pretty-looking woman, dressed in a great superabundance of finery, glittering with rings and beads,' Townsend continued. 'She was mounted astride — Indian fashion — upon a fine bay horse, whose head and tail were decorated with scarlet and blue ribbons, and the saddle, upon which the fair one sat, was ornamented all over with beads and little hawk's bells.'[76]

Many later-nineteenth-century Americans were to regard all alliances of Catherine's and Angus's type as automatically degrading to the whites involved in them. By such Americans, then, the 'squawman' and his 'squaw' were generally treated with much the same mixture of condescension and contempt as was heaped on their 'half-breed' children — children like Angus's and Catherine's son, Duncan. Such condescension and contempt, however, can seldom have been more inappropriate than in the case of Angus McDonald and his Indian wife. Both of them, after all, were the products of societies which valued an individual largely in terms of that individual's ancestry, pedigree, connections. When viewed from this standpoint, rather than from the perspective of people who reckoned human worth in terms of racial categories, the marriage of Angus and Catherine was very much a marriage of equals and of comparatively high-born equals at that – the families from which Angus was descended having occupied a very similar position among the Highland clans to the position occupied among the Nez Perce by the family to which Catherine belonged.[77]

It does not do, for all that, to assume that Highlanders like Angus McDonald – despite the Highlands having been one of the last parts of Europe to have had an Indian-like tribal structure – were universally inclined to treat Native Americans with the comparatively high regard which Angus was to show both for Catherine and for Indians more generally. More typical, perhaps, were those Highlanders who arrived in the Red River area with Archibald McDonald in 1813 and who made good the loss of their lands back in Scotland by appropriating other lands which had previously been occupied by the Metis, a mixed-blood people with whom the Kildonan settlers were soon at war. Right across the North American continent, from Nova Scotia to the Great Plains and from Glengarry County to Georgia, Highland refugees from eviction, clearance and other forms of oppression were to better themselves at the expense of the Indian peoples they casually displaced. And had they been asked to justify such conduct, which few of them ever were, North America's Highland immigrants would have done so in terms identical to those employed by all the numerous other whites to whom Indians seemed a self-evidently inferior race – a race, moreover, whose historic destiny, as the settler communities of the American West so stridently insisted, was ultimately to give way to whites.[78]

Patrick Sellar, when organising the dispossession of the Kildonan families who were to make their way to Red River, might have regarded these families as being on a par with North American 'aborigines'. But the Kildonan people, had they known of Sellar's comment, would have thought this comment every bit as insulting as Sellar intended it to be. Most of North America's Highland settlers, in other words, were no less racist in their attitude to Indians than settlers from other places. Nor did Highland fur traders, although their contacts with native peoples were far more extensive than those of most settlers, necessarily regard Indians in any more positive light.

'With respect to the fur trade,' a senior Nor'Wester commented caustically when a colleague suggested that the company inform itself more fully about the native societies with which its representatives dealt, 'whatever peculiarity each tribe of Indians may have, and however various their customs, manners and language may be, they are divided by the North West Company into two classes: those who have furs and those who have none.'[79]

There were plenty fur traders who cheated Indians, robbed Indians, raped Indians. And even when a fur trader entered into a permanent or semi-permanent relationship with an Indian woman, that relationship could easily have its exploitative aspects. 'Connubial alliances are the best security we can have of the goodwill of the natives,' one Hudson's Bay Company governor remarked by way of explaining the extent to which trade could be facilitated by a trader taking as his wife or partner the daughter, sister or other close female relative of a prominent chief. No less important than her role as intermediary and interpreter in her man's trade negotiations, moreover, were the many practical skills which such a woman always had at her command. She dressed and prepared each season's take of furs, for instance. And much more expertly than any white woman could have done, she made moccasins and snowshoes, mended canoes, trapped game, cooked food, kept house.[80]

Put like that, it is hard to see why any Indian woman should have consented to what was known to Nor'Westers and Bay Company men alike as a *mariage à la façon du pays*, a country-style wedding. This was the term applied to a fur-trade ritual devised to mark the inauguration of the family unit created when a trader and an Indian woman set up home together. But no such arrangement – as is symbolised by the fact that the ceremonials surrounding a *mariage à la façon du pays* incorporated elements of both European and Native American cultural traditions – was ever a wholly one-way street. At what was, partly as a result of the fur trade's own expansion, a time of growing impoverishment and dislocation among her own people, the Indian woman who entered into a *mariage à la façon du pays* obtained material comforts, to say nothing of physical security, of a type that would otherwise have been unavailable to her. And though many such women were jettisoned by men who had decided to abandon both the frontier and their 'country wives', or Indian partners, there were other such women whose relationships with their white menfolk were to be terminated only by death.[81]

The connection between Catherine and Angus McDonald – which was anyway slightly more formal than a *mariage à la façon du pays* and which was solemnised by a Jesuit missionary in 1854 – was to be of this latter sort. Angus, admittedly, was not always and forever faithful to his wife – as Duncan McDonald was to acknowledge when one of his correspondents asked him to explain why his father had two sons by the name of Angus, one called Angus Colville and the other called

Angus Pierre. 'The mother of Angus Pierre put up in the same bed with father when my mother was away for about one year,' Duncan wrote. 'When mother returned . . . the other woman met her with her baby in her arms and begged her [pardon] for the wrong she had committed and said, "This baby boy is the son of your husband."'[82]

Catherine and the other woman in the case – who was an Okanogan Indian – were 'always . . . kind to one another', according to Duncan. Maybe. But McDonald family tradition, whether recounted by Angus Pierre's descendants or by the descendants of Angus McDonald's other children, embodies the very definite message that Catherine – although she made Angus Pierre, in effect, a member of her family – also took steps to ensure that her straying husband was made fully aware of the error of his ways. How much heed Angus took of his wife's strictures is unclear. But he certainly showed absolutely no inclination to break permanently with Catherine – to whom, in the end, he was married for some 47 of his 73 years.[83]

Both Angus and Catherine must, on occasion, have fallen victim to the bigotry which inter-racial marriages such as theirs were capable of engendering among nineteenth-century whites – and, it must be said, among some Indians also. There is nothing in Angus McDonald's life or writings, however, to indicate that he shared anything of the feelings of one of his Montanan contemporaries, Granville Stuart, a prospector and rancher who – with a settler society gradually developing around him – clearly came to regret his youthful union with an Indian. 'My repugnance to my present mode of life increases daily,' Stuart wrote on one occasion. 'It does very well when one is young, but it don't last.'[84]

Angus McDonald's marriage did last. It resulted in twelve children being born between 1845 and 1871. These children, Duncan McDonald recalled, were given 'Indian names in Nez Perce language' by his grandmother – Catherine's mother – a year or two before she died in Mission Valley. 'I was a young man,' Duncan added ruefully, 'and I did not care about our Indian names.' He thus remembered only his own, which he set down as Tim-mi-na-il-pilp. Duncan's older brother and sister were known to him, then, by their 'English' names, John and Christina. The same was true of the nine younger members of the McDonald family: Donald, Anne, Margaret, Thomas, Alexander, Archibald, Joseph, Angus Colville and Mary.[85]

His mother's 'Indian name' had equally been forgotten by Duncan McDonald, as he noted sadly, before he began to take an active interest in his family history. But whatever that name was, it is likely that Duncan's mother was also known as Catherine from birth. This, it seems, was the name given to her by her father, Baptiste. Baptiste, however, would have pronounced his daughter's name in the French fashion because – like almost all the other mixed-blood freemen who followed the Nor'Westers and the Bay Company across the Rockies – he was French-speaking.

French was also to be the language in which Duncan's parents communicated during their several decades together. Catherine would have learned her French from her father. Angus, who was sufficiently literate in the language to have attempted at least one poem in it, may well have been taught some French when a boy in Scotland. The fur trader's spoken French, however, is likely to have been the patois of the Bay Company's Québecois and mixed-blood voyageurs. And it is this variant of the language which Angus and Catherine no doubt passed on to their children. 'I speak French not fluently but good enough to talk with a Frenchman,' Duncan McDonald observed in his old age. 'My father and mother,' he went on, 'talked all the time in the . . . French language.'[86]

Nothing of what Angus and Catherine said to each other can now be recaptured. But even when, in his surviving correspondence, Angus pokes fun at his wife, there is discernible, in his gentle jibing, an undercurrent of affection. 'Your mother was hunting and came home light,' Angus tells one of his daughters in a letter dated February 1881. 'Her hunts, you know, never paid their trouble.'[87]

CHAPTER FOUR

The old Glencoe chieftain

To glance at a relief map of the north-western corner of the United States is to see a series of mountain ranges stretching north to south across the thousand-mile-wide territory which separates the Pacific Ocean from the North American continent's enormously extensive central plains. Among the more significant such mountain chains are the Cascades, 100 or 150 miles inland from the sea, and the Bitterroots, some 250 miles further to the east. The first of these two massifs tends to strip most of the moisture from the westerly winds which blow off the Pacific. This means that the hill country between the Cascades and the Bitterroots – a place where sheltered river valleys and canyons alternate with high, more exposed, ridges – has a relatively low rainfall. Forests flourish on this region's damper slopes. But much of its terrain is naturally treeless and, especially in summer, this terrain can readily take on an arid look.

Here, spread across an area almost as large as Scotland, there lived the several thousand families who called themselves, in their own Sahaptin language, the Nimipu – a term meaning, more or less, the people. French-speaking traders – for reasons that may have had to do either with the Nimipu's habit of wearing shells in their noses or with the nose-pinching gesture by which they were denoted in the sign language of the Plains Indians far to the east – were eventually to call this people *Nez Percé*. And that name, although long since shorn of its French pronunciation, has tended to stick. But it was as Nimipu that the Nez Perce knew themselves for most of the many thousands of years which have passed since Coyote, the disruptively assertive figure at the centre of so many Indian creation myths, both brought the Nimipu into existence and put them in the places they were for so long to inhabit.[1]

The Nimipu, although a single people, owed no allegiance to a single leader. This was partly, perhaps, a function of their homeland's mountainous topography — topography which tended to result in each valley being occupied by its own self-regulating community. Rather in the manner of the MacDonalds of Glencoe — who similarly felt themselves to be both independent and part of the much wider entity that was Clan Donald — the few dozen families who constituted the typical Nimipu settlement, although they certainly acknowledged their membership of the larger whole, simply got on, for the most part, with managing their own lives. This they did in accordance with patterns dictated by the different tasks and responsibilities associated with each passing season.

There were camas roots, bitterroots, kouse, wild carrots and wild onions to be dug by Nimipu women and children in many different parts of the Nez Perce country. There were elk, deer, moose, goats, black bear, brown bear and grizzly bear to be hunted by men whose bows — made from the horns of mountain sheep — were so powerful as to be able to whip an arrow through the body of a running animal. There were rabbit, squirrel, badger and marmot to be trapped. But always more highly valued by the Nimipu than roots, game and the like were the various salmon species — the king, the sockeye, the silver and the coho — which, at predetermined times each year, came thrusting up the Columbia River and its many tributaries.

One means of taking salmon was to fix a large basket-like structure just below the rocky lip of one of the falls which the migrating fish had to leap on their way upstream. Angus McDonald, on his arrival in the Columbia country, was to be a fascinated observer of what this technique involved. 'The basket is a vessel made of stout hazel or birchen osiers hung to the lower edge of the falls by a rope of the same boughs,' he explained. 'The fish that fail in their leap are cast back and fall by scores into the ever open basket. When it is full, two strong, hardy men strip and, club in hand, go down through the drenching cold foam into the basket to knock the yet living fish in the head and heave them up, or hand them up, with the already dead. One basket has caught a thousand salmon a day in this way.'[2]

Salmon, as Angus McDonald made clear, were also speared at river falls and rapids. 'The spear at rest in the hand of a naked Indian standing on the foam-drenched cliff is a fine picture,' Angus wrote of one location where such spearing was traditionally carried on. 'As the eager fish glances to the surface of the whirlpool, looking to his leap, he is pierced and dragged quivering ashore. Now and then, however, the spearman loses his life. I have known two athletic Indians seal their fate this way. Having speared a strong fish, the sudden struggle and iron pressure of the mighty waters jerked these poor fellows from their dizzy standing-place and, falling headlong into these terrible whirlpools, they never breathed again.'³

As well as drawing on the plentiful natural resources of their home-land, the Nimipu traded with neighbouring peoples and, by this means, were able to access goods originating on the distant coast. Trading and other journeys were traditionally made on foot or by water. But Nimipu mobility was to increase enormously when the people obtained their first horses. Introduced to Mexico by that country's Spanish invaders some 200 years before, the horse reached the Columbia country in the early eighteenth century. And the Nimipu were soon to master both horsemanship and the art of selective breeding. 'Nez Perce horses are much finer than any Indian horses I have yet seen,' a United States government official was one day to comment of the resulting mounts. 'A great many are large, fine-bred . . . stock, with fine limbs, rising withers, sloping well back, and are uncommonly sinewy and surefooted.'⁴

Their horses enabled the Nez Perce massively to increase the scope of their hunting. Soon they were regularly traversing the Lolo Trail into the Bitterroot Valley and pushing on eastwards into the Great Plains where, at certain times of year, as Catherine McDonald remembered, there was 'nothing but buffalo' to be seen 'until the sky struck the earth'.⁵

Their trips into the Bitterroot Valley brought the Nimipu into closer and closer contact with this locality's Salish or Flathead people in whose company the Nez Perce often hunted buffalo and with whom, as Angus McDonald remarked, the Nez Perce also shared a number of beliefs and customs.

'The going up into some high mountain there to commune with nature and their own innermost being was a frequent practice with the Indians of this section,' Angus noted of the Salish people and of their Nez Perce neighbours. 'They had reached that stage in human progress,' Angus commented of such rituals, 'where man personifies the sublime and startling manifestations of nature.' And the 'undoubted' fact of 'the white race' having 'passed through that phase of human development', Angus added, ought to have encouraged his fellow whites to 'temper [their] judgements' on Indian religious rites.⁶

At a time when most whites were inclined to dismiss Indian spiritu-ality as so much superstitious mumbo-jumbo, this was to be excep-tionally tolerant. But Angus, not content with mere tolerance, went on to assert that Native American religions might well be superior to Christianity. 'Some learned bigots,' he commented, 'tell us that the

Jews were the only people of antiquity that worshipped the true God. How silly that assertion!' The 'simple yet profound theology' of the Indian compared favourably with 'anything of that kind . . . from . . . Jerusalem'. All 'the volumes of Christendom could not bring a more splendid dispensation' than that which Indians 'enjoyed' prior to Europeans arriving in America. 'As to their moral precepts,' Angus observed of native peoples who were routinely characterised as murderous, thieving, dishonest, lazy and untrustworthy, 'I think they are ahead of the Christian.'[7]

Prominent among the Indians from whom Angus McDonald learned about such matters was Chief Kamiakin of the Yakima people whose lands lay to the north of those of the Nez Perce. 'He was . . . a fine, well-formed and powerful Indian, standing five feet eleven in his moccasins,' Angus observed of Kamiakin, 'his hair, twisted down over his shoulders, of auburn colour at its points, but as usual darker near the roots. His weight was about two hundred pounds, muscular and sinewy.'[8]

From Kamiakin, with whom he was 'enjoying a pipe' at the time, Angus heard of how the chief, when a boy of 15, spent 'five days and nights' near the summit of the 14,410-foot-high Mount Rainier 'without food and water'. This most 'sagacious' of Indians, Angus reported, maintained that his time on Mount Rainier had been 'the severest feat of his life . . . He said that he was glad when the number of his initiating suns and nights had passed and he came down to speak again with man.'[9]

What Kamiakin thus described was the 'vision quest' which was a common rite among many of the indigenous peoples of the American West. Usually involving fasting, isolation and meditation, such a quest provided each Indian teenager with the opportunity to search out the guardian spirit – *wyakin* this spirit was called by the Nez Perce – which would henceforth watch over his or her life. Manifesting itself very often in the form of an animal, the spirit might actually appear to the anxiously waiting teenager. 'It was just like dreaming what I saw,' one of the Nimipu was to say of this most critical moment. 'It was a spirit of a wolf that appeared to me. Yellow-like in colour, it sort of floated in the air. Like a human being it talked to me, and gave me its power.'[10]

This is not to imply that the Nimipu, any more than people elsewhere, devoted themselves exclusively to the metaphysical and to the supernatural. Their lives – and in this the Nez Perce were no different from the rest of humanity – were dominated less by religious ritual than by the many mundane matters which had to be constantly attended to if their families were to have reasonable supplies of food. And on opportunity presenting itself — as happened each fall when the Nimipu ceased their summer wanderings and settled down for the winter in villages which were strung out along the valleys of the Clearwater, Salmon, Snake and Imnaha Rivers — this Indian people were by no means averse to enjoying themselves. Like the Glencoe MacDonalds, who passed the year's darkest and coldest months in much the same fashion, the Nez Perce gathered around their firesides to hear again the stories — sometimes exciting, sometimes funny, sometimes serious, sometimes scary — which constituted their people's collective memory and in which there was embodied so much of the Nimipu's strong sense of identity.

Nez Perce storytelling — and in this it was identical in its purposes to the storytelling in which the MacDonalds of Glencoe also engaged — had the effect of emphasising both the sheer continuity of this people's well-established culture and their powerful affinity with the places which had been the Nimipu's places since Coyote placed them there in a past so distant that it lay beyond man's reckoning. But what had endured for millennia, as the Nimipu were painfully to discover, could be destroyed in decades. Prior to the nineteenth century, it seems probable, the Nez Perce would scarcely have considered it possible that their lives could be so disrupted as to separate them from landscapes and locations which were integral to their whole existence. Within forty years of Angus McDonald marrying into the Nimipu, however, Nez Perce society was to be subjected to treatment of a kind it was no more able to survive than Scotland's clans had been able to survive the various upheavals which had resulted in so many Highlanders having come to North America.

In the fall of 1805, at about the time that the earliest of the coming winter's snows were falling on the Bitterroots, the Nimipu met their first whites. These whites were members of an American expedition sent westwards by President Thomas Jefferson who was determined that the United States should imitate and surpass Alexander MacKenzie's feat of some twelve years before by searching out, as the expedition's instructions put it, 'the most direct and practicable communication . . . across this continent'. Led by Meriwether Lewis, who had previously been Jefferson's private secretary, and by William Clark, a soldier, the expedition had been ordered both to explore the territories which the American government had bought from France in 1803 — territories which extended from the Mississippi River to the Rocky Mountains — and to push on to the Pacific across lands which growing numbers of

Americans already hoped their country would one day annexe.[11]

Having crossed the Continental Divide into the Bitterroot Valley at the beginning of September 1805 and having been received hospitably by that locality's Flathead inhabitants, the Lewis and Clark expedition next set out along the Lolo Trail. Here the going was as hard as any the party had so far encountered. And nowhere in 'this horrible mountainous desert', as one expedition member described the Lolo Trail's surroundings, was there any worthwhile hunting to be had. 'The men are growing weak and losing flesh very fast,' William Clark noted in his journal on 19 September. 'Several are afflicted with the dysentry, and eruptions of the skin are very common.'[12]

At the Lolo Trail's western end, however, Lewis and Clark encountered the Nimipu – from whom, as Clark commented, they were to receive 'greater acts of hospitality' than had been extended to them by any of the other tribes they had met since leaving the Great Plains. The expedition was now resupplied, brought back to health and helped by the Nez Perce to construct the boats which were to carry Lewis and Clark to the Pacific by way of the Clearwater and Columbia Rivers.[13]

'We wish to live with them as one people and to cherish their interests as our own,' President Jefferson remarked of his government's attitude to the Indian nations occupying the territories through which Lewis and Clark travelled in the course of their journey to the sea. And the president no doubt meant what he said. But Lewis and Clark were nevertheless to study the 'soil and face of the country'; to assess its agricultural potential, its mineral wealth, its forests; they were, in short, to make some estimate of the extent to which the American West might be suited to white settlement. And such settlement, of course, could hardly be other than detrimental to the interests of the Nez Perce and their neighbours.[14]

Even before Lewis and Clark came over the Lolo Trail into the Nez Perce country, that country's inhabitants had felt something of the terribly adverse impact which people of European origin seem almost always to have had on America's indigenous populations. Smallpox, measles, typhus and all the other diseases brought by whites to North America had arrived in the Columbia country some decades in advance of any actual white. And here – as had happened further east and as had happened, too, in the Aztec and Inca empires far to the south – the effect of such disease was to reduce Indian numbers so drastically as to make it even more difficult than it would otherwise have been for Indians to resist white incursions. 'The smallpox is playing a very mortal game with the poor natives of the country,' Angus McDonald was to report from one Columbia River outpost in 1853. That game, as Angus was well aware, had then been going on for a long time. And its consequences were everywhere to be seen in extraordinarily high Indian death-rates and in the despair and demoralisation which each new epidemic brought in its wake.[15]

But the Nimipu homeland, for all that it had already been badly affected by infectious illness, was anything but bereft of life in the period following the Lewis and Clark expedition's transit of the area. To a Scottish Highlander like Alexander Ross, who came here as a John Jacob Astor employee and who afterwards joined the North West Company, the Nez Perce country of the years around 1815 seemed next best thing to paradise. 'Groups of Indian huts,' Ross remembered of his time among the Nimipu, 'with their little spiral columns of smoke and herds of animals, gave animation and beauty to the landscape. The natives, in social crowds, vied with each other in coursing their gallant steeds, in racing, swimming and other feats of activity. Wild horses in droves sported and grazed along the boundless plains; the wild fowl, in flocks, filled the air; and the salmon and sturgeon, incessantly leaping, ruffled the smoothness of the waters. The appearance of the country on a summer's evening was delightful beyond description.'[16]

Nor were the Nez Perce, it must be emphasised, necessarily averse either to fur traders or to the many manufactured goods which the fur trade made available to them. White settlement, however, was something else entirely. Because it necessarily implied loss of Indian land, settlement was invariably opposed by Indians. But given the disparity of numbers and resources as between Native Americans on the one hand, and North America's rapidly swelling ranks of prospective white settlers on the other, Indian opinion was equally invariably disregarded. All that held up the white settlement of the Nez Perce country, therefore, were the difficulties which faced anyone attempting to make an overland crossing of the continent. And during the summer of 1840, the year which brought Angus McDonald from Fort Colville to Fort Hall, these difficulties were clearly beginning to be overcome.

That summer there rolled into Fort Hall from the east a wagon carrying the first white family to come west with the express purpose of setting up a home in Oregon – then delineated in such a way as to include the entire landmass to the west of the Rockies and to the north of California. Soon hundreds, even thousands, of other such families were making their way along the 2,000-mile-long Oregon Trail which began at Independence on the Missouri, swung across the Great Plains to the south of the Platte River, crossed the Rockies at the South Pass and, by way of Fort Hall, led eventually into the fertile and highly attractive Willamette Valley in the vicinity of the Bay Company's Fort Vancouver.

The men, women and children brought west by 'each hungry caravan . . . of emigrant wagons', as Angus McDonald once described the Oregon Trail's increasingly regular convoys, were collectively to transform the region they now made their place of residence. This, however, was not the reason for their coming. Most of the many folk who were to spend between 20 and 25 weeks getting from Independence to Oregon were not impelled westwards by any overarching vision of what their individual journeys cumulatively represented. 'His tone was dim, not to say subdued,' it was reported of a man of the sort one might typically have encountered on the Oregon Trail during the years which Angus McDonald spent at Fort Hall. 'His boots [were] enormous piles of rusty leather, red from long travel, want and woe.' An emigrant of that type – and there were lots of them – did not come to Oregon to engage in any scheme of national expansion. He came primarily in the hope of finding here something a little better than the less-than-satisfactory life he had left behind him in the east.[17]

Many such people were to have cause to be grateful to Angus McDonald and his Fort Hall superior, Richard Grant, who – for wholly obscure reasons – was generally known as Captain Johnny. 'Captain Grant was . . . in charge,' one Oregon-bound emigrant wrote of his arrival at Fort Hall in 1846, 'and his man of affairs was one McDonald. Both were Scotchmen and gentlemen. They treated our party with great courtesy . . . They furnished us with a written guide for the journey westward, with all the camping places specified [and] the distance from each to the next, with information as to wood, water and grass . . . which was of exceeding value.'[18]

Angus was himself to toy with the idea of setting up as an Oregon homesteader. 'As it is my wish to leave the service of the Hudson's Bay Company and feeling no desire to return to Scotland,' he wrote to John McLoughlin in 1844, 'I would beg permission, as a favour, to be allowed to go to the Willamette as a settler.' But McLoughlin's reply made clear that Angus would not be permitted to leave the Bay Company's employment for at least a year. And the promotion for which McLoughlin shortly afterwards recommended him may well have had the effect of reconciling Angus to a Bay Company career. He seems, in any case, to have been comparatively content thereafter to fall in with the company's plans for him. The shape and content of those plans, however, was to be heavily influenced by the way in which the settlement of Oregon began rapidly to undermine the Bay Company's position in the area.[19]

❦

'For nearly twenty years,' a senior representative of the United States government observed in 1839, 'the Hudson's Bay Company have exercised an almost unlimited control over the Indian tribes and the trade of the whole country west of the Rocky Mountains.' This was to state a self-evident fact. But it was also to outline a set of circumstances which the U.S. government – under pressure both from the many American settlers who were moving into Oregon and from those American politicians who wanted a frontier on the Pacific – was increasingly to challenge. The outcome, in 1846, was the internationally agreed extension of United States sovereignty into all of Oregon.[20]

That Oregon should have thus become American seems, from a late-twentieth-century perspective, utterly inevitable. It did not seem so in the early 1840s, however. A New England skipper by the name of Robert Gray may have discovered the mouth of the Columbia River in 1792, Lewis and Clark may have traversed Oregon in 1805 and John Jacob Astor may have established his Astoria trading post in 1813. But Captain George Vancouver of the British Royal Navy had mapped much of the Oregon coastline in the early 1790s, and Nor'Wester and Bay Company traders had afterwards established themselves far more solidly in the Oregon interior than any American managed to do prior to the arrival of the mountain men in the 1820s. Britain's claim to Oregon, from a Bay Company perspective at any rate, was consequently every bit as strong as the claim of the United States. And Angus McDonald was among the many Bay men who thought that Britain should, quite literally, have stuck to its guns in the face of repeated assertions along the lines of John L. O'Sullivan's much-quoted comment to the effect that it was the American people's 'manifest destiny to overspread the continent'.[21]

One of Angus McDonald's Bay Company colleagues was to note that Angus 'never missed an opportunity' of 'getting into a wordy quarrel' with Americans on the rights and wrongs of the Oregon Treaty of 1846. 'More than once', Angus's colleague added of the disputes that tended to break out every time he brought this 'very plain-spoken' Scotsman into one of Oregon's rapidly developing settlements, 'I saved him from being assaulted for talking contemptuously of decent Americans . . . But he didn't appreciate it, and continued as abusive as ever, until at last I refrained from taking him with me when I visited the adjoining towns.'[22]

'Oregon would, in '45 or '46, have fallen in one month into the hands of the British were the [British] government determined upon it,' Angus McDonald was to assert. But ministers in London, not sharing Angus's bellicose convictions, were not prepared to risk war with the United States in order merely to advance the commercial interests of the Hudson's Bay Company. As far as its operations in Oregon were concerned, therefore, the company, after 1846, found itself subject to Washington's – as opposed to London's – jurisdiction. This, from a Bay Company point of view, was bad enough. Still harder to bear was the campaign now mounted with a view to ejecting the company from what had become U.S. territory. There was no room for a 'large and powerful moneyed institution, controlled by foreigners, in the heart of this young America,' thundered one of the Bay Company's many critics. And since these critics had the ear of powerful men, both in Oregon itself and in Washington, D.C., it was clear that the company's Oregon establishments were now existing very much on borrowed time.[23]

Still more endangered by Oregon's changed political status were the Native American peoples with whom the Hudson's Bay Company and its Nor'Wester precursors had been dealing for some forty years. As already acknowledged, not every fur trader shared Angus McDonald's positive view of Indians. But every Bay man wanted, at the minimum, to maintain the trading patterns which underpinned the company's profits. And because these patterns had evolved on the basis of commercial interchange between Bay Company traders and Indians, it followed that the Bay men had an interest in sustaining traditional societies of the Nez Perce type. Settlers, on the other hand, mostly wanted Indians ejected from large areas for exactly the same reason as men like Patrick Sellar wanted Highlanders removed from places such as the Strath of Kildonan – this reason having to do, in both cases, with an incoming group's need to dispossess the occupants of the land which this incoming group wanted to take over. And since human beings are always good at cloaking their baser motives with some high-sounding justification, Oregon's white settlers were every bit as prone as Patrick Sellar had been in a Highland context to assert that the society of which they were part was innately superior to the native societies which the same settlers were all too often to destroy.

In its more intellectual manifestations, the doctrine of Indian inferiority was expressed in ways that appeared to regret those Indian extinctions which were nevertheless thought unavoidable. 'They are shrinking before the mighty tide which is pressing them away,' a Bostonian writer commented of Native Americans in 1825. 'They must soon hear the roar of the last wave which will settle over them forever.'[24]

Out on the actual frontier, however, racial prejudice was always more direct than in New England drawing-rooms. Most Westerners 'hated an Indian as they [did] a rattlesnake,' an Oregon judge confessed during the 1850s. He personally felt 'a natural repugnance towards the filthy, dirty, lazy Indians,' the judge went on. 'Almost everybody does,' he added.[25]

Such remarks – and they could be multiplied indefinitely – are virtually identical, of course, to comments which had earlier been made about Highlanders. The 'wild savages' whose 'barbarous inhumanity' ostensibly underlay King James VI's wish to 'root out' Scotland's clans are clearly the product of a mind-set which is indistinguishable from the one which dealt, two centuries later and on a different continent, in 'blood-thirsty brown animals' who, being 'incapable of civilisation', were 'best destroyed'. And just as the habitual denigration of Highlanders made it easier for otherwise reasonable men to engage in the Massacre of Glencoe, so the routine characterisation of Indians as 'a dirty array of indescribably . . . degenerate people' made it inevitable that Native American lives would be cheapened to the point at which some whites felt able to take these lives almost at will.[26]

Catherine McDonald saw something of the consequences of such attitudes in the course of her youthful travels in the Colorado country. At one point, for instance, the mountain men in charge of Catherine's party became convinced – without so much as a shred of evidence, according to Catherine – that a particular band of Indians were responsible for some 'four or five' of the party's traps having gone missing. An immediate attack was consequently mounted on the riverside camp which housed the alleged thieves.[27]

'Yells of woe from men, women and children filled the place,' Catherine commented of what happened next. 'The dead and wounded lay there. The active ran to the river . . . But they were picked off by . . . cruel marksmen. The women made every effort to swim and save their children. Women who had one or two children made, by terrible labour, a safe landing on the other side, but those who had three or four children could not get over and gradually sank with them . . . I noticed one woman, just as she landed on the other side, fall dead from a bullet that entered her back . . . The trappers, after this work, went into the deserted camp and pillaged everything they liked . . . They then came back perfectly unconcerned, and smoked and jested over the success of their revenge.'

The United States authorities, needless to say, did not approve of such conduct. In fact, the U.S. federal government and its agencies – including, at various points, the army – were thought by many settler communities to treat Indians with far more consideration than Indians were entitled to expect. But America's national politicians frequently lacked either the means or the will to enforce law and order in the West. The Indians on the receiving end of casual violence of the type decribed by Catherine McDonald, then, had little reason to trust the United States government. Indeed they had every reason to adopt an entirely opposite stance. Given the extent to which white murderers of Indians went uncharged and unpunished, for example, it would have been astonishing if Native Americans had done anything other than conclude that the U.S. government's stated concern for Indian rights was no more than the rankest hypocrisy. Besides, the government, although ostensibly opposed to the indiscriminate slaughter of Indians, was itself committed to an Indian policy which, from a Native American perspective, seemed no less destructive of Indian society than the murderous activities which were witnessed by the young Catherine McDonald.

United States Indian policy had its origins in the period prior to American independence. That was a time when the military balance as between whites and Indians had not tilted nearly as far towards the white side as it was to do later. This earlier period was also a time when Indians were able to take advantage of white divisions. When Britain and France were fighting for political supremacy in the eastern part of North America, or when Britain was warring with its American colonists, Indian peoples like the Creeks, the Cherokee and the Iroquois were eagerly courted by the contending parties. Just as the Lordship of the Isles had once sought to enhance its position by dallying with the Scottish kingdom's English enemies, then, a strategically important Indian people could similarly seek to enhance their prospects by threatening to align themselves with France against Britain or with Britain against the nascent United States. It was as an incidental result of such manoeuvres that loyalist Highland settlers in the Mohawk Valley were to fight alongside the Iroquois for the duration of the Revolutionary War – the Iroquois having concluded that Indian interests were marginally more likely to be safeguarded in a British-ruled America than in the independent nation which so many white colonists were battling to obtain. Of more general significance, however, was the fact that Indian peoples had to be treated by prospective allies – irrespective of the latter's feelings on the matter – as sovereign powers in their own right. Hence the growing tendency for all the white nations operating in North America in the eighteenth century – France, Britain and, latterly, the United States – to sign treaty after treaty with Native Americans.

The American government continued to promote such treaties well into the second half of the nineteenth century. With every decade that passed, however, the resulting documents became steadily more inequitable in content and intention. Once they had tended to be voluntary agreements of a type which assumed the essential equality of each party to them. Increasingly, they became the means by which

Indians were persuaded – or forced – to relinquish what American lawyers called the 'aboriginal title' to the localities where these Indians lived. By the time the United States took charge of Oregon, therefore, the typical Indian treaty was little more than a means of giving something of a legitimising gloss to expropriating processes made all the more painful, from the Indian standpoint, by the way in which most whites entirely disregarded Indian feelings for the land which American treaty-makers so cursorily carved up.[28]

'Tribes are like the clans of Scotland,' Duncan McDonald commented when trying to explain what it was that bound Indian peoples to their homelands. 'Each clan has a little territory of their own.' Most whites could follow Duncan's argument that far. Very few whites, however, were prepared to explore what it was that connected 'tribe' with 'territory' in the Indian mind. To have engaged in such exploration, after all, would have been to question the whole basis of treaties which depended on the assumption that Indians, just like whites, considered land to be, in essence, a commodity to be traded in much the same manner as the furs which Indians happily exchanged for pots, pans, axes, guns and other goods. The trouble was that Indians did not view land in this way. Indians did not think land was something to be bought, sold, developed, exploited, utilised. Rather like the Gaelic-speaking Highlanders with whom Duncan McDonald compared them, Indians regarded land as the embodiment of community – the physical repository of those things that provided them with their collective identity. That is what one Western chief meant when he said of his tribal territories in 1854: 'Every part of this soil is sacred in the estimation of my people. Every hillside, every valley, every plain and grove has been hallowed by some sad or happy event in days long vanished.'[29]

These were sentiments, however, which meant little or nothing to Isaac Ingalls Stevens, the politically ambitious military man who, in 1853, was made governor of the newly created Washington Territory. The territory in question consisted of the northern half of what had previously been called Oregon. It comprised, therefore, much of present-day Montana and Idaho as well as present-day Washington State. The greater part of this huge area, Governor Stevens insisted, needed to be immediately opened to white settlement. But there were, the governor recognised, serious legal difficulties in the way of such a move. 'The Indian title has not been extinguished, nor even a law passed to provide for its extinguishment, east of the Cascade Mountains,' Stevens wrote in 1854. Until this was done, the governor went on, no settler could obtain valid title to land. Hence the priority which Stevens now attached to making treaties with Washington Territory's numerous native peoples.[30]

Governor Stevens began his treaty negotiations with the Nez Perce in May 1855. Most of the ensuing debate involved Stevens and his aides on the one side and Nez Perce chiefs like Catherine McDonald's close relative, Eagle-from-the-Light, on the other. But some 2,500 of the Nimipu attended the governor's grand council in the Walla Walla Valley some 70 or 80 miles to the west of the point at which the modern states of Washington, Oregon and Idaho all intersect. And the Nimipu's entry to the council grounds was, as it was meant to be, impressive – involving, one American eyewitness reported, 'a thousand warriors mounted on fine horses and riding at a gallop, two abreast . . . their faces covered with white, red and yellow paint in fanciful designs . . . firing their guns, brandishing their shields, beating their drums and yelling their war-whoops.'[31]

Soon, however, Governor Stevens had got down to business. 'What shall we do at this council?' he asked the assembled chiefs. Then, by way of answering his own question, he outlined the U.S. government's position: 'We want you and ourselves to agree upon tracts of land where you will live; in those tracts of land we want each man who will work to have his own land, his own horses, his own cattle and his own home for his children.'[32]

Forty years before, when asked to justify the forcible removal of so many families from the Strath of Kildonan and other inland parts of the Scottish Highlands, Patrick Sellar had argued that the landed proprietors who were responsible for such clearances had actually acted in the best interest of the families who had been evicted. These families had been 'brought down to the coast and placed there in lotts under the size of three arable acres,' Sellar explained. Such 'lotts' or crofts, Sellar admitted, were on the small side – especially when compared with the large tracts of common land where the Kildonan folk had once pastured their cattle. But that was because it was essential to engender more entrepreneurial attitudes among Highlanders by extinguishing their out-of-date communalism and pastoralism and by getting them to 'turn their attention' to new ways of earning a living. Sellar concluded: 'I presume to say that the proprietors humanely ordered this arrangement, because it surely was a most benevolent action to put these barbarous hordes into a position where they could better associate together, apply to industry, educate their children and advance in civilisation.'[33]

What Isaac I. Stevens now proposed to impose on the Nez Perce was what Patrick Sellar had already imposed on the Kildonan people. The Nimipu, the governor told Eagle-from-the-Light and his fellow chiefs, were to give up their former way of life and were henceforth to confine themselves to a reservation that would be set aside for them. There Nimipu men would 'learn to make ploughs . . . learn to make wagons'; there Nimipu women would be taught how 'to spin, and to weave and to make clothes'; there Nimipu children would one day become 'farmers and mechanics . . . doctors and lawyers like white men'. None of this, to the governor's Nez Perce listeners, was in the least enticing. They were being asked, they knew, to sign away their birthrights for what, at best, were merely half-meant promises. But the Nez Perce had little alternative but to acquiesce in the plans which Stevens had made for them. They certainly did not have the Kildonan people's option of taking themselves off to another continent. And so the Nimipu's chiefs, including Eagle-from-the-Light, put their names to the governor's treaty.[34]

Next it was the turn of the Nimipu's many close acquaintances among the Salish or Flathead bands whose lands accounted for a substantial slice of what is nowadays western Montana. From Walla Walla, therefore, Isaac I. Stevens hurried across the Bitterroot Mountains. And in July 1855, at a council held in the vicinity of Hell's Gate Canyon, not far from modern Missoula, the governor fixed on the area that was to become the Flathead Reservation. This area included Mission Valley. And Mission Valley, as it happened, was the site of a Hudson's Bay Company post known as Fort Connah.

Angus McDonald left Fort Hall for the Flathead country in the summer of 1847, travelling north in the company of his wife, Catherine, their two-year-old son, John, and their baby daughter, Christina. The party's destination was Salish House where, following his recent promotion, Angus was, for the first time, to take overall command of a Hudson's Bay Company post.[35]

Finan McDonald had been stationed at Salish House in the 1820s when the place served as base to the Bay Company's Snake Country Brigade. Angus, as things turned out, never met his Knoydart-born kinsman, Finan having retired to Glengarry County with his Indian wife well before this latest McDonald fur trader first got to the West. But Angus had no doubt heard a good deal about Finan's exploits. One source of such information, it can safely be guessed, was Finan's mixed-blood daughter, Helen, who married Richard Grant, the Fort Hall bourgeois, during Angus's time in the Snake River territory. Helen and her husband, whose own family origins can be traced to the Highlands which Richard Grant's grandfather left in the 1750s, were eventually to settle in the Flathead country, an area Helen would have known during her childhood. And it is by no means inconceivable that Angus's connections both with Helen and with Finan, whose reputation remained high among his former Flathead associates, helped to facilitate the good relations which Angus seems always to have had with the Flathead, or Salish, people.[36]

Although its site had altered more than once in the intervening period, Salish House, when Angus took charge there, was located more or less where David Thompson had established the post a quarter-century before – in the vicinity of the present-day town of Thompson Falls on the Clark Fork River.[37]

There is something a little bit reminiscent of the Scottish Highlands about the hills which overlook the Clark Fork, which may be why Angus McDonald seems to have regarded this locality with a good deal of affection. Its remoteness, he admitted, was such that he and his Salish House colleagues were 'glad to hear once a year from Europe'. But 'many a fine buffalo tongue . . . and many a glass of the best cognac that ever crossed the Atlantic was served in that sylvan building', Angus went on. News of his subordinates indulging themselves in such high-living would not have pleased the Scrooge-like George Simpson who was more or less in sole control of the Bay Company's operations by the 1840s. But not even Simpson could make Bay men give up drinking. And the annual arrival of a fresh supply of cognac, which would have made its way to Salish House by way of Cape Horn and the Columbia River during Angus's time here, was no doubt the occasion for one of the noisy celebrations at which Angus – peering back, as it were, through a lingering haze of brandy fumes – remembered 'stirring' reels being danced and 'solemn' Scots songs being 'whistled and sung' by the several Highland fur traders who regularly turned up at Salish House in order to take advantage of the post's supplies of liquor.[38]

Life at Salish House was not without its complications, however. On one occasion, according to Angus, the post lost 'all its horses' to a Blackfoot 'war party' – this people, whose lands lay to the east of the Flathead country, then being in the habit of raiding westwards into the Bitterroot Valley and adjacent areas. 'We narrowly escaped . . . destruction,' Angus commented ruefully of his encounter with these raiders. 'As our horses grazed untied, however, they did not trouble themselves with taking our scalps. They were sixty, well-armed, while we were only five, with two guns.'[39]

The Blackfoot – with whom Finan McDonald, as mentioned earlier, had tangled repeatedly when in these parts – were also to have an unintended hand in determining the precise location of the post which replaced Salish House shortly after Angus took charge there. Frank MacArthur, the Bay Company man who preceded Angus at Salish House and who was afterwards to set up as an independent trader in the vicinity of Hell's Gate, had concluded that trade with the Flathead people and their neighbours would be boosted if the company's centre of operations in the Flathead country was moved to Mission Valley which lies, as the crow flies, some 50 miles due east of Thompson Falls. Angus agreed. That was why, when ranching in Mission Valley in the 1880s, Angus was able to write: 'Here there was begun by MacArthur, and finished by me, the last post established by the Hudson's Bay Company in the territories of the United States.'[40]

The growing tension between the Bay Company and the U.S. government at which Angus thus hinted – tension which was to lead not only to the company building no more posts on American territory but also to the gradual closing of those which were already there – would eventually impact directly on Angus's own career. In Mission Valley in 1847, however, the Blackfoot still exercised a more immediate influence than the American authorities who, at this point, had scarcely begun to consolidate their grip on what was shortly to become Washington Territory. Hence Angus's decision that Fort Connah, as the Bay Company's latest post came to be called, should be constructed on the open ground above Post Creek rather than on the creek's bank – where water, always an important consideration, would have been more readily to hand. A local chief, Duncan McDonald remembered hearing from Angus, 'advised my father not to build along the creek as it was covered with brush and heavy timber'. This would have made it easy for Blackfoot marauders to 'shoot and kill' the post's occupants from 'places of hiding in the brush'. Much the safer and wiser course, Angus's Indian adviser consequently counselled, was to select a site beside a convenient spring on a gently rising slope a little to the west. 'And at this place,' Duncan recorded, 'my father built the trading post.'[41]

Duncan McDonald was born at Fort Connah – 'in 1849 in the month of March about the end of the month,' he wrote nearly seventy years later. 'As my father was away and my mother was not educated,' Duncan added, 'she could not tell the day.'[42]

Some six years later, Thomas Adams – who was one of Governor Isaac I. Stevens's party when the latter negotiated with the Flathead people at Hell's Gate – described Fort Connah as 'a wooden building, about twenty-four by sixteen feet, of one storey, with a bark roof; one wooden bastion about fourteen feet square; and two storerooms, each ten feet square; also a log corral about sixty feet square.'[43]

The single-storey 'wooden building' – which Adams, a trained artist, clearly observed closely – was the house where Duncan McDonald was born and where Angus, Catherine and their steadily expanding family lived during this, their first, period of residence in Mission Valley. The bastion, as its military-sounding title suggests, probably owed its existence to the Blackfoot threat and would, no doubt, have been typical of its kind – being made from heavy logs into which there had been cut the narrow slits from which a defending party could fire on any besieging Indians. But of much more enduring significance than Fort Connah's bastion was what Thomas Adams called its 'storerooms'. One of these, in Duncan's recollection, was, as Adams suggested, a warehouse. The other, according to Duncan, was the post's 'trading house'. Here Angus would have conducted business with the many Indians who came regularly to Fort Connah to deal in furs and other goods.[44]

Although Angus certainly traded beaver pelts at Fort Connah, the post's particular role in the Bay Company's overall strategy was to allow the company to access commodities deriving from the buffalo which were to be found, on occasion, in the Bitterroot Valley and which grazed in huge numbers on the Great Plains to the east. Among the more important of these commodities was the pemmican, or dried buffalo meat, with which the Bay Company always provisioned its voyageurs and other field employees. Having purchased quantities of pemmican, tallow, buffalo robes, buffalo-hide ropes and the like from the Flathead and other local Indians who were then in the habit of travelling regularly to the Plains to hunt, Angus consequently had the responsibility of getting these materials from Fort Connah to Fort Colville where they were loaded on to boats for shipment either to the Pacific coast or to other Bay Company depots to the north of the 'medicine line' – as Indians were beginning to call the boundary between the United States and the Canadian territories which Britain had retained even after the country's abandonment of its earlier claims to Oregon.[45]

'The returns from the different outposts were brought in in the spring,' the Fort Colville bourgeois of that time, Alexander Anderson, explained. 'The outposts then received supplies and provisions and goods for the purposes of the summer trade; their parties again returned in the autumn to meet the fall brigade from the maritime depot; they then returned to their different posts with the outfit for the winter trade.'[46]

The Fort Connah 'returns' – by which Anderson meant Angus McDonald's haul of pemmican and associated items – had, first of all, to be broken down into the tightly compressed ninety-pound packs which the Bay Company always insisted upon for the simple reason that two such packs, although weighing well over a hundredweight in total, were thought to amount to a reasonable burden to impose on a voyageur when he was helping to get a trade consignment round some unnavigable set of river rapids. Other than on the Columbia River and its larger tributaries, admittedly, those Bay men who operated to the west of the Rockies relied much more on horses and mules than on canoes and boats of the sort preferred by their counterparts to the east of the mountains. But the ninety-pound pack remained standard all the same – with two such bundles being carried by each animal in the pack-trains which Angus McDonald took twice a year from Fort Connah to Fort Colville.

'The call in the morning for all men to rise should be at the dawn of day,' one Bay man commented in the course of the instructions which he helpfully compiled for the guidance of a novice in the business of organising pack-trains. At noon, the pack-train's horses were 'to be allowed to have at least three hours to eat and rest'. Care was to be taken to prevent animals straying overnight when they might readily fall victim to bears, wolves or horse-thieves. And each horse was to be provided with water 'in the evening, midday and morning'.[47]

On modern roads and by car, the journey westwards from Mission Valley to Colville can be accomplished in about eight hours. Around 1850 it took many days and could easily involve hazards of a sort which anyone making the same trip today is most unlikely to encounter.

When, for example, Catherine McDonald and her children camped on one occasion beside the Pend d'Oreille River to the west of Fort Colville and on the boundary between present-day Idaho's northern panhandle and Washington State, Christina McDonald – who had been named after her Scottish grandmother and who was then, in her father's recollection, 'a toddling babe dressed in a Glengarry tartan frock' – wandered away from her mother's tent and fell into the nearby water.[48]

Hearing her other children screaming, Catherine, as she later told Angus who was elsewhere at the time, 'rushed to the top of the bank and saw the top of the head of her little one borne rapidly away by the deep and flowing river.' The riverbank being 'a high, stepless clay cliff', Catherine 'sprang into the river from the top of it and swam in her clothes to the sinking child'. Although Christina was buoyed up by her 'tartan frock making a safety collar round her neck', she was also being swept downstream so fast that it took her mother some time to catch up with her. And even when Catherine finally did manage to lay hold of the drowning toddler, she found she could make no progress towards the riverbank when able to swim with only one hand. 'She then laid hold of the back of the head of the child in her teeth,' Angus writes, 'and thus the use of both hands was had, and required, to bring her, after a long . . . and fatiguing swim, ashore.' Christina, her father concludes, 'was apparently dead'. But 'by rolling and pressing the water out of her', Catherine soon had the little girl ready to resume the family's travels.

Overland travel, however, could have its compensations – as is clear from Angus McDonald's memories of another and later trip through the Pend d'Oreille region when Angus was accompanied not only by Christina and her younger sister, Margaret, but also by 'two fathers of the Jesuit Society'. Several members of this missionary order – who had been ministering to the Flathead people and their neighbours since the early 1840s and who eventually constructed their own mission complex in the vicinity of Fort Connah – were well known to the Bay man. One such priest, as mentioned at the end of the preceding chapter, formally married Angus and Catherine in 1854. And though Angus's own religious convictions seem to have been of a determinedly unorthodox variety, he clearly enjoyed being in the company of men who shared some, at least, of his intellectual and other interests.[49]

'One of them had his clarinet,' Angus recalled of the two Jesuits with whom he travelled through the Pend d'Oreille country, 'and, my two daughters . . . being with us, he blew on his instrument some of the best old airs of Scotland and they accompanied him with their voices.' The resulting music, Angus remembered, echoed and re-echoed from the surrounding mountains. And when the clarinet-player gave an especially spirited rendition of that most poignant of Highland emigrant airs, *Lochaber No More*, the effect seemed particularly striking to this man who was never to forget his Highland origins. 'I thought I could hear some of the fallen angels beat it out of the rocks after the father ceased,' Angus wrote of the sounds thus set rolling round and round 'the ancient Columbian forests and hills'.[50]

❀

One journey from Mission Valley to Fort Colville provided Christina McDonald with her earliest childhood memories. 'I was so small I had to be tied on to the saddle of the horse I rode,' she recalled of this trip which was made in the spring of 1852 and which was particularly unforgettable, in McDonald family circles at any rate, because it marked Angus's latest promotion. He had 'last June assumed the present charge of this district', Angus formally reported from Fort Colville to his Hudson's Bay Company superiors in September 1852. And having thus become Colville's bourgeois – the office which Archibald McDonald had held when Angus first got here in 1839 – Angus had also assumed control of a whole network of smaller posts, Fort Connah included, stretching eastwards to the Rockies, northwards into present-day British Columbia and westwards to the Cascade Mountains.[51]

Apart from a brief break in the later 1850s, Angus McDonald was to remain in charge at Colville for nearly twenty years. And as is shown by an impressively ornate warrant in the possession of one of his Flathead Reservation descendants, he was to reach, in 1856, the rank of Hudson's Bay Company Chief Trader. This was almost as high as it was possible for one of the Bay Company's field officers to rise. It meant that, for the rest of his Bay Company career, Angus McDonald, instead of earning a fixed salary of the kind on which he had to rely as a general servant or clerk, was now entitled to share in the organisation's overall profits.[52]

Angus took his Colville responsibilities very seriously. 'I have nearly rebuilt all the buildings inside the square of the fort since 1852,' he reported in the mid-1860s. Fort Colville, as a result, contained 'a large dwelling-house . . . one storey and a half high', 'a back family house of squared timber', 'a frame house . . . with two large, quartz rock chimneys', 'a file of officers' houses', a large store on two floors, a smaller store, 'a bake house', 'a poultry house', 'a pigeon house', 'a heavy square timber bastion', 'a blacksmith's shop', 'a carpenter's shop', 'a barn' and 'a cedar-rail horse park'.[53]

The fort, then, was a substantial complex – so substantial that its locking-up became something of a nightly ritual. One of Angus's subordinates, Duncan McDonald recalled, 'had a bunch of keys' which 'every night after locking-up he would bring into father's room and hang up'.[54]

To Duncan, who grew up at Fort Colville, the trading post was chiefly remarkable, in retrospect at least, for the endless opportunities it offered him and his brothers to engage in boyhood escapades of the kind that stick always in the memory. 'We used to climb up there to pull the feathers out of the pigeons' tails for our arrows,' Duncan recalled of the 'pigeon house', or dovecot, which his father had established by way of supplementing Fort Colville's food resources. With Louis Mott, the post blacksmith, Pierre Wing, the Colville carpenter, and the 'Iroquois boatmen' he remembered as 'Narcisse' and 'Grand Louis', Duncan was clearly on good terms. But he retained, even in old age, a good-going dislike of a 'post trader' by the name of Custer. 'He was a rough man,' Duncan said. 'I have seen him knock Indians around with a club . . . I am sure my father did not know of his conduct towards the Indians, as . . . he did it when father was away from home.'[55]

Neither Duncan nor the other McDonald children, it should be made clear, were left simply to run wild at Fort Colville. In 1856, the year of his advancement to chief trader, Angus McDonald — entirely at his own expense — founded the first school to exist in this part of the United States, hired a teacher for the school and insisted that his children, together with the children of such other local parents as were interested, became regular attenders.[56]

In one of his more philosophical letters, Angus McDonald was to pose this question: 'Is our memory, handed from generation to generation, our only immortality?' And if that is indeed the case, then Angus's immortality — not least as a result of his obvious affection for, and interest in, his children — is assured. Not only has 'the old Scotchman', as his Indian descendants sometimes call Angus, never been forgotten by them. His reputation, thanks to that Colville school and many similar gestures, still stands very high. 'My great-grandfather was not one of those run-of-the-mill white men who came West, got mixed up with an Indian woman, fathered children by her and deserted her,' comments Eileen Decker who is one of the Mission Valley members of what has become an enormously extended McDonald family. 'He stood by his children and he gave them as good an education as he could.'[57]

Among Angus McDonald's more prestigious visitors at Fort Colville, within a year or two of his becoming bourgeois there, were Isaac I. Stevens, newly-appointed Governor of Washington Territory, and a United States army officer called George B. McClellan. Ten years later, at the height of his country's Civil War, McClellan would be one of the American Union's principal commanders. At this stage in his career, however, McClellan — still a relatively junior officer — was assisting Stevens to survey possible routes for the railroad the governor was anxious to see constructed across the territory for which he was now responsible. And Angus McDonald, because Fort Colville constituted a convenient rendezvous for the two survey parties which Stevens and McClellan were respectively leading from the Pacific and from the Missouri, found himself with the job of entertaining two men whom the Hudson's Bay Company — given the growing political precariousness of its position on United States territory — was most anxious to impress. 'I had full instructions as to the hospitality and the discretion of it entirely entrusted to myself,' Angus remarked. And if that comment seems slightly ambiguous, there was nothing at all unclear about Angus's notion of what was to be considered appropriate in the way of hospitality – his preparations for the forthcoming visit consisting principally of laying in 'fifty imperial gallons' of spirits.[58]

On Stevens, McClellan and their parties getting to Fort Colville on 18 October 1854, this 'grog', as Angus called it, was duly dished out to all hands while Angus personally entertained McClellan and the governor to dinner. 'Mr McDonald,' Stevens reported, 'gave me a most hospitable reception . . . We sat down to a nice supper, prepared by Mrs McDonald, and regaled ourselves with steaks cooked in buffalo fat.' Afterwards, so McClellan recorded in his journal, the party 'sat up nearly all of the night talking'.[59]

Angus's account is more explicit. The governor, he notes, had shown himself 'rather fond' of brandy and had consequently gone to bed comparatively early. McClellan, who 'drank but little' prior to this point, now felt himself at liberty to unwind, sat down beside Angus on an 'old sofa' and 'began to sip the juice of the vine more freely'.[60]

'We sat on the old sofa together as closely as space allowed,' Angus writes. 'I felt my grog inviting me to go to my blankets. But I was well trained in that splendid brandy and in prime of life, too.' Rather than 'give in', therefore, Angus entertained McClellan to more of what Stevens had earlier described as 'thrilling stories and exciting legends' – some of them, no doubt, dealing with Angus's Western adventures and others, still more certainly, featuring the many military exploits of the trader's Highland ancestors. 'Suddenly,' Angus goes on, 'the general [and here Angus anticipates McClellan's later rank] put his arm round my neck and whispered in my ear, 'Mac, my proud father, too, was at Culloden.' And he quietly slipped down off the sofa to the floor.'[61]

Writing from Fort Vancouver a month or so later, one of Angus's Bay Company colleagues informed him that Governor Stevens had 'dined' there on 17 November. Stevens, Angus's informant continued, 'paid a very high encomium to the Hudson's Bay Company in general and then, with a flow of imagery that spoke highly of his poetic taste, did worthy homage to the hospitable friend who received him as a brother at Fort Colville. You stand very high there and . . . deservedly so.'[62]

When the occasion demanded, then, Angus McDonald could clearly keep his lingering anti-Americanism in check. And it is not at all surprising, given his growing reputation and standing in the company, that younger Bay men, such as Edward Huggins, a London-born clerk who met the Fort Colville bourgeois for the first time in July 1855, should have begun to regard Angus – now nearly twenty years in the fur trade – with something approaching awe.

Angus, on the occasion in question, had come down to Fort

Nisqually, one of the Bay Company's Pacific coast depots, with a pack-train containing the previous winter's take of furs. 'In the lot,' Huggins noted of this consignment, 'were upwards of 1,300 bearskins, almost all large, and 250 of them . . . grizzlies.' And that, it appears, was only the start; for Angus, according to Huggins, had also brought in the skins or pelts of 200 badgers, 2,500 beavers, twelve silver foxes, 80 'cross-silver' foxes, 334 'red' foxes, 185 lynx, 1,500 marten, 575 mink, 412 otters, 8,000 musquash, 580 wolves and 45 wolverines. So heavy was the Colville pack-train's cargo, Edward Huggins added, that it required no less than 200 horses and mules — accompanied, as Huggins put it, by 'a cosmopolitan crowd' of 'Scotchmen, French-Canadians, half-breeds and Iroquois Indians'.[63]

'I had heard a good deal about McDonald and was anxious to see him,' Huggins wrote of Angus's arrival at Fort Nisqually. 'He was rather a good-looking man, about six feet in height, straight and slim, but . . . said to be very wiry and strong. He had a dark complexion and long, jet-black hair reaching to his shoulder, and a thick, long and very black beard and moustache. He wore a dressed deerskin shirt and pants . . . and had a blackish silk handkerchief tied loosely round his neck. He had a black, piercing eye and a deep, sonorous voice, rather musical, and . . . a slow . . . manner of speaking. He was fond of telling Indian stories and legends and would sometimes keep an audience entranced when . . . telling some bloodcurdling Indian story . . . He was fairly educated and well up in the politics of the day. He was a good French linguist, but his native language was the Gaelic of the Scotch Highlands, and he was very fond of singing or chanting — in a deep, not by any means musical, voice — Gaelic songs or verses improvised by himself.'

Edward Huggins may have got wrong points of detail. McDonald family tradition, for example, insists that Angus's hair was 'reddish' and that his eyes were blue. What emerges clearly from Huggins's account of Angus, however, is the extent to which the latter — from Huggins's viewpoint — possessed more than a little of the mystique that the younger Angus had himself discerned, it seems likely, in Joe Meek and the other mountain men whom he had encountered in the course of his own early years in the fur trade. But just as those mountain men who had married Indians — a category which included Meek — were increasingly vilified during the 1850s by the many Western settlers to whom such marriages seemed little short of unnatural, so Angus, to Huggins, seemed 'excessively fond of living the life of an aborigine'. The Fort Colville bourgeois, Huggins noted critically 'would much prefer to live in a tent, or lodge, than in a house built in accordance with civilised plans'.[64]

That Angus spent a lot of time in the company of Indians – not least, of course, his wife – is undoubted. 'He could talk several Indian languages,' Edward Huggins reported of Fort Colville's chief trader. What Huggins probably underestimated, however, was the sheer effort Angus must have put into acquiring such fluency. He had 'set to in earnest to learn the Indian language,' another fur trader once commented of his own linguistic studies, 'and wrote vocabulary after vocabulary'. In similarly disciplining himself through countless winter evenings, Angus McDonald would have been motivated partly by commercial considerations. He had to trade with Indians, after all. But Angus, as has been indicated several times already, was also interested in Native American languages and cultures for their own sake. There was much 'that may be learned from the campfire stories of the . . . Indians,' as he once observed by way of preliminary to recounting just such a campfire tale which he had been told originally 'by an old Flathead chief'.[65]

This chief was almost certainly Victor – as he was known to whites – whose Salish band was resident in and around the Bitterroot Valley during Angus McDonald's first prolonged stay in the Flathead country. Such was Victor's feeling for Angus, an early Montana newspaper reported, that when the chief became mortally ill in the course of a buffalo-hunting expedition to the Great Plains in the summer of 1870, 'he requested those who surrounded his deathbed to give his old war-horse to Mr McDonald as a present from a dying friend' – the horse in question being duly gifted to Angus when the latter next visited the Bitterroot Valley in the fall of that year.[66]

Victor, it seems likely, was present in 1850 when Angus – at a spot near the present-day town of Polson on what was five years later to become the Flathead Reservation – took part in the Indian ceremonial he called the San-ka-ha. This was 'the red man's farewell,' Angus explained, 'before he leaves for battle'. To have heard the San-ka-ha song 'sung by five or six hundred voices in a calm, starry night', Angus went on, had been 'a rare thing'. And what had been still rarer was to be given the chance to participate in such an event. 'I stripped with the leading men,' Angus recalled, 'painted with vermilion the grooves and dimples of my upper body, mounted on my black buffalo charger with my full eagle-feather cap and cantered round and round . . . keeping time to the song.'[67]

More than a century after Angus's death, his Indian grandson, Charlie McDonald, said this about his grandfather: 'In all his trading and every-thing else with Indians, he was always fair with them and, I guess, more or less leaning in their favour most of the time. That's why they all respected him and why he got along so good with the different tribes wherever he went.'[68]

Among the 'different tribes' Angus McDonald dealt with regularly at Fort Colville when he became bourgeois there in 1852 were the Yakima by whose chief, Kamiakin, Angus was told of the Mount Rainier vision quest which was described at the beginning of this chapter. 'Kamiakin was a notable-looking man,' Angus's daughter, Christina, recalled. 'He used to wear — when visiting father at the fort — a coat of Hudson's Bay broadcloth with red trimmings and brass buttons. I remember father telling Kamiakin that it was hopeless for the Indians to fight the whites; that to kill a white man was like killing an ant, there would be hundreds more pour up out of the nest; that the whites would eventually overrun the Indian country; and that the more the Indians resisted or fought, the more determined and more numerous the whites would be.'[69]

If, in fact, Angus did give Kamiakin such advice, it was disregarded in the course of the widespread hostilities precipitated by the treaty-making activities on which Isaac I. Stevens embarked in 1855. The governor's evident determination to confine their people to reservations, combined with the equally unsettling impact of growing white incursions on what had always been Indian land, had the effect of convincing both Kamiakin and many other chiefs that they had little to lose by embarking on a policy of violent resistance to white claims. Actual fighting began to break out in the late summer and fall of 1855. And only his high standing among the region's Indians, according at least to Edward Huggins, prevented Angus McDonald from becoming one of this Indian war's early victims.[70]

Angus was returning to Fort Colville from Fort Nisqually — a journey which took him and his pack-train through the Yakima country — at the point when, by killing an American government official, the Yakima people effectively declared themselves at war with whites. 'Had any other man but McDonald been in charge of the pack-train,' Huggins wrote, 'the whole outfit would no doubt have been sacrificed and the men in charge murdered, for the goods would have been of great value to the already hostile Indians.' As it was, the Yakima allowed the Fort Colville pack-train — which was carrying guns and ammunition as well as other goods — to pass unmolested. 'McDonald's influence among the Indians must have been very great to have allowed him to come scatheless through such danger,' Huggins observed. 'He was looked up to by . . . all the tribes . . . and that reputation, along with the ability to talk to the Indians in their own language, permitted him to pass safely.'[71]

The fighting which thus broke out was to last, on and off, for two or three years. And Angus's continuing immunity from Indian attack was to result, during this sometimes stormy period, in him giving refuge to Major John Owen who both operated a trading post in the Bitterroot Valley and acted as the U.S. government's agent on the Flathead Reservation. Owen and his assistant, Charles W. Frush, had run into 'five hundred or six hundred hostiles' when packing trade goods eastwards from the Columbia River to the Flathead country and had consequently made for Fort Colville where Angus, as Frush reported afterwards, received them with his usual 'hospitality'.[72]

When he and Owen finally judged it safe to leave, Frush recounted, 'the major tied his fine saddle mule, Kitty, to a post in front of the chief trader's house' and went inside to make his farewells. But several Indians remained in the vicinity, Frush went on, and one of them – 'a big brave', according to Frush – 'deliberately walked up', untied the mule and walked off with it.

'Old Angus McDonald,' or so Frush's story runs, 'looking out of his window, saw this bold proceeding, rushed out of the house and across the courtyard, snatched the rope from the Indian and gave him a severe lecture in his own language relative to his conduct, unbecoming an Indian brave and more especially so in regard to the respect due to him, Angus McDonald, the chief trader of the Honourable Hudson's Bay Company post, giving him to understand that no such business would be tolerated. You should have seen the major smile when the old Glencoe chieftain led . . . Kitty back and handed her over to her owner who valued the mule and outfit at $500.'

John Owen was properly grateful for Angus's protection. But the fact that the Fort Colville bourgeois was on such good terms with so many Indians could nevertheless be viewed, from a white American perspective at any rate, as raising questions about Angus's ultimate loyalties. The Bay Company, after all, had been opposed to the United States acquiring both Washington Territory and the rest of the Columbia country in the first place. And most Bay men, including Angus McDonald, remained British citizens. Was it not more than likely, then, that the company's representatives, as alleged by one U.S. army officer in 1858, were encouraging Indians to treat 'United States officials as intruders'? Might the British, as had happened more than once in the past, be making trouble for the United States by fomenting unrest among Indians? Could the Bay Company be supplying Kamiakin and his followers with guns, gunpowder and the various other munitions they needed to sustain their war?[73]

The Americans who harboured such fears would not have been reassured by the fact that Angus McDonald co-operated closely in the later 1850s and early 1860s with the British military surveyors who had been ordered to report to London on how best to defend the British Empire's Canadian frontier with the United States. Angus was regarded by the British soldiers in question as 'a gentleman of great information' who had 'travelled much' in the mountain country traversed by the boundary between British Columbia and Washington Territory. But to help with boundary surveys – even surveys which had some underlying military purpose – was a long way from actually arming Indians. And Angus always denied that he had done so. 'He once sent me an offer of a hundred horses for seventy pounds of powder,' Fort Colville's chief trader wrote of his dealings with Kamiakin. 'But I declined acquiring wealth in that way.'[74]

If he did not actually give guns to Indians, however, Angus McDonald certainly disapproved strongly of the way that Washington Territory's Indian peoples were treated in the course of the 1855–58 fighting in the region. 'The most unrelenting barbarities are told . . . of your volunteers,' Angus informed Governor Stevens on one occasion – the 'volunteers' being the civilian militias which were then being deployed, as they were to be deployed again during the Nez Perce War of 1877, alongside the United States army.[75]

With America's regular soldiers, on the other hand, Angus seems always to have got along fairly well. One of the officers stationed at the garrison which the U.S. army established near Colville in 1859 was sufficiently friendly with the Bay man to have marked the end of his Colville posting by gifting Angus all his books. Another such officer, a Captain McKibbin, wrote to Angus with the express purpose of thanking him for 'the open-house hospitalities' on offer at Fort Colville. 'And to your wife and each of the family give my love,' McKibbin instructed Angus. 'For love it is. To each and all of you I am indebted for very many acts of kindness which I can never forget.'[76]

The attractions of Fort Colville to the nearby army post's younger soldiers, admittedly, may have had less to do with Angus McDonald than with his now-teenage daughter, Christina – 'the belle of Colville', according to one contemporary report. But the good relations which undoubtedly existed between the McDonalds and the U.S. military cannot be squared with the notion that the Fort Colville bourgeois was some sort of pro-Indian subversive. Angus, in fact, genuinely wanted peace between Washington Territory's Indians and the American authorities, his several interventions in the political and military affairs of the region being intended to curtail, rather than foster, fighting.[77]

❖

To the British surveyors who drew regularly on Angus McDonald's services in the course of their various expeditions along the line of the frontier between the United States and what were then Britain's Canadian possessions, the Fort Colville bourgeois appeared every bit as intriguing as he had done to Edward Huggins at Fort Nisqually. 'He is a great curiosity,' one of those surveyors wrote of Angus. 'He has more influence with the Indians, I suppose, than any white man ever had. Some of his hunting tales are very good. He has polished off a large number of grizzlies singlehanded, deer and buffalo innumerable.'[78]

Somebody – very possibly Angus himself – had given this surveyor, a young Englishman by the name of Charles Wilson, to understand that Angus, in his youth, had been 'the strongest man and best rifle shot on the continent'. These were big claims. But even the tallest of tall tales about the Fort Colville bourgeois gained a certain credibility as a result of Angus's always picturesque lifestyle – a lifestyle which, as is made clear by Charles Wilson's description of the McDonald family setting off on 'a hunting expedition', was as Indian as it was white.

'They went off mounted by twos and threes,' Wilson commented of the McDonalds' departure, 'Mrs McDonald . . . leading, perched high up on the curious saddle used by the women here, one of her younger daughters astride behind her and a baby swinging in its Indian cradle from the pommel. Next came Miss Christina, who is about 17, with her gaily beaded leggings and moccasins, gaudy shawl flying in the wind. She had a younger sister perched behind her and, in front, a small brother perched like a young monkey . . . Next came the boys, two and two on horseback, and last McDonald himself, on his buffalo runner, surrounded by a crowd of Indians and half-breeds . . . Add some forty or fifty packhorses and spare animals rushing wildly about, with the shouts and cries of the attendants, and you have a fine scene of excitement and confusion.'

Angus's hunting trips – especially when he had access to company of the sort provided by Charles Wilson and his colleagues – were invariably interspersed by scarcely less rigorous partying. Christmas 1860, for instance, brought 'a great spread-out of beef and plum pudding' – after which, so Wilson noted, 'Mr McDonald gave us a capital sword dance'.

Nor did his sword dance – a traditional Highland ceremonial involving intricate footwork around two broadswords lain crosswise on the ground – by any means exhaust Angus's capacity to entertain. 'We had the other day a grand ball up at the Hudson's Bay fort given by Mr McDonald,' Charles Wilson wrote on 10 February 1861. 'You have no idea of the scene. Such a wonderful collection of people . . . Songs and dances were the order of the evening. Some of the Canadian boat songs sung by a lot of voyageurs were capital. But the dancing . . . was the great thing, and, at four o'clock in the morning, I found myself dancing a reel *de deux* with an Indian squaw in a state of uncertainty as to whether I had any legs at all, having danced them clean away, and nearly dislocated them into the bargain, by trying to pick up the proper step, a kind of spasmodic kick in which the legs are doubled up and thrown out in the most extraordinary manner.'

Despite such frolics, politics – especially as they impacted on the lives of his Indian friends and relatives – continued to concern Angus McDonald. But despite his being regularly in touch with Governor Stevens of Washington Territory in the years following the latter's 1853 visit to Fort Colville, there was little that Angus or any other Hudson's Bay Company representative could do to influence the governor's Indian policy in any very direct way. The company, from the standpoint of its many American critics, might have looked like the perpetually menacing embodiment of British colonialism. In reality, though, the Bay Company's day had clearly passed – as far at least as its role in Washington Territory was concerned. The company, it should not be forgotten, was primarily a fur-trading corporation. And in the American West the fur trade was now fading steadily away.

Peter Skene Ogden, who did as much as anyone to establish the trade in Columbia country furs, once commented: 'The fur trade and civilisation can never be blended together and experience teaches us that the former invariably gives way to the latter.' Ogden inevitably equated 'civilisation' with white settlement and, to the extent that such settlement was incompatible with the maintenance of the Indian societies – to say nothing of the ecosystems – on which the fur trade relied for a great deal of its output, Ogden was clearly right. That was why North American fur traders, ever since the trade began, had always had to keep moving westwards as first one former frontier area and then another was occupied by settlers.[79]

Such settlers, of course, were not wholly to blame for the fur trade's gradual demise. The trade – as is obvious from the previously cited list of the furs conveyed by Angus McDonald from Fort Colville to Fort Nisqually in 1855 – was always terribly destructive of its own sources of supply. 'The beaver . . . is rapidly disappearing,' Archibald McDonald had written as early as 1838. And so severe was the hunting and trapping pressure on all fur-bearing animals that, even had it had no other difficulties to contend with, the Hudson's Bay Company, by the later 1850s, would have been experiencing lower and lower returns on its operations in what had become Washington Territory.[80]

The fact that the Bay Company made a net gain of only £29 from all its trading activities in the United States in 1858, however, was by no means entirely due to the growing scarcity of furs. Nor could this desperately poor performance be attributed exclusively to changes in fashion – notably a developing preference for hats made from silk – which were certainly having the effect of undermining the market in beaver pelts. The Hudson's Bay Company – as it was to prove in Canada – could live with fewer furs, even with changing fashions. What the company could not handle were the political and other pressures which, ever since the formal acquisition of Oregon by the United States, had been rendering its position on U.S. territory more and more untenable.[81]

'Fences and farms are everywhere established where our herds used to graze freely,' Angus McDonald reported from a Fort Colville which was increasingly surrounded by American settlers. Both at Colville and elsewhere, another Bay Company man complained, the American government's policy of confining native peoples to reservations was leaving the company 'no Indians to trade with'. And the Indian wars which the reservations policy had helped to cause were resulting in further disruption.[82]

One casualty of these wars was the Hudson's Bay Company post at Fort Hall which, as Angus McDonald explained, was abandoned in 1856 'on account of Indian hostilities'. Two company 'expressmen', or messengers, had been killed by Indians when riding from Fort Vancouver to Fort Hall in 1856, Angus went on. He had consequently ordered Michael Ogden – who had succeeded him at Fort Connah and who was Peter Skene Ogden's mixed-blood son as well as the husband of Catherine McDonald's half-sister, Angelina – to have the 'company's effects at Fort Hall', including its 'men and property', moved to Mission Valley which, at this time, was a place of comparative safety.[83]

Had it not been for the company's determination to insist on its entitlement to compensation in respect of what were called its 'possessory rights' in the United States, the Hudson's Bay Company would very probably have pulled out of American territory by 1860. The Oregon Treaty, however, had included clauses obliging the U.S. government, in effect, to buy out the company's longstanding interest in the region – as represented by its forts, farms and other properties. For much of the period during which Angus McDonald was in charge at Fort Colville, therefore, his function – as far, at least, as the Bay Company's London-based managers were concerned – was not so much to prosecute an increasingly non-existent fur trade as to demonstrate that the company had no intention of leaving the United States until its claims had been settled by the U.S. federal government.

This took a long time. It was not until 1863 that an international commission, comprising both American and British representatives, was given the job of settling the possessory rights issue once and for all. And the commission, even when established, worked very slowly. Angus McDonald – accompanied by his daughter, Christina – travelled down the Columbia River from Fort Colville to Portland in September 1865 to give evidence to commission members. But another four years passed before the latter agreed that the Hudson's Bay Company should receive $650,000 – to be paid, the company insisted, in gold bullion – from the U.S. government in return for its abandoning all its assets to the south of the American-Canadian frontier.[84]

The Hudson's Bay Company, having thus got its money, began to shut down the last of its posts in Washington Territory. Fort Colville – where the company's trade was now described as 'discouraging' – closed in the spring of 1871 and Angus McDonald, who both took out Anerican citizenship and retired from the Bay Company at this point, moved that year from Colville to Mission Valley where the McDonald family once again set up home.[85]

The McDonald link with Colville – which had lasted for most of the former trading post's existence – was not yet to be broken, however. 'When the Hudson's Bay Company left the Oregon territories,' Angus explained in a subsequent letter to an American friend, 'I was left in charge of their place at Colville, to be delivered that summer to the governor of Washington Territory. Seeing that the company was going away and that I had an American-born family, I became naturalized into this republic the year before they left. No governor nor any other person called for the place and, it being subject to being jumped on by citizens of the United States, I thought I had as good as right to it as any other and I held it, and hold it, under a squatter's right . . . the government never having called for it.'[86]

Although Angus's interpretation of the legal position at Colville was to be challenged more than once during the 1870s, his son Donald, who had been born at Fort Connah in 1851 and who had himself been on the company's staff at Colville for some months prior to the post's closure, remained in effective possession of at least a portion of the Bay Company's former landholdings in the Fort Colville area. Also resident there was Archibald McDonald's mixed-blood son, Ranald, who – following his Japanese and Australian adventures – had returned to Fort Colville in the 1860s. In partnership with his half-brother, Ben, another of Archibald's sons, Ranald first of all ran pack-trains from Colville into a number of the more or less remote locations, on both sides of the

Canadian-American border, where gold was discovered in this period. Then, when there were no more gold prospectors to supply, Ranald, some years before his death in 1894, took finally to farming – possibly in collaboration with Donald McDonald, Angus's son, who had fairly extensive agricultural and business interests in the vicinity of Colville towards the close of the nineteenth century.[87]

Angus McDonald, meanwhile, was rapidly re-establishing his connection with the former Fort Connah – 'the favourite spot of all he has found in his long residence in this country', as Marshall William Wheeler was to note following his conversation with Angus in 1885.[88]

Angus's Fort Connah connection, indeed, had never quite been broken. The veteran fur trader's friends among the Flathead people – friends who included, as mentioned earlier, the leading Flathead chief, Victor – had long since made clear to Angus that he would be welcome to set up home alongside them. It was to Mission Valley, where he knew they would have Flathead protection, that Angus had sent Catherine and several of their children when Fort Colville seemed at some risk of attack during the Indian wars of the 1850s. And this type of association between the McDonald family and Mission Valley – an association which dated back to Angus's founding of Fort Connah in 1847 – had been reinforced by the fact that, for the three or four years prior to the post's closure in 1871, Duncan McDonald, Angus's son, had served as the last of the Bay Company's Fort Connah clerks.[89]

Strolling around what remains of Fort Connah and looking out across Post Creek, it is not difficult to understand why Angus McDonald was so attracted to this spot. An extensive grassland gently rises to meet, at a point some three miles distant, the forested lower slopes of McDonald Peak – 'named after myself', as Angus wrote, but for many centuries before he got here, as he was careful to add, a place of spiritual significance to the many Indians who climbed the mountain's slopes in the course of their vision quests.[90]

Almost due east of Fort Connah, a steep-sided valley – the sort of valley that in Scotland would be called a glen but which Montanans call a canyon – reaches deep into the mountains. To walk into this valley, past noticeboards which warn of grizzlies, is at once to appreciate the wealth of wild landscape – to say nothing of hunting opportunities – which Angus McDonald had available to him within a few hours' ride of his front door.

That front door stood within a stone's throw of Post Creek. For it was near the creek, during 1872, that Angus constructed, on a site adjacent to his former trading post, a large family house built partly of logs and partly of adobe brick. The land in this vicinity, Angus knew, was reasonably productive. He had been instrumental, after all, in establishing in Mission Valley as far back as 1847 the 'small farm' which, as the Hudson's Bay Company had been informed that October, was then under cultivation on 'capital' soil. Early plans to make Fort Connah self-sufficient in grain had very possibly fallen victim to the low annual rainfalls to which this part of Montana is frequently prone. But Angus was convinced – correctly – that fine cattle could readily be reared hereabouts. 'A rolling plain undulates with the richest coat of bunch-grass that you ever saw for thirty by twenty miles before my window,' he wrote to an acquaintance in March 1876. And on this open range – 'graciously furnished by streams' – his stock were doing well. No fewer than 'three bulls' were noisily attending to 'their duty' within 'rifle shot' of his home while he wrote, Angus went on. And it is more than probable, as noted previously, that some McDonald cattle were included in the herd which Billy Irvine drove from the Flathead country to Cheyenne that summer.[91]

The man who had started with the Hudson's Bay Company in 1838 on £25 a year was now reckoned by Marshall Wheeler to have 'ample means' which had been 'accumulated by a lifetime of labour'. And Angus's surviving papers and correspondence corroborate the marshall's view. An 1879 letter to Angus from a former Bay Company colleague contains the comment: 'You ask me what is the best way for you to invest $5,000'. There is mention in another letter of Angus's investments in London. And in addition to marketing his cattle, Angus made clear at one point, he dabbled occasionally in freelance fur trading – despite his having no permit to engage in such activity on what had been, since 1855, an Indian reservation. 'I sometimes buy a few fur skins with cash in hand when the Indians desire it,' Angus admitted.[92]

❁

'I am doing nothing but eating my own steak,' Angus remarked to one of his correspondents in 1876. And for all that he was then sixty years of age, he clearly took no pleasure in an idle or routine existence.[93]

Angus's idea of the uneventful was not everyone's, of course. 'I kept very quiet all winter,' he wrote to one of his daughters in February 1881; 'one little spree at Christmas of twelve bottles for all.'[94]

Otherwise, books helped to pass the time. The 'very respectable library' which a visitor reported finding at Fort Colville in 1852 was no doubt transported to Mission Valley. And as well as reading, Angus wrote a lot, subjecting his acquaintances to page after page of poetry and prose. 'Received one of . . . McDonald's poetical effusions,' an especially long-suffering friend confided to his journal on getting some of Angus's verses. And since surviving specimens of these verses tend towards the sentimental, it is easy to understand why Angus's 'effusions' were not always eagerly anticipated.[95]

Angus was at his literary best when he stuck to telling stories culled from his own incident-filled life. 'The morning was heavy and fleecy and the earth had been whitened with . . . snow during the night,' one such story begins. 'The dreary, sluggish and treeless Missouri wound down its valley, completely harnessed in ice a foot thick. I invited an Indian brother-in-law of mine to take a horse and ride out to the mountains.'[96]

As his reference to the Missouri indicates, Angus is here reminiscing – twenty or more years after the event – about one of the many hunting expeditions he made eastwards, in the direction of the Great Plains, in the company of Nez Perce, Salish and other Indians. A highlight of this particular excursion to the Upper Missouri, it appears, was Angus's killing of a puma or mountain lion. The equivalent moment on a further trip occurs when Angus's hunting party – again consisting mostly of Indians – chase a group of elk across a snow-covered hillside. 'It was beautiful to see how the noble animals bore on,' Angus writes, 'pursued helter-skelter by the Indians whose hair streamed wildly behind them like the black manes of a herd of buffaloes.'[97]

Angus was accompanied on that occasion by one of his sons – possibly Duncan. And he and his 'boy', becoming somehow separated from their companions, found themselves benighted – 'about fifteen miles from camp' – in a fahrenheit temperature of around 30 degrees below zero. To protect themselves from the effects of exposure and frostbite, the two McDonalds made themselves a 'bed' from the freshly removed hides of a number of the elk they had managed to kill. And they were fortunate enough to discover 'dry and fallen scrub timbers' with which to make a fire. 'We built our fire on the body of the nearest elk,' Angus recalled. That prevented the life-preserving fire from being quenched by the melting snow which, being feet deep, would otherwise have tended to overwhelm the flames. But such was the intensity of the frost that, fire or no fire, worthwhile rest proved impossible. 'After the heat of walking through the snow,' Angus remembered, 'with torn and rock-cut moccasins and cotton-drill trousers without drawers, as I wore no flannels, I felt very cold and uncomfortable and could not sleep a wink.'[98]

The steady spread of white settlement, together with the confining of his Indian friends and relatives to reservations, meant that forays of the type which Angus thus described had become much rarer occurrences by the time the McDonald family settled permanently in

Mission Valley. Occasionally, however, there were business trips to be arranged. And these went some way to gratifying Angus's continuing zest for travel.

In the mid-1870s, for example, Angus journeyed more than once from Mission Valley to Victoria, the Vancouver Island capital of British Columbia — stopping off to visit his daughter, Christina, who had married a Highland-born fur trader, James MacKenzie, and who had gone on, following her husband's early death in 1873, to open a trading post of her own in Kamloops. It very probably pleased Angus — who, like most Bay men, was always more than slightly ambivalent about the company — that Christina traded in opposition to his former employers. 'I more than held my own with them,' Christina remarked proudly in later life, 'for I was raised in the fur trade, and had been a companion of my father so long I knew the business thoroughly.'[99]

'For all his years in the Northwest,' Christina said on the same occasion, 'father was never weaned from his Scotch habits and ways. Once when I was with him in Victoria he engaged a coach and, taking Hugh MacLean, a bagpipe player, we set off to pay a visit to . . . a fellow countryman and old acquaintance who lived near Esquimalt.' The acquaintance in question, Christina explained, was Alexander Anderson whom Angus had succeeded as bourgeois at Fort Colville and who was 'overjoyed' to see her father. 'Driving to Anderson's the woods rang with MacLean's spirited playing,' she remembered.[100]

'I believe if, at the last day, you will hear the sound of a trumpet,' Angus once wrote, 'you shall also hear the sound of the Scotch bagpipe.' Sometimes he played the pipes himself. Sometimes he favoured a jew's harp — especially the 'superior' model made for him by the Fort Colville blacksmith, James Goudie. 'I may say that few men equalled me at this unassuming instrument,' Angus commented.[101]

Catherine McDonald, according to her husband, also had 'an excellent ear for the music of the white man as well as for that of her red forefathers'. That was partly why, in the spring of 1878, Angus invested $136.50 in an 'organ' — perhaps a piano — which he installed carefully in his Mission Valley home. 'Maggie says the tone of the thing is very fine,' he assured the friend who had helped procure this instrument. And it was Maggie, his daughter, then 22, who now regularly treated Angus to a selection of Scottish tunes. 'The other night,' Angus wrote of one of his musical evenings, 'whilst the wild Rocky Mountain winds played their own solemn unrecorded ways over my humble roof, Maggie played *Old Hundred*, *Bonnie Doon* and *Annie Laurie* and, to be sure, I felt the thing. The sight was strange to me to see the . . . daughter of old America and far back Scotland playing these splendid airs.'[102]

'*Bliadhna mhath ur dhuibh*,' Angus began a letter written in a Mission Valley January. It was by such means – this Gaelic phrase being a standard new year's greeting – that Angus signalled his continuing interest in the language which would have been every bit as much a feature of his Highland upbringing as music of the sort he had clearly taught his family. Gaelic was his 'maternal tongue', Angus wrote, and a 'wonderfully expressive' tongue at that. He had consequently never missed a chance to make use of it. Hence Angus's enduring fondness for those fur-trade get-togethers where Gaelic was often to be heard more frequently than English. Hence Angus's habit, when on his fur-trade travels, of enlivening boat and canoe journeys by breaking into Gaelic songs. And hence his subscribing, when living in Mission Valley, to one of later-nineteenth-century Scotland's leading Gaelic periodicals, *The Celtic Magazine*, a copy of which, dating from May 1886, is still preserved in a McDonald family home on the Flathead Reservation.[103]

There was an element of nostalgia in this, of course. Especially during his later years in Mission Valley, Angus McDonald was inclined – as perhaps all older immigrants in any country are inclined – to dwell at times on the life he had given up nearly half a century before. In a letter sent to Mission Valley from Dingwall in 1884, Margaret, Angus's sister, is clearly striving to respond to her brother's desire for news of family members whom he had last seen in 1838. 'I am very sorry it is not in my power to find out what you want to know,' Margaret writes of one relative whom she has been unable to trace. 'I have been making enquiries about our cousin,' she adds of another relative about whom Angus has evidently been asking, 'and find that the only one of his family still living is a daughter who got married some years ago and went abroad to New Zealand.'[104]

'I frequently feel alone,' Angus confesses in one of his own Mission Valley letters, this one written on his hearing of the death of Joe Meek. He is not sure whether God will wish 'to bless or damn poor old hunters like me and my departed friend, Joseph Meek,' Angus continues. But he possibly suspects that the former fate may be more likely than the latter. He is, at any rate, more than a little bit depressed. And his attempts to keep up with the world beyond Mission Valley have been frustrated, Angus observes. 'Last winter,' he tells a friend one spring, 'I gave $2 for a New York paper.' But the subscription has not been honoured or, if it has, the paper has gone astray between New York and Montana. Neither 'paper nor dollars' have been heard of since he sent off his order, Angus writes. 'What a world!'[105]

In Mission Valley, however, there were always sources of knowledge other than the printed page. From the Indians who continued to be his regular visitors, for example, Angus gained additional insights into those Native American customs and beliefs which had fascinated him ever since his arrival on this continent. Among his favourite guests, Angus wrote, was Catherine McDonald's close kinsman, Eagle-from-the-Light, a 'most eloquent . . . old blood', as he described this ageing chief. 'From him I learned many an item about the Nez Perce,' he added. Others, too, were soon to hear a lot more about this people.[106]

CHAPTER FIVE

We had only asked to be left in our own homes

It is one of the American West's psychological oddities that its white settlers often gave to their new communities the names of the Indians on whose territories these communities were established. Thus Chief Victor of the Salish people, the man who posthumously gifted his warhorse to Angus McDonald, had his name appropriated by the founders of the town of Victor, located in a part of Montana from which Victor's tribe were expelled more than a hundred years ago. Many other Indians have been similarly commemorated. Hence the appearance on the map of Joseph, situated towards the upper end of the Wallowa Valley in the scenically splendid north-eastern corner of present-day Oregon.

Chief Joseph, the man whose name this small town bears, was a late-nineteenth-century leader of the Nez Perce band whose lands once included both the Wallowa Valley and its surrounding hills. The area was one of those included in the reservation set aside for the Nez Perce under the terms of the treaty negotiated with them by Governor Isaac I. Stevens in 1855. This treaty had guaranteed that the Wallowa Valley would remain, for all time coming, in the possession of the Nez Perce. 'Nor shall any white man,' one of its provisions stated, 'be permitted to reside upon the reservation without permission of the Indian tribe.'[1]

As agreed in 1855, the Nez Perce Reservation was very large. It extended from Oregon into the south-eastern corner of present-day Washington State. It took in, too, much of what is today north-central Idaho. An area of this size was almost bound, in the circumstances of the 1850s and the 1860s, to include at least some land which at least some whites would eventually want to occupy. And so things duly turned out.

152

Gold was discovered on the Nez Perce Reservation in 1860 by a trader and prospector called Elias D. Pierce. Soon thousands of other fortune-hunters had followed where Pierce had led. The consequences for the Nez Perce were summarised thus by one of their white sympathisers, a U.S. government official named H. Clay Wood: 'Their reservation was overrun; the enclosed lands taken from them; stock turned into their grainfields and gardens; their fences taken and used by persons to enclose lands to which they laid claim, or torn down, burned, or otherwise destroyed . . . Along the roads on the reservation to all the mines, at the crossing of every stream or freshwater spring, and near the principal Indian villages, an inn or *shebang* is established, ostensibly for the entertainment of travellers, but almost universally used as a den for supplying liquor to the Indians. The class of men that pursue this infamous traffic are, as might be expected, the most abandoned wretches of society . . . Horses or mules, only strayed from lack of herding, were supposed to have been stolen by the Indians; and the reckless owner would often indulge in rash measures for their recovery.'[2]

The people drawn westwards by such gold rushes – of which there were a whole series in Idaho, Montana and adjacent territories in the course of the nineteenth century's third quarter – were to have the effect of bringing about the permanent white settlement of whole localities where such settlement might otherwise have been a long time coming. That is what Idaho's district attorney meant in 1877 when he commented of the mining camps established on the Nez Perce Reservation some fifteen or sixteen years before: 'These camps may justly be termed the key that unlocked this country to civilised men.'[3]

By the nineteenth century's end – greatly helped along, as it happens, by Scottish investors – Western mining had become a highly organised industry. Prominent among its typical products was the Montana community of Butte – about 120 miles to the south-east of Missoula. Having begun as a collection of tents, Butte was quickly transformed by its mining company owners into a sprawling, dirty, overcrowded city of a type which – in its social composition and in its violently radical politics, at any rate – would not have been out of place on the Scottish coalfields where many of its miners were recruited.

Gold rushes of the sort which started on the Nez Perce Reservation in 1861, however, owed practically nothing to mining corporations of the Butte variety. An early gold rush was the preserve of endlessly optimistic prospectors equipped, very often, with nothing more expensive or sophisticated than a pack-mule, a pick, a shovel and an iron pan in which any likely-looking gravel could be washed in such a way as to separate out the few flecks of gold dust which it might contain.

It is, to put it mildly, a good deal less than likely that such prospectors – of whom a substantial number, incidentally, came from Scotland – thought of themselves as constituting civilisation's vanguard. Such rationalisations of their conduct they mostly left to others. But the cumulative effect of their individual actions was certainly to bring about the irreversible transformation of the Nez Perce country, where, by the fall of 1862, there were reported to be '15,000 people, mostly gold miners, on the . . . reservation'.[4]

All these people, as the U.S. military stressed, had crossed the Nez Perce Reservation's boundaries 'in defiance of the express provisions' of the treaty made with the reservation's Indian inhabitants just seven years before. But a white population of this size, the military acknowledged, could not simply be ejected. The ethical case for forcibly removing miners from the Nez Perce Reservation might have been, as some whites recognised, unanswerable. The political case for leaving the miners where they were, however, was more pressing and persuasive. And so the miners stayed – their various economic and other require-ments resulting in hosts of other whites encroaching in their wake on the still supposedly inviolable reservation.[5]

As merchants, packers, stagecoach-operators, saloon-keepers, gamblers, prostitutes, preachers, real estate spectulators and lawyers, to say nothing of more miners, poured on to the Nez Perce Reservation, then, the tented encampments of 1861 and 1862 gave way steadily to more permanent settlements consisting first of log cabins and then of timber-framed homes, stores, banks, hotels and other buildings. Nor were such towns necessarily small. Some of them, as is clear from a contemporary description of a mining settlement in Idaho, tended quickly to become substantial centres: 'The braying of the pack-mules and the clatter of the carpenters' and the blacksmiths' hammers gave zest to the hundreds of pedestrians continually moving about the streets from one place to another as fancy or some excitement attracted them. Violin music was heard in most of the saloons and gambling was an adjunct of them all. New arrivals were almost continuous and departures of prospecting parties were of daily occurrence.'[6]

As settlements of this sort both proliferated and expanded, so there emerged an enormous demand for food supplies of a type which required the establishment of farms and ranches. And since the only land on which these agricultural enterprises could be developed was – at least theoretically – the preserve of the Nez Perce, here was another reason to take the steps which were invariably taken in such circumstances. White claims on Nez Perce land having been deemed more important than the claims of the Nez Perce themselves, a new treaty was proposed. This treaty, it became clear in May 1863, would have the effect of reducing the Nez Perce Reservation to one-tenth of its original size. And among the territories – amounting, in all, to some seven million acres – of which the Nez Perce were thus to be deprived was the Wallowa Valley.[7]

Not all such treaties, of course, were automatically accepted by all the Indians whose future they were intended to shape. The Salish or Flathead bands inhabiting the Bitterroot Valley, for example, had never agreed to take themselves off to the Flathead Reservation which had been allocated to them by Governor Stevens in 1855. 'The Bitterroot is our old home,' one such Flathead commented in 1868. 'Here are the graves of our fathers, our own and our children's birthplaces, and we wish to be buried here.'[8]

But as more and more white settlers moved into the Bitterroot Valley during the 1850s and 1860s, founding towns like Stevensville as well as establishing scores of farms, the Flathead bands still living in the area came under steadily mounting pressure. 'Their passage through our settled valleys should be prohibited,' a Montana grand jury declared both of the Flathead people and their Kootenai and Pend d'Oreille neighbours. 'Ours is a contest between civilisation and barbarism,' the grand jury added. And Montana's settler newspapers, inevitably, agreed. The Bitterroot Valley's Indian inhabitants, one such newspaper argued, were not even who they said they were. The valley's native occupants, the paper went on, were nothing more than 'a band of mongrels numbering bucks, squaws, papooses and dogs only 300 or 400, not twenty of whom are Flatheads'.[9]

The Flathead people, for their part, saw things very differently. To Chief Victor, Angus McDonald's close friend, it seemed that Montana's settlers had undermined – intentionally or otherwise – the whole basis of Flathead existence. 'The country being filled up with white men has driven the buffalo off,' Victor complained. 'They are not close or plenty as they were before the white men came among us to hunt for the gold which they seem to love so much.'[10]

Chief Charlo, Victor's son, was still more bitter in his condemnation of whites. His people, he recalled, had gone out of their way to be of assistance to Lewis and Clark when they passed through the Bitterroot Valley in 1805. But this, the Flathead chief now felt, had been a bad mistake. 'Since our forefathers first beheld him,' Charlo said of the white man, 'more than seven times ten winters have snowed and melted . . . We were happy when he first came. We thought he came from the light. But he comes like the dusk of the evening now, not like the dawn of the morning. He comes like a day that has passed and night enters our future with him . . . To take and to lie should be burned on his forehead . . . His laws never gave us a blade of grass, nor a tree, nor a duck, nor a grouse, nor a trout.'[11]

Just like Victor, then, Charlo was adamant in his rejection of all suggestions to the effect that the time had come for his people to relinquish the Bitterroot Valley. And among the Nez Perce – with whom both Victor and Charlo hunted buffalo on the Great Plains – there emerged, at much the same time, another father and son who were equally resolute in their determination to hang on to their people's homeland.

The senior of this pair was the chief whom whites came to know as Old Joseph. He had adopted that name when, in the 1830s, he had been persuaded by American missionaries to become a Christian. But Joseph, by the 1860s, had torn up his New Testament and renounced Christianity with much the same vehemence as his Flathead counterpart, Charlo, to whom it seemed that no Indian owed any debt of gratitude to the white man's Jesus. Whites, Charlo remarked, claimed to have been saved by Jesus's crucifixion. 'Were all of them dead when that young man died,' the Flathead chief said bitterly of Montana's white population, 'we would all be safe now and our country our own.'[12]

Joseph, for his part, saw no future for Indians in either the white man's faith or the white man's treaties. Although not going so far as the McDonald family's Nez Perce relative, Eagle-from-the-Light, who would have liked his people to respond to the mining invasion of their reservation by killing as many miners as possible, Joseph was one of several Nez Perce chiefs who rejected the treaty of 1863 – a document which, to his enduring regret, Eagle-from-the-Light was actually induced to sign. The 'thief treaty' or 'steal treaty', as many of the Nez Perce called this 1863 agreement, was intended, among other things, to make Joseph's band quit their Wallowa Valley homes. That was something which Joseph had firmly set his face against. He thus refused to countenance any contraction in the Nez Perce Reservation, and he contemptuously rejected all offers of financial compensation in respect of any such contraction. 'Take away your paper,' Joseph is reported to have told one of the many Americans who tried to get the chief to agree to the U.S. government's plans for his people. 'I will not touch it with my hand.'[13]

Old Joseph died in August 1871. Just prior to his death, he sent for his son, Young Joseph, who, some years later, gave this account of what then passed between him and his father: 'I saw he was dying. I took his hand in mine. He said, "My son, my body is returning to my mother earth, and my spirit is going very soon to see the Great Spirit Chief. When I am gone, think of your country. You are the chief of these people. They look to you to guide them. Always remember that your father never sold his country. You must stop your ears whenever you are asked to sign a treaty selling your home. A few years more, and white men will be all around you. They have their eyes on this land. My son, never forget my dying words. This country holds your father's body. Never sell the bones of your father and your mother.'''[14]

Young Joseph, as he afterwards explained, made the requested promise: 'I pressed my father's hand and told him that I would protect his grave with my life. My father smiled and passed away to the spirit-land.'[15]

It was now Young Joseph's task to consign his father's body to the Wallowa earth: 'I buried him in that beautiful valley of winding waters. I love that land more than all of the rest of the world. A man who would not love his father's grave is worse than a wild animal.'[16]

As far as most white opinion was concerned, such sentiment counted for nothing. A majority of Nez Perce chiefs, whites pointed out, had signed the 1863 treaty. This meant, whites maintained, that each Nez Perce band — whether or not its chief had acceded to the 1863 agreement — was bound by the treaty's provisions. There could be no question, therefore, of the Wallowa Valley being left in the possession of its Indians.

Now and again, admittedly, a contrary voice was raised. One of the U.S. government's commissioners of Indian affairs, writing in the early 1870s, remarked: 'If any respect is to be paid to the laws and customs of the Indians, then the treaty of 1863 is not binding upon Joseph and his band.'[17]

This was Young Joseph's view exactly. By his own people he was known as Hinmahtooyahlatkekht, a name which signified the sound of thunder in the mountains. And he was not to be persuaded to relinquish Wallowa; not by the settlers who were moving into the valley in larger and larger numbers; not by those chiefs who had settled, with varying degrees of reluctance, on the new and much smaller Nez Perce Reservation which had been established in 1863; not by the American government, its officials or its army. 'We will not give up the land,' Hinmahtooyahlatkekht insisted. 'We love the land; it is our home.'[18]

Why was it that whites could not grasp what was very simple, Joseph wondered. 'I have been talking to the whites for many years about the land in question,' he remarked in the course of yet another discussion about his people's claims to the Wallowa Valley. 'It is strange they cannot understand me . . . I will not leave it until I am compelled to.'[19]

All the time, however, the pressure on Joseph and his people was becoming steadily more irresistible. During 1876, the year which saw Sitting Bull and Crazy Horse win their great victory at the Battle of the Little Bighorn, the American authorities made up their minds to have the Wallowa issue finally resolved. The responsibility for its resolution was entrusted to General Oliver O. Howard, then commanding the U.S. army's Department of the Columbia. Howard was regarded, by many whites at any rate, as anything but antagonistic to Indians – a reputation which derived from his having dealt more diplomatically than most settlers thought prudent with the Apache chief, Cochise. And the general certainly began by harbouring a good deal of sympathy both for Chief Joseph and for the stance he had adopted.[20]

In the course of his seemingly endless negotiations with Joseph and those other chiefs who had yet to sign the 1863 treaty, however, Howard gradually lost patience with the Nez Perce. At a council held in May 1877 at Lapwai, inside the redrawn reservation's boundaries, Howard's temper snapped and, in the heat of the moment, he gave orders that one of the more recalcitrant Nez Perce chiefs, Toohoolhoolzote, should be temporarily imprisoned by his soldiers. To Howard, Toohoolhoolzote may have been, as the general put it, an 'ugly, obstinate savage of the worst type'. But his arrest and confinement seemed outrageous to Toohoolhoolzote's colleagues. An act of vengeance was, therefore, considered by the Nez Perce. 'If I have been rightly informed,' Duncan McDonald was to write after enquiring closely into these events, 'Howard, in the council, came near to being a victim at the hands of the Nez Perce warriors.'[21]

That crisis passed. But Joseph, as even he now recognised, had been brought to a point where he had little choice other than to abandon the Wallowa country. 'I learned,' he said afterwards, 'that we were but few, while the white men were many, and that we could not hold our own with them. We were like deer. They were like grizzly bears. We had a small country. Their country was large. We were content to let things remain as the Great Spirit Chief made them. They were not and would change the rivers and mountains if they did not suit them.'[22]

❀

Chief Joseph left Lapwai knowing that he had been given thirty days to move his people from the Wallowa Valley to the Nez Perce Reservation. This would be hard to accomplish, Joseph realised. The journey from Wallowa to the reservation, many miles to the east, was a lengthy one. And it would be more than usually difficult because the Wallowa band's belongings – together with their herds of horses and cattle – would have to be got across a series of rivers which, at that time of year, were always swollen as a result of the previous winter's snows having begun to melt in the high mountains. But Joseph saw little practical alternative to complying with Howard's instructions. He could, of course, have gone to war. But war, as was remarked by Duncan McDonald who afterwards discussed these matters with the Nez Perce chief, was not at all in Joseph's mind in May 1877. Joseph, Duncan commented, thought it 'right to fight with diplomacy and to show the government was wrong in forcing him to acknowledge a treaty . . . which his tribe was against'. But violence was never on Joseph's agenda, Duncan insisted – not even when the chief's 'diplomacy' had clearly failed in its objectives.[23]

Despite the temporary successes achieved by Sitting Bull and Crazy Horse, the military odds in any conflict between Indians and whites were now so heavily stacked in favour of the latter as to make any such war a wholly reckless undertaking from the Indian point of view. This Joseph knew; just as he knew war to be out of keeping with those Nez Perce traditions which he valued so highly. The Nez Perce, in all the years since Lewis and Clark first came among them, had never embarked on armed aggression against whites. And Chief Joseph, Hinmahtooyahlat-kekht, had absolutely no intention of breaking with that practice.

In much the same melancholy mood as so many Scottish Highlanders had left places like the Strath of Kildonan, therefore, Joseph and his band prepared, as May turned into June, to abandon their Wallowa Valley homes. These, no doubt, were weeks of high emotion. But they were weeks of hard work, too. Horses and cattle had to be rounded up, belongings packed, the trek eastwards started.

Some days later, having got themselves and their animals across the Snake River, but having lost many cattle in the process, the Wallowa people came to Camas Prairie, near the present-day Idaho town of Grangeville and just outside the reservation boundary. Here Joseph's band met with those other Nez Perce bands whose chiefs – among them several individuals, such as Toohoolhoolzote, White Bird and Looking Glass, who were to have leading roles in what was soon to follow – had also been holding out against the treaty of 1863. At Camas Prairie, a longstanding Nez Perce gathering place, these bands intended to camp for the last time, as it were, in freedom. And at Camas Prairie, in a way that absolutely no one had foreseen, the Nez Perce War began.

While taking part in one of the ceremonial parades which the Nez Perce staged at Camas Prairie, a youth called Wahlitits had inadvertently ridden his horse across a scrap of canvas on which a woman was drying some hard-won kouse roots. 'See what you do!' this woman's husband reportedly shouted at Wahlitits. 'Playing brave you ride over my woman's . . . food! If you are so brave, why don't you go kill the white man who killed your father?'[24]

The killing in question had occurred two years before. It was one of several such incidents, according to Duncan McDonald. And its victim, Duncan added, was called Tipralanatzikan. According to Duncan, Tipralanatzikan – who was Eagle-from-the-Light's brother and, therefore, Duncan's own close relative – was 'a farmer . . . in good circumstances' and 'peaceably inclined to all'. But his benevolence, it appears, was to be Tipralanatzikan's undoing. 'A white man came to his house,' Duncan explained, 'and stated that he would like to take up a piece of land.' Tipralanatzikan, 'liking the appearance of the man,' as Duncan put it, 'at once granted his request' and proceeded to guide the settler, whose name was Larry Ott, to an 'unclaimed' area adjacent to his own farm.[25]

All went well for a year or so. Then Ott set about fencing a patch of ground which Tipralanatzikan considered to be his own. On Tipralanatzikan protesting, 'the white man,' Duncan wrote, 'at once became wrathy, took his rifle . . . and shot the Indian, wounding him mortally.'

For a variety of reasons, some more justifiable than others but most of them traceable to the fact that nineteenth-century whites were seldom punished for killing Indians, Ott had never been brought to book in connection with his crime. And it was this injustice which Wahlitits, the dead man's son, following the goading which he had endured at Camas Prairie, now set about remedying in his own fashion. Accompanied by two other Nez Perce teenagers, Wahlitits rode off along the valley of the Salmon River in the direction of Larry Ott's homestead. Finding the settler absent, but determined now to avenge his father's murder by one means or another, Wahlitits shot dead four other white settlers and seriously wounded a fifth.

'I could fill page after page in portraying the number and nature of outrages the Indians and their families were subject to,' one of General Howard's aides had noted earlier in 1877 when reporting to the general on Chief Joseph and his grievances. But white-perpetrated crime against the Nez Perce – and such crime included theft, assault and rape as well as murder – did not in any way mitigate or excuse, as far as the American authorities at least were concerned, the actions of Wahlitits and his friends. Nor were white Americans inclined to investigate the precise circumstances surrounding the Salmon River killings. Since the killers clearly belonged to one or other of the Nez Perce bands encamped at Camas Prairie, it followed, or so most white Americans of the time considered, that these bands were collectively responsible

Mission Valley, Montana, in winter
JAMES HUNTER

Post Creek in the vicinity of Angus McDonald's Fort Connah trading post
JAMES HUNTER

Only one building now stands at Craig, to the north of Loch Torridon in the Scottish Highlands, where Angus McDonald was born in 1816
JAMES HUNTER

Tom Branson and Stephen McDonald, Salish tribal members and great-great-grandsons of Angus McDonald, at what remains of Fort Connah, Angus's fur trading post on the Flathead Reservation, Montana
MICHAEL GALLACHER, THE MISSOULIAN

The approaches to the McDonald family ranch at
Niarada on the Flathead Reservation, Montana
JAMES HUNTER

Right: Joe McDonald, president of Salish Kootenai
College and great-grandson of Angus McDonald, at
Angus's grave, Mission Valley, Montana
JAMES HUNTER

Glencoe in the Scottish Highlands. The McDonald family were resident here for several centuries and are descended from the locality's clan chiefs

DERRICK WARNER

Two views of McDonald Lake in Glacier National Park, Montana. The lake is
named after Duncan McDonald
ABOVE: U.S. NATIONAL PARKS SERVICE; *BELOW*: JAMES HUNTER

Following Pages: Tipi frames mark the site of the Battle of the Big Hole, a defining
episode in the Nez Perce War of 1877
U.S. NATIONAL PARKS SERVICE

McDonald Peak, Mission Valley, Montana. The peak is named after Angus McDonald
JAMES HUNTER

Munial, Knoydart, in the Scottish Highlands. Finan McDonald, a kinsman of Angus and
one of the first fur traders to cross the Rocky Mountains, was born near here
in the late eighteenth century
TERRY ISLES

for what had occurred. Every member of every Nez Perce band at Camas Prairie, in other words, was construed to be at war both with locally resident whites and with the United States government to which these whites looked for protection. Oliver O. Howard, the senior military man in the vicinity, duly ordered the nearest available army units to take the field against a people who, as a result of the activities of Wahlitits and his companions, were now designated 'hostile'.[27]

White Bird, to whose band Wahlitits belonged, was one of the Nez Perce chiefs to whom the McDonald family were related as a result of Angus's marriage to Catherine. 'A handsome man,' Angus McDonald called White Bird, 'of about five feet nine in his moccasins, square-shouldered, long-waisted and of clean, sinewy limbs.' Just how long this obviously striking individual had been a chief is a little unclear. But White Bird is known to have succeeded another McDonald relative, Eagle-from-the-Light, when the latter — who seems never to have ceased regretting that he signed the hated treaty of 1863 — settled permanently in the Flathead country rather than watch his Salmon River homeland being overrun by whites.[28]

White Bird, who was around seventy when the Nez Perce War began, was subsequently to tell his McDonald kin that his band's initial shedding of white men's blood was something he would certainly have prevented if he could. And even when a U.S. army detachment under Captain David Perry approached the canyon to which White Bird and his band had moved in the aftermath of the Salmon River killings, the chief attempted to open negotiations with the soldiers. 'But before White Bird had a chance to speak,' so Duncan McDonald heard later, 'the soldiers opened fire.'[29]

'You have been looking for a fight with the white men,' White Bird tells his people in Duncan McDonald's account of what happened next, 'and now you have got it. Fight . . . to the last! I want my warriors shot in the breast, not in the back!'[30]

Perry had expected an easy victory. Within minutes, however, it was clear that the U.S. army — as was to happen on more than one further occasion in the months ahead — had hopelessly underestimated the fighting capabilities of its opponents. Soon Perry and his troops were in full retreat — the magnitude of their defeat apparent in a casualty list which featured more than thirty American dead and just two Nez Perce wounded.[31]

What occurred next was a classic demonstration of the extent to which the Americans — to whom the Nez Perce always seemed a single grouping — failed to appreciate the political complexities of the situation they now found themselves confronting.

Looking Glass, one more of the McDonald family's Nez Perce kin, had begun by being outraged both by White Bird's apparent failure to keep his young men under control and by Joseph's apparent readiness to accept the ensuing drift to war. 'My hands are clean of white men's blood,' Duncan McDonald records Looking Glass as saying to White Bird and to Joseph. 'I want you to know they shall so remain. You have acted like fools in murdering white men. I will have no part in these things . . . If you are determined to fight, go and fight yourselves and do not attempt to embroil me or my people.'[32]

In the early part of July, however, the U.S. army gratuitously brought Looking Glass into the war by attacking and looting his village. Now the Nez Perce 'hostiles', in the careful estimation of Angus McDonald who took time to write his own account of these events, had no less than three leaders of stature: Joseph, White Bird and Looking Glass. The first of these, as Angus noted, was the chief whom most whites believed to be in overall charge of the military operations which the Nez Perce were now to conduct with such skill. But this, Angus thought, and here he foreshadowed the verdict of most modern historians, was to make a mistake. Joseph, Angus conceded, was a 'persistent politician'; a tireless negotiator; a man who was superbly skilled with words. But Looking Glass, Angus went on, was 'the leading patriarch of the camp'; a chief to whom the Nez Perce always listened. And as regards the formulation both of tactics and of strategy, Angus McDonald concluded, the 'unassuming but undaunted' White Bird stood head and shoulders above any of his compatriots. He might not have had the chance to shake empires in the way that the classical world's greatest general had done, Angus acknowledged of White Bird. But this Nez Perce chief, in Angus's opinion, was nevertheless as close as Indians ever came to producing their own Hannibal.[33]

❁

Having once more outfought and outwitted Howard's forces, the Nez Perce, in the manner described earlier, crossed the Lolo Trail into Montana, moved up the Bitterroot Valley, traversed the Continental Divide and camped beside the Big Hole River where, in the early hours of Thursday, 9 August 1877, they were attacked by U.S. troops under the command of Colonel John Gibbon.

As Angus McDonald subsequently commented, Gibbon, that morning, had every reason to anticipate success. The 'time and place' of the Big Hole engagement, Angus pointed out, were of Gibbon's 'sole choosing'. White Bird, Looking Glass and Joseph, Angus admitted, might have had 'a few more men than Gibbon', but the latter had 'more effective weapons' in the shape of repeating rifles and a ready supply of ammunition. The Nez Perce, for their part, were desperately short of ammunition and reliant, all too often, on muzzle-loading firearms which 'had long ago gone out of date'. Indeed a number of the guns wielded by the Nez Perce fighters at Big Hole — or so Angus McDonald asserted on the basis of information which came to him, no doubt, from his own Nez Perce contacts — were 'utterly worthless' and were 'only carried for impression or as a club of last resort.'

Nor were these the sum total of the American commander's advantages, Angus declared. The Nez Perce had to look all the time to the defence of their old people, their women and their children. Gibbon, on the other hand, 'was not encumbered by anything whatever'. And even if the immediate balance of forces was not in the American officer's favour, Angus continued, 'Gibbon knew that the country moved, was moving, to support him with endless means'.

To be on the Nez Perce side at Big Hole, in contrast, was to be utterly isolated. The Nez Perce fighter's U.S. army opponents were well aware that, sooner or later, they would be reinforced. 'But the Indian,' Angus McDonald remarked sadly, 'had no such favourable knowledge, or even hope. He was there a forlorn, driven, scorned, shunned, hunted, condemned thing.' So why, then, were the Nez Perce not rapidly obliterated? Because the Indian, Angus McDonald observed, 'was under every disadvantage save one'. Each Indian fighting man's sole strength was his own courage. He could 'conquer or die', as Angus put it; and 'he resolved to die rather than give up his camp to the assailants.'

At first, however, this was far from obvious. Both the unexpectedness and the sheer ferocity of Gibbon's initial onslaught had the effect of throwing the Nez Perce into turmoil. And it was only as a result of their mounting their own surprise counter-attack that the Indians, as Duncan McDonald was to comment in his narrative of the Nez Perce War, 'plucked a victory from the very jaws of defeat'[34]

Absolutely central to this Nez Perce rally was the leadership supplied by White Bird. That, at least, was the conclusion reached by both Angus and Duncan McDonald on the basis of what they heard, in due course, from the battle's Nez Perce survivors.

With Gibbon's men moving in strength into the Nez Perce camp, and with many Indian fighters abandoning womenfolk and children in their panic-stricken haste to get to safety, White Bird's voice, as Duncan McDonald reported, was suddenly heard to rise above the constant din of gunfire and of screaming: 'Why are we retreating? Since the world was made, brave men fight for their women and children. Are we going to run to the mountains and let the whites kill our women and children before our eyes? It is better we should be killed fighting . . . Fight! Shoot them down! We can shoot as well as any of these soldiers!'[35]

This last point, at least, was no more than a statement of fact. Among the Nez Perce were men whose marksmanship, thanks to their buffalo-hunting exploits on the Great Plains, was second to none. And once these men had been persuaded to stand and face Gibbon's troops, they discovered, no doubt to their suprise, that the battle was not, after all, beyond recovery. Finding themselves subjected to a remarkably accurate crossfire, Gibbon's men began pulling out of the Nez Perce camp where some of them had been hopelessly diverted by largely vain attempts to burn captured tipis and where practically all of them were becoming more and more disorganised. Soon the Nez Perce encampment was back in Indian hands and it was Gibbon's turn to find himself encircled and besieged on the nearby piece of rising ground to which he and his soldiers had been forced to withdraw.[36]

The Nez Perce, who had already lost a lot of men, mounted no final assault on Gibbon's position. Instead they simply kept the Americans pinned down through a long, hot day – using the time thus gained to get their surviving old people, women and children safely away to the south and to the east. When General Howard and several hundred more U.S. troops – troops who had meanwhile been making their own crossing of the Lolo Trail – reached the Big Hole River on 10 August, therefore, the Nez Perce were long gone and Gibbon's badly mauled soldiers were simply waiting to be rescued. 'We found a horrible state of affairs,' one of Howard's doctors reported of the sight that greeted him when he reached the remnants of Colonel Gibbon's unit. 'There were 39 wounded, without surgeons or dressings, and many of them suffering intensely.'[37]

Gibbon promptly claimed the Battle of the Big Hole as his victory. 'We cannot but congratulate ourselves,' the colonel told his men, 'that . . . we inflicted upon a more numerous enemy a heavier loss than our own.' Others, however, were more sceptical. Eastern public opinion was already beginning to conclude, as the *New York Times* was to comment some weeks later, that 'the Nez Perce War was, on the part of our government, an unpardonable and frightful blunder . . . whose victims are alike hundreds of our gallant officers and men . . . and the peaceful bands who were goaded by injustice and wrong to take the war path'. Nor were the U.S. military inclined to endorse Gibbon's boasts. With almost half of the colonel's force either dead or wounded and with the Nez Perce still at large, the Battle of the Big Hole, whatever else it might have been, was no American triumph.[38]

'It was lucky for him,' Angus McDonald remarked caustically of Gibbon, 'that Howard was so close behind him and that the Nez Perce . . . decided to let him live.' Nor was Angus impressed by the attention which white Montanans lavished on Gibbon's troops in the Big Hole battle's aftermath. 'I see their care for the soldiers of Big Uncle Sam,' Angus commented in a letter to a friend. 'I also see a little girl, away in the grass, lying and moaning in her blood.'[39]

❀

The Nez Perce had suffered hugely at Big Hole. More than thirty of their fighting men had been killed. Between thirty and sixty of their women and their children had died also. But still the Nez Perce kept ahead of their pursuers. First they pushed south into Wyoming. Next they headed north; re-entering Montana; making their way on to the Great Plains; fighting off still more soldiers; managing to get across the Missouri River; coming, at the end of September, to the rounded, grassy hills known as the Bear's Paw Mountains.[40]

In the course of the three and a half months which had passed since they left Camas Prairie, the Nez Perce had travelled the better part of 2,000 miles. And despite the United States government having invested more than $1 million in its army's pursuit of these few hundred Indians, the Nez Perce, for all their many difficulties, were still at liberty. Some forty miles to the north, just two days' march away, was the Canadian border. Across the border, the Nez Perce knew, was the semi-permanent camp which, ever since Sitting Bull slipped into Canada in May 1877 rather than surrender to the American troops who were then closing in on him, had been home to the Sioux war leader and many of his people.[41]

The Nez Perce, when they camped beside a Bear's Paw Mountain stream called Snake Creek, believed – correctly – that General Oliver O. Howard, whom they had been evading so successfully for so long, was still far behind them. What the Nez Perce did not know was that Howard, realising that his adversaries were heading for Canada, had contacted General Nelson A. Miles, stationed at Fort Keogh, well to the east of the Nez Perce line of march, and asked Miles to do what he could to stop the Nez Perce joining Sitting Bull. Miles, who had been many months in the field against the Sioux and who was thus well acquainted with the geography of the Great Plains, moved very fast. A mounted force was sent racing north-westwards across the prairie grasslands. And on the morning of Sunday, 30 September, before the Indian camp at Snake Creek was properly aroused, three companies of the U.S. army's Seventh Cavalry – the dead George A. Custer's regiment – came crashing down upon the Nez Perce.[42]

Among the casualties arising from that cavalry charge was Chief Toohoolhoolzote whom General Howard had imprisoned briefly in distant Idaho. But neither Toohoolhoolzote's loss, nor the loss of several other skilled fighters, had any very noticeable impact on Nez Perce morale. In a manner that was wholly uncharacteristic of Indian wars, which were almost always hit-and-run affairs, the Nez Perce dug themselves into the prairie earth and, for day after day, first in an icy rain and then in snow, held off the U.S. army. 'Thoughts came of the Wallowa where I grew up,' the then youthful Yellow Wolf was to say much later of this battle. 'Thoughts came . . . of my own country when only Indians were there. Of tipis along the bending river. Of the blue, clear lake, wide meadows with horse and cattle herds . . . Then with rifle I stood forth, saying in my heart, "Here I will die, fighting for my people and our homes."'[43]

General Miles brought up a mortar and began to shell the Nez Perce lines. But these lines were held as determinedly as ever. 'They fight with more desperation than any Indians I have ever met,' a reluctantly admiring Miles remarked.[44]

Gradually, however, the Nez Perce were worn down. More and more of their men fell victim to sniper fire. Women and babies, too, were dying. The cold, meanwhile, was intensifying steadily, and supplies were running so low that children were heard to cry from hunger. It is perfectly understandable, therefore, that Joseph, always the leading politician among the various Nez Perce chiefs, should have agreed to talks with General Miles. But it is equally understandable that White Bird and Looking Glass – whose roles, ever since the Nez Perce War began, had been much more military than political – were immediately suspicious of where such talks might lead. By 5 October, nearly a week into the Bear's Paw fighting, Joseph had secured both from Miles and from General Howard – who had at last caught up with the Nez Perce – a promise that, if his people laid down their arms, they would be permitted, in due course, to return to the reservation towards which they had been heading when the war began. Neither White Bird nor Looking Glass were in any way impressed. 'White Bird and Looking Glass,' Duncan McDonald wrote, 'refused Chief Joseph point blank to surrender after Joseph told them that the army officers offered good promises.'[45]

This was not because White Bird and Looking Glass were necessarily averse to settling on the Nez Perce Reservation. They had reconciled themselves to that some months before. Nor did White Bird or Looking Glass expect now to win their latest battle with the U.S. army – despite

White Bird remarking afterwards to Duncan McDonald that, 'if Joseph only held out another hour or two', Miles, Howard and their men could have been 'wiped worse than General Custer'. What really concerned both White Bird and Looking Glass was the possibility that the whites might be lying – as whites, they pointed out to Joseph, had often previously lied to Indians. Nor did White Bird – according at least to his McDonald relatives – change his mind on this point even after Looking Glass had taken a bullet in the chest and joined the lengthening list of Nez Perce dead. 'Your heart is at peace,' White Bird tells Joseph in Angus McDonald's account of the Bear's Paw Mountain fighting. 'You are making a peace and you give ear to their promises . . . I will not surrender my arms while I know not our fate . . . Make the peace you wish to make. I leave you here.'[46]

Joseph, then, had no alternative but to make his solitary way on horseback to the waiting American officers. 'I am tired of fighting,' he told General Miles. 'Our chiefs are killed. Looking Glass is dead. Toohoolhoolzote is dead . . . It is cold and we have no blankets. The little children are freezing to death. My people, some of them, have run away into the hills . . . No one knows where they are . . . I want time to look for my children and see how many of them I can find. Maybe I shall find them among the dead . . . I am tired. My heart is sick and sad. From where the sun now stands, I will fight no more forever.'[47]

White Bird, meanwhile, in a last act of generalship, managed somehow to get through the American lines with several dozen men, women and children who were as disinclined as he was to trust the U.S. army's word. His goal, White Bird told this fragmented remnant of the people who still called themselves Nimipu, was Sitting Bull's Canadian refuge. 'I felt that I was leaving all that I had,' one of the women who followed White Bird through the snow was afterwards to comment. 'But I did not cry. You know how you feel when you lose kindred and friends through sickness . . . You do not care if you die. With us it was worse. Strong men, well women and little children killed and buried. They had not done wrong . . . We had only asked to be left in our own homes, the homes of our ancestors. Our going was with heavy hearts, broken spirits. But we would be free . . . All lost, we walked silently on into the wintry night.'[48]

In much the same way, and in much the same cheerless state of mind, the survivors of the Glencoe massacre, nearly 200 years earlier, had slipped away into the snow-covered hills above their devastated townships. And just as the MacDonalds who survived that night of terror were taken in by the Stewarts of Appin, so White Bird and his people were to be cared for by the Sioux.

It was well into their journey's 'second sun', according to Yellow Wolf who had escaped with White Bird from the Bear's Paw Mountains battlefield, when the party 'crossed the border into Canada'. There they bivouacked. 'Next morning,' Yellow Wolf remembered, 'we had not gone far when we saw Indians coming.' These Indians were Sitting Bull's men. They warmly welcomed the Nez Perce refugees and led them into Sitting Bull's camp where the arrival of White Bird's people – who, as one of them later recalled, had gone 'five suns without food' – was watched, not uncompassionately, by an officer of the Royal Canadian Mounted Police. Hunger and frostbite had added terribly to the sufferings of the many members of White Bird's group who had been more or less seriously wounded, this officer reported. 'Some were badly shot through the body, legs and arms,' he observed. One woman, the mounted policeman added, had been 'shot in the breast and the ball had turned upward, passing through the side of her head. Despite her condition, she valiantly rode a small pony with a child strapped on her back.'[49]

The Sioux were by no means among the natural allies of the Nez Perce, the two peoples having warred more than once in the century or so since the Nimipu had begun coming east to the Great Plains in search of buffalo. But Sitting Bull, it appears, was more than ready to forget all such enmities in the face of the growing white threat to the last vestiges of Indian independence. 'We, too, have lost our country by falsehood and theft,' the Sioux chief told White Bird. 'If I had known you were surrounded by soldiers at [the] Bear's Paw Mountains,' Sitting Bull continued, 'I certainly would have helped you. What a pity that I was not there with my warriors. But now you are here and, as long as you are with me, I will not allow the Americans to take even a child from you without fighting for it.'[50]

All this, and much more besides, White Bird was to tell the young kinsman with whom he was afterwards to discuss the events of the Nez Perce War, as the kinsman in question put it, 'by our campfires in the Sioux camp'. White Bird's confidant was Duncan McDonald whose Nez Perce relatives were now the victims of a disaster even more cataclysmic in its impact than the one from which Duncan's great-great-great-grandfather had escaped that February morning when he fled from the soldiers whose mission it was to kill Glencoe's MacDonald chief and all his clan.[51]

❁

'Just as human beings make their own history,' a leading modern theorist of such matters has remarked, 'they also make their cultural and ethnic identities.' So it was with Duncan McDonald. 'From my mother and from my long association with the Indians,' Duncan said when an old man, 'I have learned to have a thorough understanding of Indian things. Today I think of and view things about me with Indian eyes.' This did not mean that Duncan's outlook was uninfluenced by his father. 'To Duncan,' observed a close acquaintance of the McDonald family, 'his father was a remarkable man, learned in the ways of the frontier and a source of information on the history he helped to make.' But it is clear, all the same, that Duncan, in becoming 'Indian' rather than 'white', had exercised an element of choice — and that he had exercised this choice in such a way as to align himself with North America's native peoples.[52]

Another of Angus and Catherine McDonald's children, Christina, had married a white man and had gone on to make a determinedly success-ful career in white society. While it is certainly true — for unappealingly atavistic reasons which need not be gone into here — that white racists, whose views did so much to determine what was and what was not acceptable in the late-nineteenth-century American West, were marginally more tolerant of a mixed-blood woman marrying a white man than they were of a mixed-blood man marrying a white woman, Duncan McDonald could, in principle, have organised his life in such a way as to follow the same sort of path as his sister. Indeed one person who knew Duncan in his twenties — and who remembered him as 'a handsome young man' — was firmly of the opinion that, until the early 1870s at least, Duncan was 'anxious to appear to be a full-blooded Scotchman like his father'. Ambiguities of this kind were, in some measure, to surround Duncan McDonald all his life. But by 1875, when Duncan became the husband of one of the Flathead Reservation's Indian residents, he was sufficiently 'Indian' in outlook as to have married in the traditional Salish fashion. 'We were wed with the usual Indian ceremony,' Duncan said long afterwards. 'Two years later we were remarried by Christian ceremony.'[53]

Duncan was enormously attached to his wife whose Americanised name was Louisa Quill and whose Salish designation was Red Sleep. 'They were pals in every sense of the word,' a friend wrote after Louisa's death in 1928. 'A deep affection existed between them. Duncan never left home on a journey without taking her picture with him.'[54]

One of Angus McDonald's correspondents, a Montana judge called Hiram K. Knowles, made this comment about Duncan in the period following his marriage: 'As he has taken to himself an Indian girl, the only hope for his posterity is locked up with that of the Indians. Their destiny must be that of his children.'[55]

In the event, both the children born to Duncan and Louisa were to die before them – their daughter at the age of four, their son at the age of 22. But another of Judge Knowles's thoughts retains its original relevance to Duncan's story. He hoped, Knowles wrote to Angus, that Duncan 'would . . . become a sort of leader . . . among these Indian friends of his'.[56]

This aspiration, of course, can itself be construed as more than slightly racist. Because Duncan McDonald – his father being entirely white and his mother partly white – was more white than Indian by descent, then, from the standpoint of anyone given to categorising human beings in accordance with such terms, Duncan, for all the racist abuse that came his and most other mixed-blood people's way, could be considered 'superior' to a pure-blooded Indian. That, then, may be why Judge Knowles looked to Duncan to adopt something of a leadership role among those Indians with whom his marriage to Louisa had symbolically identified him. It is by no means necessary to attach such a wholly uncharitable interpretation to the judge's comments, however. He may simply have wanted Duncan McDonald to assert himself inside his chosen culture. Nor would Duncan have broken any new ground in so doing. There had already been, after all, a number of outstanding Indian leaders whose descent was very similar – almost, one could say, identical – to that of Duncan McDonald.

Most prominent among this group were Chief Alexander McGillivray of the Creek nation and Chief John Ross of the Cherokee. McGillivray, whose Creek mother's people occupied much of present-day Georgia, was the son of a Highland-born trader who came to America in 1735. Ross, whose Highland ancestors included MacDonalds, was the second-generation product of a series of marriages between Highland soldiers and merchants on the one side, and women of the Cherokee nation – whose historic territories were in present-day Tennessee and Georgia – on the other.[57]

McGillivray, a superbly talented diplomat who negotiated personally with President George Washington in 1790, succeeded over several decades in maintaining Creek independence by constantly switching his support from one to another of the three white powers – Spain, Britain and the United States – which then had strategic interests in the country of the Creeks. Ross, who was first elected the Cherokee nation's principal chief in 1828 and who retained that office until his death in 1866, confronted the much more difficult circumstances created by the nineteenth-century U.S.A.'s increasingly unrivalled continental dominance. In the face of growing white demands for the removal westwards of all Indians living east of the Mississippi, Ross and his Cherokee people devised their own alphabet, established their own schools, wrote their own democratic constitution and generally adopted the 'civilisation' which was forever being urged upon them. All this, however, was to no avail. In 1838, the Cherokee were forcibly rounded up by the American authorities and placed in hastily constructed 'stockades', or prison camps, as a prelude to their being forced to trek overland to what was then called Indian Territory in present-day Oklahoma.[58]

'Men working in the fields were arrested and driven to the stockades,' an American who took part in this operation was one day to recall. 'Women were dragged from their homes by soldiers whose language they could not understand. Children were often separated from their parents . . . In one home death had come during the night. A . . . child had died and was lying on a bearskin couch and some women were preparing the little body for burial. All were arrested and driven out, leaving the child in the cabin. I don't know who buried the body.'[59]

In the course of the Cherokee nation's ensuing march westwards – a march which this Indian people remember as their 'Trail of Tears' – several thousand people died of cold, hunger, whooping cough, cholera, measles, dysentry and influenza. Among the dead was John Ross's wife, Quatie. And if Ross had never subsequently shown the least regard for whites, that would have been wholly understandable. But just a few years on from the Trail of Tears, this most remarkable man – struggling then to re-establish the Cherokee nation in the utterly alien prairie setting in which he and his people now found themselves – took time to urge the Cherokee to contribute to a fund 'for the relief,' as Ross wrote, 'of those who are suffering by the famine in Scotland'.[60]

The famine in question was caused by the failure in 1846 of the Highland potato crop – a crop on which more and more Highlanders had become almost totally reliant as a result of the continuing spread of sheep farms and the confining of more and more families to utterly inadequate scraps of land by the seashore. 'Have the Scotch no claim upon the Cherokees?' asked John Ross when he heard, in early 1847, of the difficulties then being experienced by so many Highlanders. 'Have they not a very especial claim? They have.' Thus it came about that the fund then being raised in Scotland to buy food for starving Highlanders received a contribution of $190 from a Native American people whose humanitiarian gesture was all the more astonishingly generous in the context of their own appalling problems.[61]

❦

Hiram A. Knowles, it seems likely, would not have taken kindly to Duncan McDonald exercising his own version of the leadership displayed by men like Alexander McGillivray and John Ross. And

171

Duncan, as things turned out, was never to operate on anything like so wide a stage as the one available to those Creek and Cherokee chiefs. But Duncan seems, for all that, to have wanted something of a public role – his various involvements in the Nez Perce War and its aftermath being, at the minimum, suggestive of a young man who keenly wanted to do something to advance the interests of the Indian people to whom he was linked by blood and with whom he evidently wished more and more to be identified.

Duncan appears first to have tried, as noted a lot earlier, to offer his services as a guide to Joseph, Looking Glass and White Bird at the point when these three chiefs, together with the other leading men of the Nez Perce, were debating the fateful issue of whether to turn north or south at the eastern end of the Lolo Trail. And though Duncan took no further part in the affairs of the Nez Perce prior to Joseph's surrender and White Bird's escape to Canada, he was to devote a lot of time, during 1878, to ensuring that the Nez Perce case got, if not a fair hearing, then at least an airing in print.

That was the purpose of the long journey which Duncan made, in the summer of 1878, from his Flathead Reservation home to Sitting Bull's camp in present-day Alberta. This journey was undertaken partly at the instigation of Captain James H. Mills – mentioned in this book's opening paragraphs as a result of Governor Benjamin F. Potts having sent the captain to Missoula in July 1877 with instructions to report on the military preparations made necessary by the Nez Perce threat to western Montana. Mills, as well as being one of the Montana governor's aides, owned a newspaper, *The New Northwest*, published weekly in Deer Lodge, some sixty or seventy miles to the south-east of Missoula. And he became sufficiently embroiled in the 1877 crisis, it appears, to feel that his newspaper ought to carry some account of the Nez Perce War as the war seemed to its Indian participants.

Mills, Duncan McDonald explained subsequently, 'wanted to write up the cause of the war from the Indian point of view'. And on making enquiries as to who might be best equipped to get 'information' from the 'Indian side', Duncan went on, Mills 'was told to give the job to Duncan McDonald living on the Flathead Indian Reservation'.[62]

By far the best way 'to get the facts', Duncan now decided, was to seek out White Bird who, some nine months after Chief Joseph's surrender, was continuing to keep himself out of reach of the American authorities by remaining with Sitting Bull in Canada. Hence the six-week trip which Duncan McDonald made to Sitting Bull's Canadian refuge. And hence the numerous conversations which Duncan had there both with White Bird himself and with White Bird's two brothers.[63]

As was equally true of Chief Eagle-from-the-Light and as had been true of the now dead Looking Glass, these three men – because of their kinship links with Catherine McDonald – would have considered Duncan to be a member of their own extended family. And as is demonstrated by the detailed description which Angus McDonald was able to provide of the chief's physical appearance, White Bird, if not his brothers, must also have had dealings in the past with Duncan's father – one white who seems always to have been regarded highly by the Nez Perce. Thanks to his parentage, therefore, Duncan was trusted by White Bird in a way that a stranger would never have been. That was why White Bird was so willing to go into such detail with him – not just about the actual fighting which had gone on in the summer of 1877 but about the much more distant origins and causes of the Nez Perce War.

Since White Bird died some months after his discussions with Duncan, there is a sense in which the articles which Duncan McDonald produced for *The New Northwest* – articles which were based largely on his talks with White Bird – constitute the chief's last testament. That testament, however, found no very sympathetic audience among whites. And Angus McDonald, it is clear, had feared as much. 'I think the object of his tour to White Bird should for a while be delayed,' Angus wrote on hearing that Duncan was planning an excursion to Canada. 'The country is now too sore about the Nez Perce. At least I think so.'[64]

'I made many enemies among the whites,' Duncan himself commented of his contributions to *The New Northwest*, 'because I corrected them about their stories.' Not the least important of these white 'stories', as Duncan well knew, was the one dealing with the circumstances surrounding Chief Joseph's surrender to General Miles and General Howard at the Bear's Paw Mountains battleground in October 1877. Central to these circumstances, as already emphasised, was Joseph's faith in the promise made to him – more particularly by Miles – that he and his people were to be returned to Idaho. This, of course, was the promise which both White Bird and Looking Glass, as Duncan McDonald's published account of the Bear's Paw Mountain episode made clear, immediately categorised as one more of the white men's lies. 'I know we will never see our country again,' Looking Glass had remarked bitterly to White Bird on hearing Joseph state that a Nez Perce surrender to Miles would be a prelude to their all going home.[65]

Duncan's publication of such comments would not have offended white opinion had the guarantees extended to Chief Joseph by General Miles been honoured. But they were not. And possibly because many of them felt more than slightly uneasy about the implications of this fact, the white Montanans who read Duncan McDonald's articles seem to have resented the way in which these articles highlighted the breaking of the promise which Nelson A. Miles made to Joseph.

That his word was not honoured, to be fair, was certainly not Miles's fault. Having something of the typical fighting soldier's respect for a courageous enemy, and having formed a high opinion of Joseph personally, Miles undoubtedly meant what he said in the course of the Bear's Paw Mountains negotiations. But above Miles in the U.S. army's command structure was General William T. Sherman. And Sherman did not share Miles's attitude to the Nez Perce.

Whether or not Sherman ever actually said – as has long been alleged – that the only good Indian is a dead Indian, he was definitely of the opinion in 1877 that the Nez Perce had to be punished as severely as possible for having had the temerity to go to war with the United States. On Sherman's orders, therefore, Miles's promises to Joseph were promptly countermanded. Instead of being returned to the Nez Perce Reservation – which was at least in the same area as their homeland – Joseph and his people were placed in military custody and conveyed down the Missouri as a prelude to their being deposited in that same Indian Territory to which Chief John Ross and the Cherokee had been sent some forty years before.[66]

There are few more telling measures of the extent to which the Native American world was disrupted in the nineteenth century than the fact that the Nez Perce and the Cherokee, who had previously lived some 2,000 miles apart, thus found themselves occupying much the same patch of prairie in a part of North America with which neither people had ever previously had any connection. It is as if Scots and Albanians, who actually live a good deal closer to each other than the Cherokee did to the Nez Perce, were to be deprived of their homes at the two ends of Europe and dumped together in, say, the Ukraine.

It was not so much their sending of his wife's people to Indian Territory which caused Angus McDonald to accuse the American authorities of 'infamy', however. It was the sheer duplicity involved which rankled. 'Although Joseph was . . . warned by experience that the white man was trained to falsehood,' Angus wrote, 'yet he believed.' Like Duncan, therefore, if rather more circumspectly, Angus took up the cause of the Nez Perce. 'They were always in hope,' he commented in 1878 of the exiled Nimipu, 'that some place, if not in their own country at least nearer to it than has been decided, would be given to them.'[67]

But Angus McDonald, by the later 1870s, no longer possessed even the modest political influence which had been his when, twenty or more years previously, he was able to communicate directly with men like Governor Isaac I. Stevens. It was as well, therefore, that others – including, it should be registered, Nelson A. Miles – began insistently to press for the remedying of the injustices to which both Angus and Duncan McDonald, in their different ways, had sought to draw attention.[68]

The result was that Joseph and those of the Nez Perce who had survived their stay in Indian Territory were finally returned, in 1885, to the western side of the Rocky Mountains – not to Idaho, for that would have been to concede too much to a people still regarded by most white Westerners with deep suspicion, but to Washington State's Colville Reservation which, as its name suggests, is located in the general vicinity of the spot which had been Angus McDonald's introduction to the American West.

Joseph, who died on the Colville Reservation in 1904, campaigned tirelessly throughout his last years to be permitted to settle again in the Wallowa Valley. No such permission was granted. But Joseph, just three or four years before his death, was at least allowed, for the first time since his enforced departure in 1877, to visit the Wallowa. There Joseph stood beside his father's burial place and wept. It is not clear whether the now elderly chief had been informed that his father's grave had been robbed by one of the Wallowa Valley's settler families and Old Joseph's skull placed, by way of decoration, in a local dental surgeon's waiting-room. It is much to be hoped, however, that Joseph never heard of this last humiliation.[69]

'Treat all men alike,' Chief Joseph once urged a white audience. 'Give them all the same law. Give them all an even chance to live and grow. All men were made by the same Great Spirit Chief. They are all brothers. The earth is the mother of all people, and all people should have equal rights upon it. You might as well expect the rivers to run backwards as that any man who was born a free man should be contented while penned up and denied liberty to go where he pleases . . . Let me be a free man – free to travel, free to work, free to trade where I choose, free to choose my own teachers, free to follow the religion of my fathers, free to think and talk and act for myself – and I will obey every law or submit to the penalty.'[70]

This was as powerful a critique as was ever made by any Indian of the policy that resulted in Native Americans being universally confined, by the nineteenth century's end, to reservations of the Colville or the Flathead type. It was a critique, however, which altered absolutely nothing.

CHAPTER SIX

As long as our songs are sung

The Nez Perce War of 1877 was one of the final episodes of its kind. Just nine years later, in 1886, Geronimo, the Apache chief who was the last Indian to engage in armed resistance to white settlement, surrendered to the American military and was promptly imprisoned. Four years after that, Sitting Bull – who had long since been forced to leave Canada and to move on to a reservation – was killed while being arrested on charges arising from his supposed complicity in the Ghost Dance movement which was then gripping the Sioux people. The Ghost Dance, a religious revivalism which was more the product of its adherents' despair than of their faith in a better future, promised both that the now virtually extinct buffalo would shortly reappear on the Great Plains and that whites, in turn, would vanish from the earth. But the Ghost Dance brought no salvation to the Sioux. On a cold and snowy December day in 1890, at a place called Wounded Knee on South Dakota's Pine Ridge Reservation, 146 Ghost Dancers – including 44 women and 18 children – were shot dead by the U.S. army.

'I did not know then how much was ended,' a former Ghost Dancer called Black Elk was to remark long afterwards of what occurred at Wounded Knee. 'When I look back now from the high hill of my old age, I can still see the butchered women and children lying heaped and scattered . . . as plain as when I saw them with eyes still young. And I can see that something else died there in the bloody mud, and was buried in the blizzard. A people's dream died there . . . The nation's hoop is broken and scattered. There is no centre any longer, and the sacred tree is dead.'[1]

What was hardest to grasp, perhaps, was the terrible rapidity of the

176

Indian collapse. In 1839, when Angus McDonald came to the Columbia country, he and the few other whites then resident in the region dealt with dozens of Native American societies which – although they were even then being altered by the fur trade – remained, in their essentials, self-governing and intact. In 1889, when Angus died at his home in Mission Valley, this Indian-dominated world had vanished, if not beyond recall, then certainly beyond recovery. In the contiguous and continental U.S.A. – meaning all of the United States except the detached possessions of Hawaii and Alaska – there had once been several million Indians. Now there were fewer than 250,000. And practically none of them had the freedoms which Chief Joseph had so eloquently sought when asking that he be allowed to live and work and travel where he pleased.

In 1878, the year during which Duncan McDonald published his articles on the Nez Perce War, the *Daily Missoulian* – as if to underline the difficulties in the way of anyone attempting to get whites to respond positively to Indian grievances – gave space to calls for the expulsion of all Missoula's Indians. 'The presence of Indians in town has not only been tolerated but encouraged,' the newspaper commented, 'for the reason that they have made themselves useful in washing and scrubbing, in sawing wood, carrying water in the winter and pulling weeds from gardens in the summer.' But the time had come, the paper continued, for Missoulians to ask themselves 'whether the continued presence of Indians about town is wholly beneficial'. Nor would the ejection of the town's Native Americans deprive Indians of anything to which they were entitled: 'It is certain that there is not an Indian on the face of the earth that belongs to the town of Missoula . . . A decent regard for the welfare of the settlements in this city teaches us that the Indians must go.'[2]

In the Bitterroot Valley, it appears, much the same sentiments were increasingly to be heard. The citizens of Stevensville might have entertained Chief Charlo and his Flathead band to a community dinner in the immediate aftermath of the chief's refusal to join the Bitterroot Valley's Nez Perce invaders. But the strict neutrality which Charlo observed throughout the Nez Perce War was to secure him no long-term benefit. Whites continued to insist that all the Bitterroot Valley's Indians, Charlo included, be removed to the Flathead Reservation. And though Charlo – who 'was treated worse than a yellow dog', in Duncan McDonald's opinion – held out against this pressure for another decade, he and his band left finally for the reservation in October 1891.[3]

If it was not literally the case that Charlo 'died with grief', as Duncan McDonald was to claim, then it was undoubtedly true that he had good cause to be bitter. So, too, had the Nez Perce chief, Eagle-from-the-Light, once Angus McDonald's frequent guest and a man who, despite his earlier advocacy of armed action against whites, had kept firmly out of the 1877 fighting. 'I am very poor now,' Eagle-from-the-Light complained before he died. 'I have lost all my children, all my brothers, all my women in the war, although I took no part in it.'[4]

Eagle-from-the-Light was one of a number of Nez Perce who, as the nineteenth century drew to a close, found themselves resident on the Flathead Reservation — theoretically the preserve of the Salish, or Flathead, people and their Kootenai neighbours. Some such individuals arrived on the reservation as refugees in the months and years following the Nez Perce War. Others had much more longstanding links with the locality. Catherine McDonald, who remained in Mission Valley until her death in 1902, was in this latter category. So, too, were those of Catherine's children who made homes in the area — among them Joseph Alexander McDonald, Angus Pierre McDonald, Margaret McDonald, Angus Colville McDonald and, of course, Duncan McDonald. The latter, described by an American official in 1893 as 'a meddlesome half-breed . . . who desires to shine as a man of influence and who properly belongs to the Nez Perce Reservation', clearly continued to irritate the authorities. But there was little or nothing that Duncan or any other Indian could now do to change the fundamentals of the situation created by the reservation system.[5]

Most of the time, in fact, Duncan McDonald was obliged to concentrate on earning a living. Because of his detailed knowledge of western Montana's mountainous terrain, he was employed as a guide by the survey crews who, towards the end of the 1870s, were mapping the route that was afterwards to be followed — through the southern part of the Flathead Reservation, as it turned out — by the Northern Pacific Railway. Later he was one of the contractors who provisioned the railroad construction crews with beef — some of it supplied, no doubt, by Duncan's brothers, Angus Pierre and Angus Colville, who had followed Angus Senior into cattle-ranching. At other times, Duncan ran pack-trains, helped operate a steamer service on the Flathead Lake and even attracted statewide attention as a boxer — one of his fights, at Butte in 1884, lasting for a gruesomely punishing two hours and thirteen minutes.[6]

On one trek north into Canada with a pack-train in the fall of 1878, not long after he had returned from Sitting Bull's encampment, Duncan accidentally ensured his permanent commemoration on the map of Montana. He had paused for an hour or two, as he explained years later, to wait for one of his assistants. 'There was a tree standing near,'

Duncan explained. 'I took an axe and blazed it and put my name on the tree, and the date, just to pass the time.' The tree, as luck would have it, overlooked a mountain-enclosed stretch of water – which, thanks to Duncan's name now being displayed so prominently beside it, became known as McDonald Lake. Later the lake and its surrounding mountains, which include some of North America's most striking peaks, became part of Glacier National Park. And when, in 1932, the park authorities inaugurated their Going-to-the-Sun Highway, a cliff-clinging road which crosses the Continental Divide at an altitude of almost 7,000 feet, Duncan McDonald was one of the U.S. National Park Service's official guests – looking, in a photograph taken that day, more than a trifle stern and forbidding.[7]

'We stayed pretty quiet around him', Duncan's nephew, Charlie McDonald, remembered of his uncle. But if Duncan, in his later years, seemed a slightly intimidating figure – as Charlie, ironically, was to do in his turn – to ensuing generations of the McDonald family, he was increasingly sought out by writers and historians looking to draw on his knowledge of western Montana's Indian peoples. Most such writers treated Duncan with the same wary deference shown to him by his younger relatives. Some, however, were offensively patronising. One journalist, for instance, made a great deal of Duncan's literacy and still more of his 'remarkable intelligence' – these attributes, by implication, being newsworthy in a 'half-breed'.[8]

Possibly in reaction to such treatment, Duncan, for his part, was inclined to stress repeatedly – more particularly, perhaps, when in white company – that he was an educated man. He was certainly a complex one; always straddling the boundary between the two cultures to which his ancestry and upbringing had given him access; looking first to one side of that boundary, then to the other, for the respect which he evidently felt to be his due. Duncan McDonald, as one of his white acquaintances observed, was undoubtedly 'much more Indian than Scotch by inclination and sympathy'. But when the same acquaintance went on to claim of Duncan that the latter knew more of the 'old customs' of Montana's Indians than 'any other man', this was the most blatant of flatteries. There were, then and afterwards, many full-blood Indians – whether Flathead, Nez Perce or otherwise – who were much more immersed in tribal tradition than Duncan McDonald ever was. But Duncan – unlike many, maybe most, of his full-blood contemporaries – was both fluent in English and comparatively comfortable in white society. 'His mind is stored with rare stories of historic value,' one of Duncan's numerous white visitors remarked. And so it was. But what really distinguished Duncan McDonald's tales was not so much their

179

rarity as this mixed-blood storyteller's ability – an ability which numerous Indians of his time did not, and could not, possess – to connect with English-speaking audiences.[9]

This, it should be stressed, is not to detract from Duncan McDonald's posthumous reputation. It is simply to make the point that Duncan, in his old age, was inclined to revel just a little bit – and he would have been less than human had he not done so – in some white Montanans' tendency to portray him as a uniquely unrivalled authority on all things Indian. 'People come here and expect me to tell them in a couple of hours all that has happened to me in a lifetime,' Duncan once complained of someone whom he clearly felt had not been sufficiently respectful. 'That is not the way. They should stay and talk with me.'[10]

Duncan McDonald, of course, had much to say that was worth hearing. He had spoken, after all, with White Bird in the camp of Sitting Bull. And his repertoire of Indian lore – if probably less comprehensive than some of his white admirers thought – was by no means contrived or spurious. 'Duncan talked good Indian,' Charlie McDonald recalled of his uncle – the latter's understanding of Indian custom and belief being enormously enhanced by his undoubted fluency in the Salish of the Flathead country.[11]

As to Duncan's English, while it would clearly have been, in its essentials, the standard speech of the American West, it almost certainly bore some trace of Angus McDonald's influence on his children's upbringing. Because Catherine, Duncan's mother, seems to have known little English prior to her meeting Angus, and because she continued to prefer the French she had learned from Baptiste, her father, the chances are that practically all the English spoken in the McDonald family home during Duncan's childhood was the sort of English which the originally Gaelic-speaking Angus would have learned back in Scotland. 'My dad had a lot of Scotch accent when he talked,' Charlie McDonald said of his father who, of course, was Duncan's brother. And though Charlie himself knew no Gaelic, he had a clear recollection of occasional Gaelic phrases, picked up orginally from Angus, having featured in the conversation of McDonalds of his parents' generation.

The opening decades of the twentieth century, when Duncan McDonald was getting old and when Charlie McDonald was young, were not good times for Indians. Charlie, born in 1897 at the family home which Angus McDonald had earlier built in Mission Valley, preferred, towards the end of his long life, to talk about his childhood's happier moments.

He remembered gathering berries, riding a horse round and round what remained of Fort Connah, fishing in Post Creek, listening intently while his father, Joe McDonald, played a set of bagpipes which had once belonged to Angus. But the grim realities of their people's subordinate status could all too readily intrude on the lives of the Flathead Reservation's children. Charlie, when growing up, was well aware of how his mother, whose name before her marriage to Joe McDonald was Lucy Deschamps, had been among the Salish people who were expelled from the Bitterroot Valley in the years following the Nez Perce War. The miseries and humiliations endured by Lucy Deschamps in the course of her family's trek north to the Flathead Reservation are recalled to this day by her descendants. And Charlie McDonald, of course, heard of these things at first hand – just as he experienced, in a direct and personal way, what it meant to be on the receiving end of white attempts to eradicate Indian distinctiveness.

The European Jesuits who helped staff the mission at St Ignatius, within an hour or two's ride of Post Creek, were among the folk who tried – or so Charlie McDonald thought – to make Indians more like whites. 'These foreign priests,' Charlie said, 'they'd come to your house and they'd start right in on the youngsters there with the catechism and stuff like that. And they'd say if you didn't do this or you didn't do that, you'd burn in hell and all that stuff. But you could always tell a good way off that they were coming – because of the way they rode a horse and because of their flat hats. So us kids, we'd spot one of them guys coming and we'd head for the brush. It was the same way with the government police. They'd drive around in a buggy and find the Indian kids that should have been in school and weren't in school. And lots of the time these kids were sent away to some government school someplace. And so, when we saw the police coming, we'd kind of hide out along the creek till they'd all leave.'

Priests and police alike, if they had been asked to explain what it was that they were about, would have replied, no doubt, that they were engaged in 'civilising' the Flathead Reservation's Indian inhabitants. It was in Indian children's own interest, both churchmen and policemen would have argued, that they become Christians; that they shake off the alternative faiths and beliefs to which some at least of their parents were still stubbornly attached; that they be taken, as Charlie McDonald once feared might happen to him, to one of the distant boarding-schools – maintained either by the federal government or by one of the U.S.'s many Christian denominations – where Indian children were educated in such a way as to divorce them from their own culture.

'We read a history book about "the savages",' Rose Mary Barstow, an Ojibwe born in 1915, remarked of her time in just such a school. 'The pictures were in colour. There was one of a group of warriors attacking white people – a woman held a baby in her arm. I saw hatchets, blood dripping, feathers flying. I showed the picture to the Sister. She said, "Rose Mary, don't you know you're Indian?" I said, "No, I'm not." She said, "Yes, you are." I said, "No!" And I ran behind a clump of juniper trees, and cried and cried.'[12]

D'Arcy McNickle – born at St Ignatius on the Flathead Reservation in 1904 and the eventual author of a novel, *The Surrounded*, which is as good an evocation as any of how it felt to be a reservation Indian in the early part of the twentieth century – was sent to another such boarding-school at Chemewa, Oregon. There, McNickle remembered, he and his schoolmates were punished if they lapsed from English into their Native American languages – a state of affairs, incidentally, which was very similar to that prevailing in the many Highland schools which, in the nineteenth century and later, made it their business to insist on English at the expense of Gaelic.[13]

Neither McNickle nor his parents had wanted him to leave home. And Charlie McDonald, who was of McNickle's Flathead Reservation generation, seems to have avoided the same fate only because his father – no doubt recalling how he and his brothers and sisters had been provided with schooling by Angus, Charlie's grandfather – took care to ensure that no charge of neglecting his children's education could ever be levelled against him. 'My dad had a teacher come to our place,' Charlie recalled.

While they could thus do something to mitigate the impact of the U.S. government's Indian policy on their own families, neither Joe McDonald nor other Flathead Reservation residents could exert any meaningful influence on the various measures which the government took to dilute Indian control of even the comparatively tiny area of land which remained in Indian occupation. Among the most far-reaching of these measures was the Allotment Act or Dawes Act – the latter title deriving from this statute's principal promoter, Senator Henry Dawes of Massachusetts – which Congress passed in 1887.

Presented as an essentially benevolent attempt to get Indians to adopt white attitudes to land, the Dawes Act was intended to transform Indian families into approximations of the homesteading households which were the basic building blocks of settler society in the West. Instead of being treated as its Indian population's common asset, which was how most reservations were regarded initially by their Native American occupants, a reservation was, from this point forward, to be divided between all the families residing on it – with each family getting, in effect, its own farm. This sounded, as the earlier and rather similar insistence on providing Highland families with their own crofts or smallholdings had also sounded, entirely reasonable. But just as crofts were made so small as to ensure that most of the available land on the typical Highland estate became the preserve of sheep farmers rather than crofters, so the typical reservation was divided, or allotted, in such a way as to make it inevitable that a great deal of land would, so to speak, be left going begging at the end of the allotting process. Much of this land was then thrown open to white settlement. The result was that, between 1887 and the adoption of a new policy in 1934, the amount of U.S. territory in Indian occupation fell by well over half.[14]

Colorado congressman James Belford encapsulated white opinion on these developments when he commented that 'an idle and thriftless race of savages' ought not to be permitted to retain control of any worthwhile proportion of America's natural resources. And in western Montana – where the expansion of Missoula County's population from around 2,500 in 1880 to more than 14,000 in 1890 is testimony to the region's growing attractiveness to settlers – the prospect of whites gaining access to remaining Indian lands was particularly well received. An 1895 contributor to the *Daily Missoulian* set the tone for much that was to follow. Why should Indians and 'half-castes' have a monopoly on the 'fine tract' of land that was the Flathead Reservation, he asked, 'to the detriment of thousands of willing and anxious homesteaders?' Eight years later, the paper was still hammering at the same theme: 'The Indian must take his place with the white man. He must sink or swim, survive or perish, with the paleface. The natural owners of the soil may object to the advance of civilisation, but they cannot stop it.'[15]

Through their chiefs, and by such other means as were available to them, the Confederated Salish and Kootenai Tribes – as the Flathead reservation's Indian occupants were, and are, formally known – consistently opposed the proposed allotment of the Flathead Reservation. 'I won't sell a foot,' declared the Flathead chief, Charlo – who, having already been forced out of the Bitterroot Valley, had no intention of giving up any part of such land as remained in Flathead possession. The Kootenai people's Chief Isaac was equally adamant. He was particularly contemptuous of the notion – much canvassed by Missoula's politicians – that it would be in his people's financial interest to sell tribal land to whites. 'You told me I was poor,' Isaac commented in the course of his discussions with representatives of the U.S. federal government. 'But I am not poor. What is valuable to a person is land, the earth, water, trees . . . and all these belong to us.'[16]

All such objections, inevitably, were overruled by the U.S. authorities and allotment of the Flathead Reservation duly went ahead. Each Indian family was allocated its own farm of either 80 or 160 acres — the smaller units being theoretically cultivable, the larger ones being intended for stock-rearing. Since the reservation's Indian population was relatively small, this left — as it had always been intended to leave — the bulk of the Flathead Reservation's 1.25 million acres available for the white homesteaders who, in 1910, were permitted to settle in the area. Soon much of the Flathead Reservation was in the ownership of whites. Soon the Salish and Kootenai peoples, as they have ever since remained, were in a minority in what was, and is, ostensibly their homeland.

By way of compensation for the large acreage thus lost to them, the Confederated Salish and Kootenai Tribes received $1,783,549. Much later, in 1971, the U.S. Court of Claims, adjudicating on a case raised by the Flathead Reservation's Indian inhabitants, found that, on the basis of 1910 land values, the tribes should actually have received more than four times what they got. 'The forced sale of assets at less than their market value,' as the Indian authors of the introduction to a modern historian's account of these events have pointed out, 'is commonly defined as theft or larceny.' It is no wonder, then, as these same authors add, that the white settlement of the Flathead Reservation has 'left a reservoir of hard feelings'.[17]

❀

Writing some five years prior to Angus McDonald's death at Post Creek, Mission Valley, on 1 February 1889, and making mention of two men whom Angus had known well, one of the first historians of the American West, Hubert H. Bancroft, delivered this verdict on white fur traders who, as Angus McDonald had done, became the partners of Indian women: 'It has always seemed to me that the heaviest penalty the servants of the Hudson's Bay Company were obliged to pay for . . . wealth and authority . . . was the wives they were expected to marry and the progeny they should rear. What greater happiness to the father, what greater benefit to mankind than noble children. I never could understand how such men as John McLoughlin and James Douglas could endure the thought of having their name and honours descend to a degenerate posterity. Surely they were of sufficient intelligence to know that by giving their children Indian mothers, their own Scotch, Irish or English blood would be greatly debased . . . Perish all the Hudson's Bay Company thrice over, I would say, sooner than bring upon my offspring such foul corruption, sooner than bring into being offspring of such a curse.'[18]

The notion that a man like Angus McDonald might actually have chosen – rather than have been forced by his employers – to marry an Indian; the notion that such a man might actually have taken pride in the mixed-blood children whom he educated and trained to the best of his ability; the notion that these children possessed the same capabilities as any other set of human beings: all such thoughts, presumably, were so totally at odds with Hubert H. Bancroft's outlook that they did not even occur to him. And it was Bancroft's attitudes, of course, not those of Angus McDonald, which were typical of their time and place. It followed, as can readily be gathered by talking to present-day representatives of the McDonald family on the Flathead Reservation, that Angus McDonald's children, and the children of these children, encountered more than their due share of difficulties.

'There has been a lot of pain,' acknowledges Gyda Swaney, Angus McDonald's great-great-granddaughter and a clinical psychologist working on a mental health programme organised by the Flathead Reservation's tribal council. No small part of that pain, originally anyway, was bound up with the consequences of the Flathead Reservation having been first allotted and then opened to white settlement.

Angus McDonald, prior to his death, had made such arrangements as he could to provide for the future well-being of those of his children who were settled in his vicinity. 'Old Angus left details of how his stock was to be divided,' remarks Joe McDonald, Angus's great-grandson and president, as mentioned earlier, of the Flathead Reservation's Salish and Kootenai College. 'There were as many as a couple of thousand head of cattle involved. And Duncan McDonald had the job, I understand, of executing this part of old Angus's will. Two or three hundred cows went to this son or daughter. Another two or three hundred went to the next. And so it went on until all Angus's stock had been dispersed.'

Among the beneficiaries was Duncan's half-brother, Angus Pierre McDonald, whose mother, of course, was the Okanogan woman with whom Angus Senior had briefly become involved at Fort Colville.

At some point in the 1880s, in partnership with his half-sister Margaret, or Maggie, Angus Pierre – whom his father, preferring the Gaelic equivalent of Peter to the French one, called Angus Padruig – established a ranching business near Niarada in the north-western corner of the Flathead Reservation.

This McDonald Ranch is still in existence. It is operated today by Maggie Goode, a granddaughter of 'Angus P.' – as the McDonald family invariably refer to Angus Pierre – and a great-granddaughter of the man whom Maggie calls 'the old fur trader'.

At first sight, the hill country around the McDonald Ranch – where

Charlie McDonald, as a young man, learned from his uncle, Angus P., the riding and roping skills which made Charlie a talented cowboy – has about it something of the appearance of the Scottish Highlands. But those Niarada hills, if in Scotland, would run most of the time with water. And this, as can be seen from the tumbleweed that blows constantly across Niarada's dirt roads, is semi-arid terrain, collecting under ten inches of rain, on average, each year.

Maggie Goode, whose first name has turned up in successive generations of her family ever since the old fur trader's grandmother was born in eighteenth-century Glencoe, runs some 250 head of cattle on her Niarada ranch. This ranch, she says, extends to 1,500 acres – a fair proportion of it visible from the windows of a ranch-house dating from the time of Angus P. And in winter – when the searingly cold winds which blow into Montana from Canada can quickly freeze a new-born calf's ears and legs – Maggie's cows are kept close to the ranch-house and looked after very carefully. But in summer, in much the same way as her Highland ancestors drove their cattle to the high hills in May or June in order to take full advantage of these hills' transient crop of grass, Maggie pastures much of her stock on a 30,000-acre range leased from the Flathead Reservation's tribal council.

Recent years have not been kind to America's family ranchers – many of whom have sold out to the big corporations which now control much of the country's farming industry. The McDonald Ranch has had its bad times with the rest. But nothing she has lived through, Maggie Goode insists, has in any way matched the difficulties faced here by her grandfather, Angus P.

Angus Pierre McDonald was one of a number of mixed-blood ranchers who were hit particularly hard both by the allotting of the Flathead Reservation and by the subsequent opening of the reservation to white homesteaders. The maximum amount of land such a rancher could obtain by way of a family allotment from the U.S. government in the the years around 1910 was 160 acres – nothing like enough for a halfway reasonable cattle-rearing enterprise. Allotment and white settlement, therefore, tended rapidly to impoverish a number of reservation families who had previously been doing reasonably well financially. And Angus Pierre was not the only McDonald to be among the losers.[19]

Very definitely in this category, for instance, was Angus Pierre's half-brother, Joe McDonald, who had taken over Angus Senior's ranching business at Post Creek following his father's death. Eileen Decker, Joe's granddaughter, remembers her grandfather, just a week or two before his death in 1944, looking out from his Post Creek home and lamenting what had been done to the Flathead Reservation more than thirty years before. 'Grandpa Joe just didn't like the division of the reservation,' Eileen Decker comments. 'He hated the barbed wire that had gone up all over.'

That barbed wire, of course, made it impossible for Joe McDonald to retain cattle numbers of the sort which his father had owned in Mission Valley in the 1870s and 1880s. And although Angus Pierre was rather less hemmed in by homesteaders than his half-brother, for the simple reason that the land around Niarada was relatively unattractive to white settlers, his position, too, was inherently vulnerable. That was one reason why, in the period following the allotment of the Flathead Reservation, Angus P. McDonald made a concerted attempt to obtain the U.S. citizenship rights which, despite their father having been an American citizen for most of the last twenty years of his life, were denied to Angus Pierre, to his half-brothers and to his half-sisters on the grounds that this latest McDonald generation consisted of reservation Indians – all such Indians being officially regarded, until the twentieth century was fairly well advanced, as 'wards', or dependents, of the U.S. federal government's Department of the Interior.

'I will first explain in as short a space as I can my exact status in order that you may better understand my standpoint,' Angus P. McDonald wrote in the course of a letter which he sent directly to the Secretary of the Interior. 'My father a Highlander of Scotland. My mother Native American. Love of parents: equal. Love of parents' country: slightly in favour of mother's country. Love of race: equal.'[20]

So prevalent was 'race prejudice' in the United States, Angus Pierre told the Secretary of the Interior, that 'no Indian of mixed-blood . . . may . . . hope to obtain equal justice as against his white cousin'. He had once before applied for citizenship, Angus Pierre added, but this had resulted only in his 'bitter humiliation . . . when pointed at as the Indian who was vain enough to think himself the equal of anyone in manhood'. That was why Angus Pierre had – as it turned out, correctly – little hope of being any more successful on this occasion. But he felt it right to try.

It was around this time that Angus P. McDonald – and the trip may have been made partly in the belief that an authenticated white family background would help sustain his citizenship claims – both travelled to Scotland and sought out some of his Highland relatives. No family tales of Angus Pierre's Scottish experiences have survived among his descendants, but some impression of how he fared in the country which his father had left in 1838 can be derived from correspondence still preserved at the McDonald Ranch – correspondence in the shape of letters to Angus P. McDonald from several of the Highlanders with whom he had managed to get in touch.

An elderly cousin in Dingwall wrote thus of Donald McDonald who, at Craig in 1816, had become the father of the future fur trader, Angus McDonald: 'I remember our grandfather. I was a little girl when he died. He was a dear, good man.'[21]

From Torridon, a man called John MacDonald wrote: 'I am told that I am one of your nearest relatives . . . I am told that your grandfather [Donald MacDonald] was my great-grandfather.'[22]

What is most striking about this second letter, however, is not so much its genealogical content as the laboured way in which its writer apologises repeatedly to Angus Pierre for his not having received the Niarada rancher with the warmth due to a family member. Angus P. McDonald, of course, was the mixed-blood product of an extramarital relationship. And it is easy enough to imagine that, in the early-twentieth-century Highlands, where people tended both to be intensely puritanical and to think of 'coloureds' only in relation to the seemingly endless colonial wars in which the British army's Highland regiments played such a prominent part, Angus Pierre may well have been regarded by those kinsfolk whom he was able to track down as the sort of relative those kinsfolk would have preferred to be without. The contact which Angus Pierre succeeded in re-establishing between the Highland and the American branches of the McDonald family was not, at all events, to be maintained.

❁

Despite his failure to become an American citizen, Angus P. McDonald, by a variety of devices which are possibly best left unexamined, managed to keep control of rather more land than might have been expected. Other McDonalds, then and later, were less fortunate. It would consequently be possible – although this book does not undertake any such exercise – to dwell at some length on the way in which the experiences of this single family serve as an all too depressing introduction to the darker features of life on a twentieth-century Indian reservation. As is revealed by conversation after conversation with the family's current representatives, individual McDonalds have been touched – and sometimes more than touched – by unemployment; by alcoholism; by drug-abuse; in short, by all the unlovely manifestations of the economic, social, cultural and psychological dislocation caused by the disintegration of those Indian societies which, from the moment he first encountered them in the years around 1840, Angus McDonald of the Hudson's Bay Company so evidently admired.

To focus exclusively on the Indian as victim, however, is not necessarily to do any very great service to the McDonald family, to the generality of Native Americans or, for that matter, to the many other tribal peoples, all around the globe, who are presently endeavouring to cope with the consequences of their own invariably shattering collisions with the complex of forces which our planet's ruling orders, for a long time now, have dignified with the title 'civilisation'.

That Indians have had a lousy deal is evident enough from the story which this book has tried to tell. But what Indians require today from whites, if they require anything, is not so much sympathy as some understanding of what it is that Indians are presently attempting to do on their own behalf. It is in relation to this requirement that a final connection can arguably be made between the two widely separated localities – the Scottish Highlands and the Rocky Mountain West – to which the McDonald family can trace their origins.

As emphasised in earlier chapters, the part of the world where Angus McDonald was born in 1816 was among the first to be subject to disruption of the sort which Angus was afterwards to witness in the American West. The destruction of the Lordship of the Isles; the Glencoe massacre; clearance and eviction of the sort which occurred in the Strath of Kildonan: these events were to affect Highlanders in a way that was analagous to the impact on Native Americans of occurrences like the Nez Perce War. There is, of course, nothing in the Highland experience – certainly not in the recent Highland experience – on a par with the confining of entire tribes to reservations. But to travel today from the Scottish Highlands to the Flathead Reservation is immediately to be struck by the extent to which the reservation's Indian residents are grappling with issues of a kind which, in essence if not in detail, are recognisably akin to issues with which Highlanders have long been familiar.

Both on the Flathead Reservation and in the Scottish Highlands, for example, people whose language and traditions have long been under threat are presently making strenuous efforts to ensure that these key aspects of their collective identities are safeguarded and regenerated. Indian distinctiveness and Highland distinctiveness are consequently beginning to be asserted in all sorts of parallel ways. Thus the Gaelic-medium primary schools which have been established widely in the Highlands since the mid-1980s will shortly have their Flathead Reservation counterparts in Salish-immersion classes. And to talk to the Indians who are advocating such initiatives is at once to be exposed to arguments which have become increasingly familiar in a Highland context. Only by valuing and sustaining what is unique to them, these

189

Indians assert, will Native Americans regain the self-esteem and the self-confidence which have been so badly eroded as a result of what has occurred over the last hundred years or more. And only by regaining such self-esteem and self-confidence, these same Indians continue, will their people acquire the capacity to take charge once more of their own lives, their own futures, their own destinies.

Julie Cajune, Catherine and Angus McDonald's great-great-granddaughter and curriculum co-ordinator in the Flathead Reservation's Tribal Education Department, is one of the Indian people – as Native Americans customarily describe themselves – now pressing hard for the measures needed to ensure the survival of the Salish language. 'So much of what it means to be Salish is bound up with our language,' Julie says. 'Those of us who can't properly speak our language – and that includes me – just can't understand fully how our people traditionally perceived the world and their own place in it. And the fact that we can't understand these things, I feel, adds to the awful sense of loss, the sense of cultural disorientation if you like, that so many Indian people experience all the time.'

Gyda Swaney, another of Angus and Catherine McDonald's great-great-granddaughters, agrees with much of this analysis. As one of only a handful of Native Americans to have qualified in clinical psychology, and one of the still smaller number of such clinical psychologists working on a reservation, Gyda deals professionally with many men and women for whom the stresses and strains of their existence as Indians have simply become intolerable. 'There is an obvious link between individual problems of the sort that I come up against every day,' Gyda comments, 'and the much wider dislocations which have come about because of what has happened to our society.'

Nobody in her position could be anything other than personally affected by the constant parade of human tragedy with which Gyda Swaney has to cope. Possibly because of her training, however, there is about Gyda a dispassionateness which encourages the raising of a question that is as delicate as it is obvious. What is it about the McDonald family which has enabled so many of its members both to avoid the more appalling of the hardships to which Indian people have for so long been subject and, having evaded such hardships, to take on the numerous public roles in which present-day McDonalds loom so very, very large?

Gyda smiles at this. 'Oh, we McDonalds are everywhere around this reservation,' she says. And then, more seriously, Gyda lists McDonalds in positions of some influence in the Flathead Reservation's political and administrative structures. There are, she comments, a lot of such

McDonalds. And the family, she continues, is not universally popular as a result.

As mentioned earlier and as Gyda Swaney now stresses once again, various McDonalds have been casualties, too: casualties not simply of the still all too prevalent white bigotry and racism which no Indian can escape; but casualties also of the innumerable personal disasters – so frequently involving alcohol-addiction – of which the larger Indian disaster has been composed. 'There has been a lot of pain,' Gyda repeats. But in spite of that pain, she adds, there has also been, on the part of successive McDonalds, a continuing commitment to something which has been integral to this family ever since Angus McDonald established his Fort Colville school back in the 1850s. That something, Gyda says, is education: 'We McDonalds have been what we have been because we have been educated.'

Speaking in his office at the Salish Kootenai College, Joe McDonald, the college's president and Catherine and Angus McDonald's great-grandson, makes exactly the same point. 'My Grandpa Joe, Angus's son, could read and write,' he says. 'So could Grandpa Joe's children, my dad included. That was no common thing on the Flathead Reservation in the first half of the twentieth century.'

But if the fact of their having been better educated than many of their neighbours helps to explain why members of the McDonald family – from the time of Duncan McDonald onwards – have been among the Flathead Reservation's public or semi-public figures, that fact in itself does not explain why such a high proportion of the McDonald family continue to make their careers on the reservation. In any disadvantaged society, a good education can very readily – and understandably – be seen primarily as a means of escape. That is why Highland schools for so long tended to channel the more able Highlanders out of the Highlands. That is why relatively few of the Native Americans who have managed to acquire professional skills are deploying these skills on reservations.

Gyda Swaney, when asked about this, says simply that she likes to live among her people. There can be no quarrel with that. And it is certainly not this book's intention to attribute to the McDonald family some overriding sense of mission. In view of the family's history, however, it is not difficult to believe that the McDonalds – or some of them at any rate – have almost instinctively tended to act, on the requisite opportunity presenting itself, as their people's spokespersons. So it was with Duncan McDonald at the time of the Nez Perce War. So it was with the late Charlie McDonald who, in 1935, became one of the founding members of the Flathead Reservation's tribal council.

So it is – one might, at the minimum, postulate – with a number of present-day McDonalds also.

From an Indian perspective, of course, there can appear to be a certain ambiguity about this habitual McDonald role. There are Indians who feel strongly, for instance, that tribal councils of the sort established on the Flathead Reservation in the 1930s – despite these councils being theoretically intended to promote a measure of Indian autonomy – have been no more than a means of hopelessly enmeshing Native Americans in white society by ensuring that such councils, like reservation Indians generally, are kept reliant on an independence-sapping flow of U.S. government grants, subsidies and hand-outs of one kind or another. There can be neither overlap nor compromise, it is insisted by the Indians who hold such views, between what is Native American and what is white. And it is a small step, as the relevant literature readily reveals, from political advocacy of such a doctrine to personal disavowal – by the doctrine's advocates – of the non-Indian elements which, for better or worse, are nowadays present in the family backgrounds of most Native Americans.

No such rejection of their non-Indian heritage has been contemplated by the present-day McDonalds who are featured in this book. Joe McDonald's comment quoted in an earlier chapter to the effect that people ought ideally to be comfortable with all aspects of their ethnicity might constitute something of a family motto in this regard. And to accompany Joe on a tour of the Salish Kootenai College, the tribally controlled facility which he has run since it was founded in 1976, is immediately to be convinced that here is one Native American who manages to combine his pride in every aspect of his family background with a wholehearted commitment to advancing the interests of Indian people.

In the forty years prior to SKC's establishment, Joe McDonald points out, only around forty of the Flathead Reservation's tribal members succeeded in obtaining college degrees. Now hundreds of tribal members have obtained degrees from SKC. And SKC courses, it goes almost without saying, emphasise the importance of Native American history, tradition and culture in a way that more conventional college courses never did. 'We are giving Indians access to opportunities that Indians previously did not have,' Joe McDonald comments.

Among the individuals who have benefited as a result is one of Angus and Catherine McDonald's great-great-grandsons, Tom Branson. His two years at SKC were followed by his graduating in forestry from the University of Idaho. Now he helps manage the Flathead Reservation's extensive forests – forests which are among the reservation's principal sources of tribal finance.

Only one topic rivals forestry in the animation with which Tom Branson speaks about it. That topic is the future of Fort Connah, Angus McDonald's fur trading post. Tom Branson is a member of a committee which has been formed with a view to looking after what remains of the fort. And he clearly sees no need to apologise to anyone for his thus being indentified so closely with the preservation of a building which, from one standpoint, could conceivably be regarded as a monument to processes which culminated in the white conquest of the American West.

'I guess there are Indians around here who think of Angus McDonald, if they think of him at all, as just another white man who took away Indian land,' Tom Branson comments. 'But that is not the way it was. Angus McDonald identified with Indians, defended Indians, married an Indian. He should be remembered. And so should his wife. Between them, Catherine and Angus McDonald represented something that deserves to be commemorated.'

❋

Just two or three miles from Fort Connah, in a restaurant which offers its customers picture-postcard views of McDonald Peak, Gyda Swaney is speaking about the way the world seems to Indian people. What she has to say is far from cheering. And Gyda's words, as a result, are steadily undermining one of her listeners' faith in his ability to conclude his version of the McDonald story in the way he had originally planned.

This book was begun in the naïve conviction that it would have an unrelievedly happy ending. Its comparisons between the modern Scottish Highlands and the modern Flathead Reservation, it was anticipated, would be such as to allow the book's closing paragraphs to contend that Highlanders and Indians, two otherwise disparate peoples linked by the McDonald family, are today overcoming the legacies of their respective pasts in ways which will allow both Highlanders and Indians to reinvigorate their cultures, their languages and much else besides.

That may still happen. But to spend even a few days on the Flathead Reservation is quickly to discover that the task of linguistic renewal – to take a single example of the many such distinctions which have clearly to be made – is enormously more daunting here than in the Scottish Highlands. Despite the fact that Gaelic – spoken currently by not much more than 60,000 people – has long been in decline as a result of its deliberate marginalisation by a state which has only recently begun to modify its traditionally anti-Gaelic posture, Gaelic's contemporary position is immeasurably stronger than that of a language such as Salish which few, if any, children or young people now speak fluently. And though there are many Highlanders who feel that, in trying to ensure their language's survival, they are engaged in a most unequal struggle, no such Highlander confronts obstacles anything like as daunting as those facing the Indians who are endeavouring to sustain Salish.

The Flathead Reservation, by the standards of other such reserves, is relatively resource-rich and comparatively prosperous. But many of its Indian families nevertheless live permanently with deprivation of a kind long since eradicated in the Scottish Highlands – a region which, for all that it remains economically underprivileged in comparison with the rest of Britain, contains nothing approximating to the desperate poverty which is still to be encountered on the Flathead Reservation. In such circumstances, it can easily seem insensitive, indeed insulting, to tell Indian people that they ought to be giving a high priority to – and investing scarce finance in – the upkeep of a language which, for a century or more now, has been associated rather less with Indian advancement than with want, with hunger and with misery.

Outside the Mission Valley restaurant where these topics are being so assiduously debated, the sunset's afterglow is highlighting McDonald Peak. Inside, in response to yet another question from their Scottish guest, Gyda Swaney and the friends she has arranged to meet here are making the point that their modest affluence – although newly gained in some instances – makes them, by definition, untypical of Indian people. For that reason, Gyda and her friends say, their views are not necessarily representative. It follows, they add, that they are quite possibly mistaken in their belief that, despite the numerous difficulties confronting them, Indians can – at one and the same time – maintain their cultural uniqueness and secure their economic betterment. But, mistaken or not, that is clearly this Indian gathering's collective opinion. 'We have a saying,' one man – a Salish-speaker – comments, 'that as long as our songs are sung our people will remain here. And our songs are being sung today more than they have been sung for many years.'

❁

On a Sunday afternoon in the Salish Cultural Committee's longhouse – a kind of community hall – at St Ignatius, Ellen Swaney, Gyda's sister and thus another of Angus McDonald's great-great-granddaughters, has organised a family dinner with a view to helping this book's author meet as many as possible of the Indian people who are descended from the man who was born at Craig in 1816 and whose ancestors included some of the most notable figures in the history of the Gaelic-speaking Scottish Highlands.

The occasion is a relaxed one. There is a lot to be talked over. There is a great deal of home-cooked food to be eaten. And it is not at all surprising, therefore, that – well before the dinner has finished – the latest McDonald generation, in the shape of several small children, slip away and begin playing energetically in a corner of the room. Watching these children's games, and reflecting on the various layers of meaning inherent in the notion of making a people's survival depend on the singing of their songs, it seems suddenly appropriate to think of the McDonald story as a song to which all the many McDonalds mentioned in this book have added – or are adding – their few notes. That song has been heard for an extraordinarily long time already. It deserves to be heard for a long time to come.

Thirty-six McDonald generations

This book deals primarily with the McDonald family as the family has existed in North America and Scotland during the last 300 years. As demonstrated in the course of the book's main text and in the relevant footnotes, the family's descent through these 300 years can be documented and proved beyond any reasonable doubt. As stated earlier, however, the McDonald family's descent can also be traced, in principle at any rate, through a further 900 years. The chain of descent in question is outlined here, generation by generation.

1. Charles Duncan McDonald, to whose memory this book is dedicated, was born in Mission Valley on the Flathead Reservation, Montana, on 17 November 1897. Charlie, who was – among many other things – a founding member of the Tribal Council of the Confederated Salish and Kootenai Tribes, died aged 97 on 2 January 1995, at his home in St Ignatius on the Flathead Reservation. Charlie was the son of:

2. Joseph A. McDonald who was born at Fort Colville in what is now Washington State in 1866. Joseph was the younger brother of Duncan McDonald who features very largely in this book as a result of his involvement in the Nez Perce War of 1877. Duncan and Joseph were the sons of:

3. Angus McDonald who was born at Craig on the north shore of Loch Torridon, Scotland, in October 1816 and who died at his Mission Valley home on the Flathead Reservation in February 1889. Angus came to North America in 1838 and, in 1842, married Catherine whose father was part Mohawk and whose mother was Nez Perce. Catherine was both descended from and related to a number of Nez Perce chiefs. Angus, for his part, was the son of:

4. Donald MacDonald who was resident at Craig in 1816 and who appears to have had subsequent connections with the Dingwall and Strathconon areas. Donald was the son of:

5. Margaret MacDonald who was born in Glencoe in 1763 and who was an elder sister of the leading Hudson's Bay Company fur trader, Archibald McDonald. The

first name of Margaret's husband and Donald's father is unknown. His surname, however, was MacDonald. This man had family links with the Knoydart area and was related in some way (possibly as cousin) to Finan McDonald who was born in Knoydart in the 1770s and who, as a North West Company fur trader, became one of the first white men to enter present-day Montana. Margaret, for her part, was daughter of:

6. Angus MacDonald who was born in Glencoe in 1730. Angus fought at the Battle of Culloden in 1746 and afterwards became tacksman or tenant of the Glencoe farm of Inverigan. Angus was the son of:

7. John MacDonald who was born in Glencoe around 1680 and who, as a small boy, escaped with his mother and his brother, Donald, from the massacre perpetrated by Scottish government troops in Glencoe in February 1692. John was the son of:

8. Aonghas mac Ailean Dubh (Angus son of Black Allan), or Angus MacDonald, who served as a young man with the Marquis of Montrose during the latter's campaign of 1644–45 and who personally guided Montrose's army into Argyll in November 1644. Angus was the son of:

9. Ailean Dubh (Black Allan), Allan MacDonald, who held lands, in the early seventeenth century, at Laroch, near Glencoe. Allan was the son of:

10. Iain Dubh (Black John) who was the second son of:

11. Iain Og (Young John), eighth chief of Glencoe. Iain Og, who lived towards the end of the sixteenth century, was the son of:

12. Iain, seventh chief of Glencoe, who was the son of:

13. Iain, sixth chief of Glencoe, who was the son of:

14. Iain, fifth chief of Glencoe, who was the son of:

15. Iain, fourth chief of Glencoe, who was the son of:

16. Iain, third chief of Glencoe, who was the son of:

17. Iain, second chief of Glencoe, who was the son of:

18. Iain Og an Fhraoich (Young John of the Heather) who, in the early fourteenth century, became first chief of the Glencoe MacDonalds. Iain Og was the son of:

19. Aonghas Og (Young Angus) of Islay who served with Robert Bruce, King of Scots, at the Battle of Bannockburn in 1314 – this being the key victory in the war which Scotland fought with England to establish its independence. Angus was the son of:

20. Aonghas Mor (Big Angus) who was the son of:

21. Donald who was the son of:

22. Ranald who was the son of:

23. Somerled who was born around 1100 and who made himself the effective ruler of an extensive realm which comprised the south-western portion of the Highland mainland and most of the islands off Scotland's west coast. Somerled, who died in 1164, is said traditionally to have been the son of:

24. Gilla-Brigte who was the son of:

25. Gilla-Adomnain who was the son of:

26. Solam who was the son of:

27. Meargaige who was the son of:

28. Suibne who was the son of:

29. Niallgus who was the son of:

30. Maine who was the son of:

31. Gofraid who came to Scotland from Ireland in 835 and who was the son of:

32. Fergus who, some twelve centuries ago, was the chief of a tribe, clan or kindred whose homeland was in the vicinity of present day County Derry in the northern part of Ireland.

The late Charlie McDonald was survived by children, grandchildren, great-grandchildren and great-great-grandchildren. The chain of descent outlined here, therefore, has been extended – on and around the Flathead Reservation – by a further four generations, making 36 in total.

This chain of descent, as made clear in Chapter Two, ought not to be considered totally reliable. The first slight point of doubt arises at Generation 5. The identity of Margaret McDonald, as explained in Chapter Two, is partly conjectural. The only possible replacement for Margaret, however, would be one of her sisters. Even if Margaret has been misidentified, then, the chain of descent is not broken.

From Generation 7 to Generation 11, as explained in much more detail in Chapter 2, the chain depends partly on MacDonald family history as outlined by Archibald McDonald – who appears at Generation 5 – and partly on material derived from a wide range of other sources identified in the footnotes to the first part of Chapter Two. It is by no means impossible that there are errors of detail here. It is conceivable, for example, that a generation has been omitted between Generations 7 and 8. There is no very strong reason, however, to doubt that the Angus MacDonald who appears in Generation 6 was directly descended from a sixteenth-century chief of the Glencoe MacDonalds.

Between Generation 11 and Generation 18, the chain depends on the standard genealogy of the Glencoe chiefs. This genealogy, although long accepted as probably authentic, cannot be proved accurate. Occasional contemporary references to one or two of the chiefs in question do not, of themselves, prove the existence of the remainder. And it is by no means inconceivable, for example, that the chieftainship of Glencoe was sometimes transferred between brothers – or even between more distant relatives. However, there is no good reason to question the overall thrust of the Glencoe family's age-old claim that they were descended from a son of Angus Og of Islay who is cited in Generation 19 and who was a historically verifiable figure of considerable contemporary importance. This is all the more likely in that Angus is known to have been granted lands in the vicinity of Glencoe by King Robert Bruce – to whom Angus extended valuable support during Scotland's early-fourteenth-century war of independence.

Generations 19 to 23 are certainly authentic. The generations which antedate Somerled, the major twelfth-century figure who constitutes Generation 23, depend on the traditionally-transmitted genealogy of Somerled. Although Somerled's father and grandfather are mentioned in contemporary sources, that genealogy will never be proved correct at this remove in time. As stated in Chapter Two, however, scholarly investigators have concluded that the genealogy is probably authentic as far back as the genealogy is reproduced here – that is to a father and son, Fergus and Gofraid, who lived some 1,200 years ago.

References

Chapter One: Nez Perce outriders!

1. M.H. Brown, *The Flight of the Nez Perce*, Lincoln, 1982, 222–23; R.I. Burns, *The Jesuits and the Indian Wars of the Northwest*, New Haven, 1966, 441; J. Fahey, *The Flathead Indians*, Norman, 1974, 194; A. Haines, *An Elusive Victory: The Battle of Big Hole*, Glacier, 1991, 21.
2. The origins of the Nez Perce War are explored more fully in Chapter Five.
3. Fahey, *Flathead Indians*, 189.
4. Burns, *Jesuits and Indian Wars*, 421.
5. Burns, *Jesuits and Indian Wars*, 422; Fahey, *Flathead Indians*, 188–89.
6. Brown, *Flight of the Nez Perce*, 222; Fahey, *Flathead Indians*, 194; D. Lavender, *Let Me Be Free: A Nez Perce Tragedy*, New York, 1993, 276–77; R. Wooster, *The Military and United States Indian Policy, 1865–1903*, New Haven, 1988, 34.
7. Burns, *Jesuits and Indian Wars*, 441; Lavender, *Let Me Be Free*, 273–74; M.D. Beal, *I Will Fight No More Forever: Chief Joseph and the Nez Perce War*, New York, 1971, 94–95.
8. B. Hampton, *Children of Grace: The Nez Perce War of 1877*, New York, 1994, 138–41; Brown, *Flight of the Nez Perce*, 223.
9. L.V. McWhorter, *Yellow Wolf: His Own Story*, London, 1977, 80.
10. L.V. McWhorter, *Hear Me, My Chiefs: Nez Perce Legend and History*, Caldwell, 1992, 355.
11. Haines, *Elusive Victory*, 31–32.
12. Haines, *Elusive Victory*, 31–32; *Dictionary of American Biography*, 22 Volumes, New York, 1928–58, XV, 135–36; Hampton, *Children of Grace*, 133; M.P. Malone and R.B. Roeder, *Montana: A History of Two Centuries*, Seattle, 1976, 83–86.
13. McWhorter Papers: D. McDonald to McWhorter, 11 December 1931. Also, C.M. Drury, *Chief Lawyer of the Nez Perce Indians*, Glendale, 1979, 213–14.
14. McWhorter Papers: D. McDonald to McWhorter, 1 February 1928.
15. C.A. Schwantes, *The Pacific Northwest: An Interpretive History*, Lincoln, 1989, 113; T. Morgan, *Wilderness at Dawn: The Settling of the North American Continent*, New York, 1993; B.W. Dippie, *The Vanishing American: White Attitudes and U.S. Indian Policy*, Middletown, 1982, 257–62.
16. Haines, *Elusive Victory*, 19; D. McDonald, 'Through Nez Perce Eyes', in L. Loughy (ed), *In Pursuit of the Nez Perces*, Wrangell, 1993, 252.
17. McWhorter Papers: D. McDonald to McWhorter, 1 February 1928; McWhorter, *Hear Me*, 354–55.
18. Burns, *Jesuits and Indian Wars*, 98.
19. Fahey, *Flathead Indians*, 145; Burns, *Jesuits and Indian Wars*, 435–36; Hampton, *Children of Grace*, 147.
20. Fahey, *Flathead Indians*, 188–89.
21. Fahey, *Flathead Indians*, 172–74, 188–89; Burns, *Jesuits and Indian Wars*, 434–36;

Lavender, *Let Me Be Free*, 274–76.

22. Burns, *Jesuits and Indian Wars*, 422; Hampton, *Children of Grace*, 137.

23. Haines, *Elusive Victory*, 16; Lavender, *Let Me Be Free*, 158; McDonald, 'Through Nez Perce Eyes', 223.

24. Burns, *Jesuits and Indian Wars*, 436; Fahey, *Flathead Indians*, 190–93.

25. Hampton, *Children of Grace*, 136.

26. Fahey, *Flathead Indians*, 197.

27. Hampton, *Children of Grace*, 142–49; Fahey, *Flathead Indians*, 196.

28. McWhorter Papers: D. McDonald to McWhorter, 14 September 1928; Fahey, *Flathead Indians*, 196–98; Hampton, *Children of Grace*, 142–49.

29. McDonald, 'Through Nez Perce Eyes', 247; McWhorter, *Yellow Wolf*, 81.

30. Lavender, *Let Me Be Free*, 279; McWhorter, *Yellow Wolf*, 81.

31. Hampton, *Children of Grace*, 138, 155–56.

32. Hampton, *Children of Grace*, 64–66; Haines, *Elusive Victory*, 155–58.

33. Haines, *Elusive Victory*, 44–45; Burns, *Jesuits and Indian Wars*, 450–51; Lavender, *Let Me Be Free*, 280–81.

34. McWhorter Papers: D. McDonald to McWhorter, 29 January 1930.

35. Lavender, *Let Me Be Free*, 281; Haines, *Elusive Victory*, 53.

36. McDonald, 'Through Nez Perce Eyes', 260.

37. McWhorter, *Yellow Wolf*, 86–87.

38. McWhorter, *Hear Me*, 373; McDonald, 'Through Nez Perce Eyes', 261.

39. Hampton, *Children of Grace*, 163–64.

40. McDonald, 'Through Nez Perce Eyes', 262. See also Beal, *Fight No More Forever*, 124–42; Haines, *Elusive Battle*, 51–69; Lavender, *Let Me Be Free*, 280–91.

41. A. Garcia, *Tough Trip Through Paradise*, London, 1977, 251.

42. Garcia, *Tough Trip*, 191.

43. Garcia, *Tough Trip*, 251.

44. McWhorter Papers: D. McDonald to McWhorter, 1 February 1928 and 14 September 1928.

45. The McDonald family's links with Post Creek are examined more fully in later chapters.

46. S. Bergman, *The Fabulous Flathead: The Story of the Development of Montana's Flathead Reservation*, Polson, 1988, 42–45; Duncan McDonald Papers: D. McDonald to T.D.

Duncan, undated.

47. N. Tirrell, *Montana*, Oakland, 1995, 238.

48. Burns, *Jesuits and Indian Wars*, 424.

49. A. McDonald (edited by F.W. Howay, W.S. Lewis and J.A. Meyers), 'A Few Items of the West', *Washington Historical Quarterly*, 8, 1917, 190.

50. I am grateful to George A. Knapp of the Fort Connah restoration project for information about aerial photographs.

51. Hiram Knowles Papers: A. McDonald to Knowles, 7 October 1877; Lavender, *Let Me Be Free*, 278.

52. Duncan McDonald Papers: Note in Angus McDonald's hand, commencing 'Died 3rd November', undated.

53. Hiram Knowles Papers: A. McDonald to Knowles, 7 October 1877.

54. McWhorter, *Hear Me*, 460; Hiram Knowles Papers, A. McDonald to Knowles, undated and incomplete.

55. McWhorter Papers: D. McDonald to McWhorter, 14 September 1928; McWhorter, *Hear Me*, 357–58; Hampton, *Children of Grace*, 146–47.

56. Duncan McDonald Papers: Note in Angus McDonald's hand, headed 'Nez Perce Campaign', undated.

57. Hiram Knowles Papers: A. McDonald to Knowles, 7 October 1877; Duncan McDonald Papers: Note in Angus McDonald's hand, commencing 'Died 3rd November', undated.

Chapter Two: Put all to the sword under seventy

1. Joe McDonald in conversation with the author.

2. A.J. Partoll, 'Angus McDonald: Frontier Fur Trader', *Pacific Northwest Quarterly*, 42, 1951, 138; 'Parish Register for Applecross', OPR 58/1. The Montana Historical Society (Fullerton Collection) holds a photograph showing Partoll attending Duncan McDonald's 88th birthday party.

3. Decker Papers: M. McDonald to A. McDonald, 20 July 1845; Wheeler Papers: Biographical Note on Angus McDonald, 20 May 1885. Margaret McDonald's age is given as 60 in the census returns for 1881. This suggests that she was some five years younger than Angus. See 'Census Returns,

1881, Dingwall'.

4. Wheeler Papers: 'Biographical Notes on Angus McDonald', 1885.

5. 'Parish Register for Applecross'.

6. Partoll, 'Angus McDonald', 139; footnotes by Howay, Lewis and Meyers, in McDonald, 'Items of the West', 188–89; W.S. Lewis (ed), 'Christina M. Williams: The Daughter of Angus McDonald', *Washington Historical Quarterly*, 13, 1922, 109–10; W.S. Lewis (ed), 'Narrative of Benjamin McDonald', *Washington Historical Quarterly*, 30, 1939, 186, 190.

7. Decker Papers: A. McDonald to A. McDonald, 5 April 1852.

8. J.M. Cole, *Exile in the Wilderness: The Biography of Chief Factor Archibald McDonald*, Don Mills, 1979, 6. A copy of Archibald's note on his family history is held by Norman H. MacDonald, President of the Clan Donald Society of Edinburgh and clan historian. I am grateful to Mr MacDonald for permitting me to copy this document, referred to below as McDonald, 'Family Note'. The main text of the note appears in W.S. Lewis, 'Archibald McDonald: Biography and Genealogy', *Washington Historical Quarterly*, XI, 1918, 94.

9. For information as to the Glencoe-born Donald McDonald's whereabouts in 1816, I am indebted to Iain S. Macdonald, Falkirk, who has been researching Glencoe families for a number of years and whose researches are further referred to below. See also McDonald, 'Family Note'.

10. McDonald, 'Items of the West', 194.

11. J. Hunter, *A Dance Called America: The Scottish Highlands, the United States and Canada*, Edinburgh, 1994, 73–95; M McLean, *The People of Glengarry: Highlanders in Transition, 1745–1820*, Montreal, 1991, 35, 108–11. This paragraph also draws on information communicated personally to me by Marianne McLean, Ottawa, author of *The People of Glengarry*.

12. McDonald, 'Family Note'.

13. Deady Papers: A. McDonald to Deady, 31 January 1877.

14. McDonald, 'Family Note'. Also, Cole, *Exile in the Wilderness*, x.

15. Sources dealing with Angus MacAllan Dubh are cited later in this chapter. For further detail on the genealogical information in this and the following paragraph, see MacDonald of Castleton Papers: Schematic Genealogy of the Glencoe MacDonalds and notes on the significance of McDonald, 'Family Note'; A. MacDonald and A. MacDonald, *The Clan Donald*, 3 Volumes, Inverness, 1896–1904, 3, 216–26.

16. This paragraph depends largely on the generally accepted genealogy of the Glencoe chiefs as that genealogy appears in the clan histories cited in these footnotes. A recent writer has challenged some of the detail given here. He would make Iain Dubh not the son of the eighth chief of Glencoe but the son of one of the seventh chief's sons. This, however, does not alter in any substantial way the line of descent traced in this book. See A.G. Morrison, 'The MacDonalds of Glencoe', *West Highland Notes and Queries*, July 1995, 9–13.

17. This paragraph depends on generally accepted MacDonald genealogies and on standard histories of the period. See. in particular, J.W.M. Bannerman, 'The Lordship of the Isles: Historical Background', in K.A. Steer and J.W.M. Bannerman, *Late Medieval Monumental Sculpture in the West Highlands*, Edinburgh, 1977, 201–13; MacDonald and MacDonald, *Clan Donald*, 3, 212–16; D.J. Macdonald, *Clan Donald*, Loanhead, 1978, especially, 195–226.

18. W.D.H. Sellar, 'The Origins and Ancestry of Somerled', *Scottish Historical Review*, 45, 1966, 123–42; Bannerman, 'Lordship of the Isles: Historical Background', 201.

19. For a concise summary of the early history of Scotland's Gaels, see J.W.M. Bannerman, 'The Scots of Dalriada', in G. Menzies (ed), *Who Are the Scots?*, London, 1971, 66–79. See also A.A.M. Duncan, *Scotland: The Making of the Kingdom*, Edinburgh, 1975; A.P. Smyth, *Warlords and Holy Men: Scotland, AD80–1000*, London, 1984.

20. For further details on the Lordship of the Isles, see J.W.M. Bannerman, 'The Lordship of the Isles', in J.M. Brown (ed), *Scottish Society in the Fifteenth Century*, London, 1977, 209–40; A. Grant, 'Scotland's Celtic Fringe in the Late Middle Ages', in R.R. Davies (ed), *The British Isles, 1100–1500: Comparisons, Contrasts and*

Connections, Edinburgh, 1988, 118–41; J. Munro and R.W. Munro (eds), *Acts of the Lords of the Isles*, Edinburgh, 1986.

21. Munro and Munro, *Acts of the Lords of the Isles*, 7–8; J.R.N. MacPhail (ed.), *Highland Papers*, 4 Volumes, Edinburgh, 1914–1934, I, 23; MacDonald and MacDonald, *Clan Donald*, II, 190–92.

22. D.S. Thomson, *An Introduction to Gaelic Poetry*, London, 1974, 30–31.

23. R. Nicholson, *Scotland: The Later Middle Ages*, Edinburgh, 1974, 205–06.

24. Bannerman, 'Lordship of the Isles: Historical Background', 210; Munro and Munro, *Acts of the Lords of the Isles*, lxxiii–lxxiv.

25. D.H. Willson, *King James VI and I*, London, 1956, 119; P. Hopkins, *Glencoe and the End of the Highland War*, Edinburgh, 1986, 18; W.C. MacKenzie, *History of the Outer Hebrides*, Edinburgh, 1974, 174–96.

26. Hopkins, *Glencoe*, 19; A. I. MacInnes, 'Scottish Gaeldom, 1638–1651', in J. Dwyer, R.A. Mason and A. Murdoch (eds), *New Perspectives on the Politics and Culture of Early Modern Scotland*, Edinburgh, 1982, 62.

27. McDonald, 'Family Note'.

28. For full accounts of Montrose's Highland involvements, see D. Stevenson, *Alasdair MacColla and the Highland Problem in the Seventeenth Century*, Edinburgh, 1980; E.J. Cowan, *Montrose: For Covenant and King*, London, 1977.

29. MacDonald and MacDonald, *Clan Donald*, II, 204–05.

30. A. Cameron, *Reliquiae Celticae*, 2 Volumes, Inverness, 1892–1894, II, 181; Stevenson, *Alasdair MacColla*, 145–46; Cowan, *Montrose*, 173–75.

31. Cameron, *Reliquiae Celticae*, II, 181; Stevenson, *Alasdair MacColla*, 145–48.

32. W. Gillies, 'The Prince and the Gaels', in L. Scott-Moncrieff (ed.), *The Forty-Five: To Gather an Image Whole*, Edinburgh, 1988, 62; J.L. Campbell, *Highland Songs of the Forty-Five*, Edinburgh, 1933, 8–19.

33. C. O'Baoill, *Gair nan Clarsach: An Anthology of Seventeenth-Century Gaelic Poetry*, Edinburgh, 1994, 106–09.

34. MacDonald and MacDonald, *Clan Donald*, III, 225.

35. J. MacKechnie (ed.), *The Dewar Manuscripts*, Glasgow, 1964, 237–50.

36. A. Mitchell (ed.), *MacFarlane's Geographi-cal Collections*, 3 Volumes, Edinburgh, 1906, II, 157.

37. B. Devlin, 'In Spite of Sea and Centuries', in R.J. Ross and J. Hendry (eds), *Sorley MacLean: Critical Essays*, Edinburgh, 1986, 86.

38. MacKechnie, *Dewar Manuscripts*, 154–60.

39. A. Lang (ed.), *The Highlands of Scotland in 1750*, Edinburgh, 1898, 77–78; MacDonald and MacDonald, *Clan Donald*, II, 198.

40. McDonald, 'Family Note'.

41. P. Hopkins, *Glencoe and the End of the Highland War*, Edinburgh, 1986, 328. This is the most comprehensive account of the circumstances surrounding the Massacre of Glencoe. For a much more readable, and in many ways more understanding, account of the Glencoe episode, see J. Prebble, *Glencoe*, London, 1968.

42. Hopkins, *Glencoe*, 331; Prebble, *Glencoe*, 203.

43. J. Gordon (ed.), *Papers Illustrative of the Political Condition of the Highlands of Scotland, 1689–1696*, Glasgow, 1845, 105.

44. MacDonald and MacDonald, *Clan Donald*, III, 216.

45. MacDonald and MacDonald, *Clan Donald*, III, 225; McDonald, 'Family Note'. Because of what is known about Ranald's descendants, incidentally, Archibald McDonald's descent from Ailean Dubh cannot be by way of Ranald.

46. Prebble, *Glencoe*, 203.

47. Prebble, *Glencoe*, 211–20.

48. Gordon, *Political Condition of the Highlands*, 106–07; Prebble, *Glencoe*, 213–14; Hopkins, *Glencoe*, 336–37.

49. McDonald, 'Family Note'; Hopkins, *Glencoe*, 338; J. Drummond (ed.), *Memoirs of Sir Ewen Cameron of Locheil*, Edinburgh, 1842, 321.

50. Campbell, *Songs of the Forty-Five*, 80–81; A. Livingstone, C.W.H. Aikman and B.S. Hart (eds), *Muster Roll of Prince Charles Edward Stuart's Army, 1745–46*, Aberdeen, 1984, 146.

51. C.W.J. Withers, *Gaelic Scotland: The Transformation of a Culture Region*, London, 1968, 82; A.J. Youngson, *After the Forty-Five: The Economic Impact on the Scottish Highlands*, Edinburgh, 1973, 45; P. Womack, *Improvement and Romance: Constructing the Myth of the Highlands*, London,

1989, 4; B. Lenman, *The Jacobite Clans of the Great Glen, 1650–1784*, London, 1984, 26; B. Lenman, *The Jacobite Risings in Britain, 1689–1746*, London, 1980, 262.

52. McDonald, 'Items of the West', 218–22; Prebble, *Culloden*, 60.

53. McDonald, 'Items of the West', 222; Campbell, *Songs of the Forty-Five*, 176–85.

54. Angus's tombstone gives his age, in 1815, as 82. This is at variance with Archibald McDonald's statement that his father was born in 1730. A person's date of birth, of course, was often a matter of some inexactitude before our own bureaucratic age. See McDonald, 'Family Note'; B. Fairweather and D.C. Cargill, *Pre-1855 Tombstone Inscriptions at Eilean Munda*, Inverness, 1969, 2.

55. J. Fergusson, *Argyll in the Forty-Five*, London, 1951, 193.

56. Fergusson, *Argyll in the Forty-Five*, 196.

57. For a full account of these processes and their consequences, see J. Hunter, T*he Making of the Crofting Community*, Edinburgh, 1976.

58. See J. Hunter, *A Dance Called America: The Scottish Highlands, the United States and Canada*, Edinburgh, 1994, especially 39, 90.

59. D. McNicol, 'United Parishes of Lismore and Appin', in D.J. Withrington, *The Statistical Account of Scotland*, Wakefield, 1983, XX, 351–52; I.S. Macdonald, 'Alexander MacDonald of Glencoe: Insights into Early Highland Sheep Farming', *Review of Scottish Culture*, forthcoming, 1996. I am grateful to Mr Macdonald for providing me with a typescript copy of this article.

60. National Trust for Scotland, *Glencoe and Dalness*, Edinburgh, 1975, 38–39; A. Russell, *The History of St Munda*, Glencoe, 1990, 13.

61. Macdonald, 'Alexander MacDonald of Glencoe'.

62. Macdonald, 'Alexander MacDonald of Glencoe'; C.F. MacKintosh, *Antiquarian Notes: Second Series*, Inverness, 1897, 7–11.

63. MacDonald of Dalilia Papers: Selkirk to MacDonald of Dalilia, 14 August 1811.

64. MacDonald of Dalilia Papers: Selkirk to MacDonald of Dalilia, 9 July 1812.

65. E. Richards, *A History of the Highland Clearances: Emigration, Protest, Reasons*, London, 1985, 392–408.

66. Hunter, *Dance Called America*, 182–83.

67. Hunter, *Dance Called America*, 184.

68. Cole, *Exile in the Wilderness*, 87–99.

69. Lewis and Murikami, *Ranald MacDonald*, 118

70. See Lewis and Murikami, *Ranald MacDonald*. Also, Cole, *Exile in the Wilderness*, 229; *Dictionary of American Biography*, XII, 18–19.

Chapter Three: A parcel of upstart Scotchmen

1. Decker Papers: M. McDonald to A. McDonald, 20 July 1845.

2. Angus McDonald Papers: 'Death of Lady Mary Stewart MacKenzie'; Angus McDonald (Missoula) Papers: 'I Saw Thee but Never Embraced Thee'; Partoll, 'Angus McDonald', 144. Also, *HBC Archives: Commissioned Officers' Indentures and Agreements*. This latter material was supplied by Philip Goldring.

3. Deady Papers: A. McDonald to Deady, 31 January 1877; McDonald, 'Family Note'. Much of my information as to the whereabouts of the Inverigan McDonalds, and all my information as to their financial circumstances, derives from Iain S. Macdonald's personal communication to me of 21 August 1995. In this letter Mr Macdonald cites a number of court cases involving McDonald debts.

4. E.E. Rich (ed), *The Letters of John McLoughlin*, 3 Volumes, Toronto, 1941–44, II, 394. This paragraph also makes use of information supplied to me by Philip Goldring, Ottawa, who has studied Hudson's Bay Company recruitment patterns in Scotland. See, for example, P. Goldring, 'Lewis and the Hudson's Bay Company in the Nineteenth Century', *Scottish Studies*, XXIV, 1980.

5. The late C. McDonald in conversation with the author.

6. Decker Papers: M. McDonald to A. McDonald, 20 July 1845.

7. U.K. Census Returns, 1881; Decker Papers: M. McDonald to A. McDonald, 21 August 1884.

8. J. Barron, *The Northern Highlands in the Nineteenth Century*, 3 Volumes, Inverness, 1903–1913, II, 196.

9. T. Coleman, *Passage to America*, London,

1972, 108.

10. Newman, *Company of Adventurers*, 197–98.

11. J. West, *The Substance of a Journey During a Residence at the Red River Colony*, London, 1828, 6–7.

12. HBC Archives: Log of the *Prince Rupert*, 1838. I am grateful to Philip Goldring for supplying log extracts.

13. D. Gunn, *Manitoba from the Earliest Settlement*, Ottawa, 1880, 81.

14. Newman, *Company of Adventurers*, xxx, 187–95.

15. Barron, *Northern Highlands*, II, 215–20; Wheeler Papers: Biographical Note on Angus McDonald, 20 May 1885; Partoll, 'Angus McDonald', 138–39.

16. Angus McDonald Papers: Untitled and undated note on Angus's 1839 itinerary; Burns, *Jesuits and Indian Wars*, 3; Deady Papers: A. McDonald to Deady, 31 January 1877.

17. McDonald, 'Items of the West', 198.

18. McDonald, 'Items of the West', 215–17.

19. McDonald, 'Items of the West', 198.

20. *Report of the British and American Joint Commission for the Settlement of the Claims of the Hudson's Bay Company*, 7 Volumes, Washington, 1868, I, 155; Cole, *Exile in the Wilderness*, 173; McDonald, 'Items of the West', 196–98; P.H. Overmeyer, 'George B McClellan and the Pacific Northwest', *Pacific Northwest Quarterly*, 32, 1941, 44; *Further Papers Relative to the Affairs of British Columbia*, London, 1860, 87. Fort Colvile, named after a Bay Company financier, was originally spelled as here. The modern spelling has been adopted to avoid confusion.

21. Cole, *Exile in the Wilderness*, 181, 188.

22. P. Newman, *Caesars of the Wilderness*, London, 1988, 236.

23. W.S. Lewis, 'Boyhood Days at Old Fort Colville', *Spokesman-Review*, 28 April 1929.

24. Decker Papers: A. McDonald to A. McDonald, 5 April 1852; Cole, *Exile in the Wilderness*, 217–26; Goode Papers: C. Morrison to A.P. McDonald, 27 October 1915.

25. *British and American Joint Commission*, 155; Partoll, 'Angus McDonald', 140; Deady Papers: A. McDonald to Deady, 31 January 1877; HBC Archives: 'Post History: Fort Hall'.

26. M.W. Campbell, *The North West Company*, Vancouver, 1983, 170–77;

Newman, *Caesars of the Wilderness*, 87–88.

27. Hunter, *Dance Called America*, 159; Newman, *Caesars of the Wilderness*, 85–91; Schwantes, *Pacific Northwest*, 56. Also, J. Nisbet, *Sources of the River: Tracking David Thompson across Western North America*, Seattle, 1994.

28. R. Cox, *Adventures on the Columbia River*, 2 Volumes, London, 1831, I, 348–49.

29. Cox, *Adventures on the Columbia*, I, 349; J.A. Meyers, 'Finan McDonald: Explorer, Fur Trader and Legislator', *Washington Historical Quarterly*, XIII, 1922, 196–208.

30. Newman, *Caesars of the Wilderness*, 278; Fahey, *Flathead Indians*, 28; Malone and Roeder, *Montana*, 35; *Dictionary of Canadian Biography*, 12 Volumes, Toronto, 1966–1991, VIII, 583–84; Cox, *Adventures on the Columbia*, I, 355–57; D.L. Morgan, *Jedediah Smith and the Opening of the West*, Lincoln, 1953, 122.

31. See, among other sources, Duncan's obituary in *Northern Idaho News*, 22 October 1937. Also, Campbell, *North West Company*, 180–83.

32. Campbell, *North West Company*, 183–84.

33. D. Wilson, *The Astors, 1763–1992*, London, 1993, 1–25; W. Irving, *Astoria: Adventures in the Pacific Northwest*, London, 1987, 21–23; J.P. Ronda, *Astoria and Empire*, Lincoln, 1990, 2; W.H. Goetzmann, *New Lands, New Men: America and the Second Great Age of Discovery*, New York, 1987, 129–30.

34. A. Ross, *The Fur Hunters of the Far West*, Chicago, 1924, xxxviii.

35. D. Lavender, *The Fist in the Wilderness*, Alburquerque, 1979, 110–12; Irving, *Astoria*, 26; C.W. MacKenzie, *Donald MacKenzie: King of the Northwest*, Los Angeles, 1937, 21–23; A. Ross, *Adventures of the First Settlers on the Oregon or Columbia River*, Chicago, 1923, 9–13; Ronda, *Astoria and Empire*, 88–93.

36. MacKenzie, *Donald MacKenzie*, 26; Ross, *Adventures of the First Settlers*, 183–95; Irving, *Astoria*, 99.

37. Ross, *Adventures of the First Settlers*, 77.

38. Irving, *Astoria*, 57; Ross, *Adventures of the First Settlers*, 93; *Dictionary of Canadian Biography*, V, 532–34.

39. *Dictionary of Canadian Biography*, V, 526; Irving, *Astoria*, 386; Newman, *Caesars of the Wilderness*, 103–04; Ronda, *Astoria and*

Empire, 288–91.

40. W.H. Goetzmann, *Exploration and Empire: The Explorer and the Scientist in the Winning of the American West*, New York, 1966, 83–85; G.G. Cline, *Peter Skene Ogden and the Hudson's Bay Company*, Norman, 1974, 51; Newman, *Caesars of the Wilderness*, 275.

41. Newman, *Caesars of the Wilderness*, 275.

42. Irving, *Astoria*, 9; Ross, *Adventures of the First Settlers*, 85–86.

43. Ross, *Adventures of the First Settlers*, 86.

44. Ross, *Fur Hunters*, 126–27.

45. J.S. Galbraith, *The Little Emperor: Governor Simpson of the Hudson's Bay Company*, 11–15; Cole, *Exile in the Wilderness*, 105.

46. Galbraith, *Little Emperor*, 79.

47. Newman, *Caesars of the Wilderness*, xx, 251–52; Burns, *Jesuits and Indian Wars*, 20.

48. Cline, *Peter Skene Ogden*, 3–13, 53–54; D.J. Wishart, *The Fur Trade of the American West, 1807–1840*, London, 1979, 128–29; Goetzmann, *Exploration and Empire*, 89–91.

49. Cline, *Peter Skene Ogden*, 46, 53; E.E. Rich, *The Fur Trade and the Northwest to 1857*, Toronto, 1967, 272.

50. D. Lavender, *The Penguin Book of the American West*, London, 1969, 166–67; Goetzmann, *New Lands, New Men*, 128, 132–46; M. Clark, *Eden Seekers: The Settlement of Oregon, 1818–1862*, Boston, 1981, 21–23. See also L.R. Hafen, *The Mountain Men and the Fur Trade of the Far West*, 8 Volumes, Glendale, 1965–1972.

51. F. Parkman, *The Oregon Trail*, London, 1982, 185–86.

52. M. Ridge and R.A. Billington (eds), *America's Frontier Story: A Documentary History of Westward Expansion*, New York, 1969, 393–94.

53. Ridge and Billington, *America's Frontier Story*, 394.

54. H.E. Tobie, 'Joseph L. Meek', in Hafen, *Mountain Men*, I, 313–15; M.R. Porter and O. Davenport, *Scotsman in Buckskin: Sir William Drummond Stewart and the Rocky Mountain Fur Trade*, New York, 1963, 160–61.

55. Deady Papers: A. McDonald to Deady, 30 March 1876.

56. Deady Papers: A. McDonald to Deady, 30 March 1976; Rich, *Letters of John McLoughlin*, III, 135.

57. Rich, *Letters of John McLoughlin*, III, 135; Newman, *Company of Adventurers*, 225–26.

58. *British and American Joint Commission*, 151–2; Rich, *Fur Trade and the Northwest*, 274; Clark, *Eden Seekers*, 46; Newman, *Caesars of the Wilderness*, 285–89; J.S.H. Brown, 'A Parcel of Upstart Scotchmen', *The Beaver*, 68, 1988, 4.

59. Rich, *Letters of John McLoughlin*, III, 37; Schwantes, *Pacific Northwest*, 62–63.

60. Rich, *Letters of John McLoughlin*, III, 37–41.

61. *British and American Joint Commission*, 151–52; F.C. Robertson, *Fort Hall: Gateway to the Oregon Country*, New York, 1963, 14–16, 108–10.

62. *British and American Joint Commission*, 152–53.

63. *British and American Joint Commission*, 151–53; Robertson, *Fort Hall*, 15; L.S. Grant, 'Fort Hall Under the Hudson's Bay Company', *Oregon Historical Quarterly*, XLI, 1940, 34–39. Fort Hall's connection with the Oregon Trail is examined in Chapter 4.

64. Partoll, 'Angus McDonald', 139.

65. Partoll, 'Angus McDonald', 142; Duncan McDonald Papers: Note in Angus McDonald's hand, commencing 'Died 3rd November', undated. Catherine McDonald's tombstone at Post Creek gives her age in 1902 as 75. This would mean that she was 15 at the time of her marriage.

66. W. Adams (ed), 'An Indian Girl's Story of a Trading Expedition to the Southwest about 1841', *The Frontier*, X, 1930, 338, 343; R. Wright, *Stolen Continents: The Indian Story*, London, 1992, 224–40.

67. Hiram K. Knowles Papers: A. McDonald to Knowles, 1 May 1878.

68. The original of Catherine's story is in Angus McDonald (Missoula) Papers. The version cited here, edited by Winona Adams, appeared in *The Frontier* in 1930.

69. Adams, 'Indian Girl's Story', 338–39, 349; Lavender, *Penguin Book of the American West*, 167.

70. Adams, 'Indian Girl's Story', 339.

71. Adams, 'Indian Girl's Story', 339–40.

72. Adams, 'Indian Girl's Story', 340.

73. Cline, *Peter Skene Ogden*, 71–72.

74. This and the following three paragraphs are based on Adams, 'Indian Girl's Story', 341–43.

75. Adams, 'Indian Girl's Story', 346; P.C. Phillips, *The Fur Trade*, 2 Volumes, Norman, 1961, II, 529; Rich, *Letters of John*

McLoughlin, II, 82.

76. Lavender, *Let Me Be Free*, 76–77; A.M. Josephy, *The Nez Perce Indians and the Opening of the Northwest*, Lincoln, 1979, 110–11.

77. Dippie, *Vanishing American*, 257–60.

78. Hunter, *Dance Called America*, 235–40; D.E. Walker, *Indians of Idaho*, Moscow, 1978, 136–37.

79. L.O. Saum, *The Fur Trader and the Indian*, Seattle, 1965, 46.

80. Newman, *Caesars of the Wilderness*, 261–63. Also, S.V. Kirk, *Many Tender Ties: Women in Fur Trade Society in Western Canada, 1670–1870*, Winnipeg, 1983; J.S.H. Brown, *Strangers in Blood: Fur Trade Company Families in Indian Country*, Vancouver, 1980.

81. Kirk, *Many Tender Ties*, 4–5.

82. Duncan McDonald Papers: D. McDonald to J.S. Nevin, 6 February 1931; Burns, *Jesuits and Indian Wars*, 140.

83. Partoll, 'Angus McDonald', 139; Duncan McDonald Papers: D. McDonald to J.S. Nevin, 6 February 1931.

84. Dippie, *Vanishing Indian*, 261; *Dictionary of American Biography*, XVIII, 168–69.

85. Partoll, 'Angus McDonald', 139; McWhorter Papers: D. McDonald responding to McWhorter enquiry dated 15 December 1931.

86. Angus McDonald Papers: 'La Mort de Béranger'; McWhorter Papers: D. McDonald to McWhorter, 11 December 1930.

87. Goode Papers: A. McDonald to M. McDonald, 27 February 1881.

Chapter Four: The old Glencoe chieftain

1. This and ensuing paragraphs draw on several studies of the Nez Perce, among them, H. Aoki, *Nez Perce Texts*, Berkeley, 1979; C.E. Trafzer, *The Nez Perce*, New York, 1992; Walker, *Indians of Idaho*; Lavender, *Let Me Be Free*; McWhorter, *Hear Me, My Chiefs*; Hampton, *Children of Grace*.

2. McDonald, 'Items of the West', 198–99.

3. McDonald, 'Items of the West', 198.

4. Hampton, *Children of Grace*, 21–22.

5. Adams, 'Indian Girl's Story', 340.

6. A. McDonald, 'A Flathead Tradition', *The New Northwest*, Deer Lodge, 11 April 1879.

7. Hiram Knowles Papers: A. McDonald to Knowles, 1 July 1878; McDonald, 'Items of the West', 208; Duncan McDonald Papers: Note in Angus McDonald's hand, commencing 'Died 3rd November', undated. Also G.R. Lothrop (ed), *Recollections of the Flathead Mission*, Glendale, 1977, 121.

8. McDonald, 'Items of the West', 228.

9. McDonald, 'Items of the West', 228–29.

10. McWhorter, *Yellow Wolf*, 29; R.M. Daugherty, 'People of the Salmon', in A.M. Josephy (ed), *America in 1492: The World of the Indian Peoples Before the Arrival of Columbus*, New York, 1992, 78; Walker, *Indians of Idaho*, 158–63; O.W. Johnson, *Flathead and Kootenay: The Rivers, the Tribes and the Region's Traders*, Glendale, 1969, 84–89. Also, A.P. Slickpoo, *Noon Nee-Me-Poo: We, the Nez Perces*, Lapwai, 1973.

11. Goetzmann, *New Lands, New Men*, 111–12.

12. J.P. Ronda, *Lewis and Clark Among the Indians*, Lincoln, 1984, 157; Beal, *Fight No More Forever*, 95.

13. Hampton, *Children of Grace*, 23; Ronda, *Lewis and Clark*, 157–62; Trafzer, *The Nez Perce*, 14–16.

14. Hampton, *Children of Grace*, 19; Goetzmann, *New Lands, New Men*, 112–13.

15. HBC Archives: A. McDonald to Governor of Northern Department, 26 September 1853. See also R. Thornton, *American Indian Holocaust and Survival: A Population History since 1492*, Norman, 1987; A.W. Crosby, *Ecological Imperialism: The Biological Expansion of Europe*, Cambridge, 1993.

16. Ross, *Fur Hunters*, 165–66.

17. HBC Archives: A. McDonald to Governor of Northern Department, 28 September 1852; D. Brown, *The American West*, New York, 1994, 32. See also J.D. Unruh, *The Plains Across: Emigrants, Wagon Trains and the American West*, London, 1992.

18. T.C. Elliott, 'Richard (Captain Johnny) Grant', *Oregon Historical Quarterly*, XXXVI, 1935, 5.

19. HBC Archives: A. McDonald to J. McLoughlin, 19 February 1844; HBC Archives: McLoughlin to McDonald, 19 February 1844.

20. F.E. Ross, 'The Retreat of the Hudson's Bay Company in the Pacific Northwest',

Canadian Historical Review, XVIII, 1937, 263.

21. C.A. Milner, C.A. O'Connor and M.A. Sandweiss (eds), *The Oxford History of the American West*, New York, 1994, 165–67.

22. Huggins Papers: 'The Story of the Hudson's Bay Company Brigade', undated.

23. Deady Papers: A. McDonald to Deady, 31 January 1877; J.S. Galbraith, *The Hudson's Bay Company as an Imperial Factor*, 1821–1869, Berkeley, 1957, 252.

24. Dippie, *Vanishing Indian*, 15.

25. Burns, *Jesuits and Indian Wars*, 26.

26. R.F. Berkhofer, *The White Man's Indian: Images of the American Indian from Columbus to the Present*, New York, 1978, 12–22; A. Calder, *Revolutionary Empires: The Rise of the English-Speaking Empires from the Fifteenth Century to the 1780s*, London, 1981, 110–14; R.A. Billington, *Land of Savagery, Land of Promise: The European Image of the American Frontier in the Nineteenth Century*, New York, 1981, 124–27, 139–40.

27. Adams, 'Indian Girl's Story', 347–48.

28. P. Nabokov (ed), *Native American Testimony: An Anthology of Indian and White Relations*, New York, 1979, 148–49.

29. McWhorter Papers: D. McDonald to McWhorter, 2 January 1930. See also J. Hunter, *On the Other Side of Sorrow: Nature and People in the Scottish Highlands*, Edinburgh, 1995.

30. Fahey, *Flathead Indians*, 91.

31. Trafzer, *The Nez Perce*, 41–42.

32. Trafzer, *The Nez Perce*, 44.

33. R.J. Adam (ed), *Papers on Sutherland Estate Management*, 2 Volumes, Edinburgh, 1972, I, 156.

34. Trafzer, *The Nez Perce*, 44–45; Lavender, *Let Me Be Free*, 148–54.

35. *British and American Joint Commission*, 166; Partoll, 'Angus McDonald', 140; Fahey, *Flathead Indians*, 31–36.

36. Elliott, 'Richard Grant', 2–5; Johnson, *Flathead and Kootenay*, 202, 242.

37. A.H. Smith, 'The Location of Flathead Post', *Pacific Northwest Quarterly*, XLVIII, 1957, 47–54.

38. McDonald, 'Items of the West', 193.

39. McDonald, 'Items of the West', 192.

40. McDonald, 'Items of the West', 191; A.J. Partoll, 'Fort Connah: A Frontier Trading Post, 1847–1871', *Pacific Northwest Quarterly*, XVI, 1925, 160.

41. Duncan McDonald Papers: D. McDonald to C.N. Kessler, copy letter dated 1918.

42. Duncan McDonald Papers: D. McDonald to C.N. Kessler, copy letter dated 1918.

43. Partoll, 'Fort Connah', 400.

44. Decker Papers: 'Duncan McDonald Describes Trading Posts', Extract from *Ronan Pioneer*, 11 September 1925.

45. Partoll, 'Fort Connah', 404–05.

46. Partoll, 'Fort Connah', 404–05.

47. Overmeyer, 'McClellan and the Pacific Northwest', 18. See also *British and American Joint Commission*, 155.

48. McDonald, 'Items of the West', 206.

49. McDonald, 'Items of the West', 193; Burns, *Jesuits and Indian Wars*, 85–86.

50. McDonald, 'Items of the West', 193.

51. Lewis, 'Christina M Williams', 108; *British and American Joint Commission*, 164–65; HBC Archives: A. McDonald to Governor of Northern Department, 28 September 1852; S. Dunbar (ed), *The Journals and Letters of Major John Owen*, 2 Volumes, Portland, 1927, I, 44.

52. *British and American Joint Commission*, 155; Decker Papers: HBC Warrant, 22 December 1856.

53. *British and American Joint Commission*, 156–57.

54. Lewis, 'Boyhood Days'.

55. Lewis, 'Boyhood Days'.

56. R.F. Steele, *An Illustrated History of Stevens, Ferry, Okanogan and Chelan Counties*, Spokane, 1904, 173.

57. Hiram Knowles Papers: A. McDonald to Knowles, 24 March 1878; Eileen Decker in conversation with the author.

58. McDonald, 'Items of the West', 196–97. See also Overmeyer, 'McClellan and the Pacific Northwest'.

59. H. Stevens, *The Life of Isaac Ingalls Stevens*, 2 Volumes, Boston, 1900, I, 393–94; Overmeyer, 'McClellan and the Pacific Northwest', 44–45.

60. McDonald, 'Items of the West', 196–97.

61. McDonald, 'Items of the West', 196–97; Partoll, 'Angus McDonald', 140.

62. Decker Papers: J. Miles to A. McDonald, 28 November 1853.

63. Huggins Papers: 'The Story of the Coming of the Hudson's Bay Company Brigade', undated.

64. Huggins Papers: 'Hudson's Bay Company Brigade'; Tobie, 'Joseph L Meek', 333–34.

65. Huggins Papers: 'Hudson's Bay Company

Brigade'; Ross, *Adventures of the First Settlers*, 159; A. McDonald, 'A Flathead Tradition', *The New Northwest*, 24 May 1878.

66. 'The Dying Chief's Souvenir', *Missoula and Cedar Creek Pioneer*, 3 November 1870.

67. McDonald, 'Items of the West', 191–92; Bergman, *Fabulous Flathead*, 17.

68. Charlie McDonald in conversation with the author.

69. Lewis, 'Christina M Williams', 108.

70. The Indian wars of the mid-1850s, together with Kamiakin's role in them, are examined in detail in Burns, *Jesuits and Indian Wars*. See also Lavender, *Let Me Be Free*, 145–57; Schwantes, *Pacific Northwest*, 118–19.

71. Huggins Papers: 'Hudson's Bay Company Brigade'.

72. C.W. Frush, 'A Trip from the Dalles of the Columbia to Fort Owen', *Contributions to the Historical Society of Montana*, II, 1896, 337–40; Partoll, 'Fort Connah', 404; Burns, *Jesuits and Indian Wars*, 249–50.

73. Dunbar, *Journals and Letters of John Owen*, I, 181, 285; Burns, *Jesuits and Indian Wars*, 173; E.E. Rich, *Hudson's Bay Company, 1670–1870*, Glasgow, 3 Volumes, 1960, III, 744–45.

74. *Further Papers Relative to British Columbia*, 79; McDonald, 'Items of the West', 229. Also I.M. Spry (ed), *The Papers of the Palliser Expedition, 1857–1860*, Toronto, 1968, 32, 39, 491, 531.

75. Burns, *Jesuits and Indian Wars*, 140–41. Also K.D. Richards, *Isaac I. Stevens: Young Man in a Hurry*, Provo, 1979, 300.

76. Lewis, 'Christina M Williams', 109; Decker Papers: Captain McKibbin to A. McDonald, incomplete and undated.

77. Huggins Papers: 'Hudson's Bay Company Brigade'; Burns, *Jesuits and Indian Wars*, 29–30, 134–40; J. Miller (ed), *Mourning Dove: A Salishan Autobiography*, Lincoln, 1990, 152; R.H. Ruby and J.A. Brown, *The Spokane Indians*, Norman, 1970, 97–103.

78. This and subsequent paragraphs depend on Charles W. Wilson Diary: 1 August 1860, 25 December 1860, 10 February 1861, 1 November 1861. I am grateful to William E. Farr for drawing the diary to my attention.

79. Newman, *Caesars of the Wilderness*, 377.

80. Cole, *Exile in the Wilderness*, 182.

81. Galbraith, *Hudson's Bay Company*, 278–79.

82. Ross, 'Retreat of the Hudson's Bay Company', 272; *British and American Joint Commission*, 165; Galbraith, *Hudson's Bay Company*, 273; Rich, *Hudson's Bay Company*, III, 744–45.

83. *British and American Joint Commission*, 161–62; Adams, 'Indian Girl's Story', 338; J.B. Brown, *Fort Hall on the Oregon Trail*, Caldwell, 1932, 326–27.

84. Rich, *Hudson's Bay Company*, III, 747; Galbraith, *Hudson's Bay Company*, 280–81; Lewis, 'Christina M Williams', 111.

85. Partoll, 'Fort Connah', 413; Deady Papers: A. McDonald to Deady, 9 December 1875.

86. Deady Papers: A. McDonald to Deady, 9 December 1875.

87. Knowles Papers: A. McDonald to Knowles, 7 October 1877; Deady Papers: A. McDonald to Deady, 9 December 1875; Lewis, 'Benjamin McDonald', 189–95; Lewis, 'Christina M Williams', 117; Steele, *Illustrated History*, 201.

88. Wheeler Papers, 'Biographical Notes on Angus McDonald', 20 May 1885.

89. Partoll, 'Angus McDonald', 144–45; Partoll, 'Fort Connah', 144; Johnson, *Flathead and Kootenay*, 328; HBC Archives: 'Post History: Fort Connah'.

90. McDonald, 'Items of the West', 191.

91. Partoll, 'Angus McDonald', 145; Partoll, 'Fort Connah', 402; Deady Papers: A. McDonald to Deady, 30 March 1876; Wheeler Papers: 'Biographical Notes on Angus McDonald', 20 May 1885.

92. Wheeler Papers: 'Biographical Notes on Angus McDonald', 20 May 1885; Angus McDonald Papers: A. Munro to McDonald, 24 August 1881; Knowles Papers: A. McDonald to Knowles, 12 August 1878; Knowles Papers: A. McDonald to Knowles, incomplete and undated.

93. Deady Papers: A. McDonald to Deady, 30 March 1876.

94. Goode Papers: A. McDonald to M. McDonald, 27 February 1881.

95. G.F. Weisel, *Men and Trade of the Northwest Frontier as Shown by the Fort Owen Ledger*, Missoula, 1955, 12; Dunbar, *Journals and Letters of John Owen*, II, 91.

96. Angus McDonald (Missoula) Papers: 'Death of the Rocky Mountain Puma'.

97. Angus McDonald (Missoula) Papers: 'An

Elk Hunt in the Rocky Mountains'.

98. Angus McDonald (Missoula) Papers: 'An Elk Hunt in the Rocky Mountains'.

99. Lewis, 'Christina M. Williams', 114–15. Also, Deady Papers: A. McDonald to Deady, 30 March 1876.

100. Lewis, 'Christina M. Williams', 115.

101. Deady Papers: A. McDonald to Deady, 31 January 1877; McDonald, 'Items of the West', 220; Partoll, 'Angus McDonald', 144.

102. Knowles Papers: A. McDonald to Knowles, 24 March 1878, 26 April 1878 and 20 May 1878.

103. Deady Papers: A. McDonald to Deady, 31 January 1877; McDonald, 'Items of the West', 209, 224. One of Angus's copies of *The Celtic Magazine* is preserved by his great-granddaughter, Maggie Goode, at the McDonald Ranch, Niarada.

104. Decker Papers: M. McDonald to A. McDonald, 21 August 1884.

105. Deady Papers: A. McDonald to Deady, 30 March 1876; Knowles Papers: A. McDonald to Knowles, 20 May 1878.

106. Knowles Papers: A. McDonald to Knowles, 7 October 1877.

Chapter Five: We had only asked to be left in our own homes

1. Maps and notes at the start of McWhorter, *Hear Me*.

2. F. Haines, *The Nez Perce*, Norman, 1972, 157; Brown, *Flight of the Nez Perce*, 30–32.

3. Brown, *Flight of the Nez Perce*, 46.

4. Brown, *Flight of the Nez Perce*, 33. Also, L. Mercier and C. Simon-Smolenski, *Idaho's Scots-Americans*, Boise, 1990; W.R. Paul, *Mining Frontiers of the Far West, 1848–1880*, New York, 1963.

5. Brown, *Flight of the Nez Perce*, 33–35.

6. Paul, *Mining Frontiers*, 138–39.

7. Lavender, *Let Me Be Free*, 179–85; Trafzer, *The Nez Perce*, 62–63.

8. Fahey, *Flathead Indians*, 148.

9. Fahey, *Flathead Indians*, 104, 145–53.

10. Fahey, *Flathead Indians*, 152.

11. V.I. Armstrong (ed), *I Have Spoken: American History through the Voices of the Indians*, Chicago, 1971, 99. Also W. Kittredge and A. Smith (eds), *The Last Best Place: A Montana Anthology*, Seattle, 1991,

397–99.

12. Lavender, *Let Me Be Free*, 98–99; Trafzer, *The Nez Perce*, 70; Armstrong, *I Have Spoken*, 99.

13. Josephy, *Nez Perce Indians*, 396; Trafzer, *The Nez Perce*, 62–63; Lavender, *Let Me Be Free*, 190–92; Hampton, *Children of Grace*, 32; Loughy, *Pursuit of the Nez Perces*, 281.

14. Loughy, *Pursuit of the Nez Perces*, 283.

15. Loughy, *Pursuit of the Nez Perces*, 283.

16. Loughy, *Pursuit of the Nez Perces*, 284.

17. Trafzer, *The Nez Perce*, 64.

18. Trafzer, *The Nez Perce*, 70.

19. Lavender, *Let Me Be Free*, 225.

20. Trafzer, *The Nez Perce*, 67; Lavender, *Let Me Be Free*, 208–09. Also O.O. Howard, *My Life and Experience Among Our Hostile Indians*, New York, 1972; W.S. McFeely, *Yankee Stepfather: General O.O. Howard and the Freedmen*, New Haven, 1968.

21. McDonald, 'Through Nez Perce Eyes', 232; Trafzer, *The Nez Perce*, 73–76.

22. Loughy, *Pursuit of the Nez Perce*, 285.

23. McWhorter Papers: D. McDonald to McWhorter, 2 January 1930; Brown, *Flight of the Nez Perce*, 44; Lavender, *Let Me Be Free*, 234–45.

24. Hampton, *Children of Grace*, 2.

25. This and the following two paragraphs are based primarily on McDonald, 'Through Nez Perce Eyes', 217–18; Hampton, *Children of Grace*, 2–4; Brown, *Flight of the Nez Perce*, 64–65.

26. Brown, *Flight of the Nez Perce*, 45; Haines, *The Nez Perce*, 208–11.

27. Duncan McDonald Papers: Note in Angus McDonald's hand, headed 'Nez Perce Campaign', undated; Lavender, *Let Me Be Free*, 228; McDonald, 'Through Nez Perce Eyes', 224.

28. Duncan McDonald Papers: Note in Angus McDonald's hand, headed 'Nez Perce Campaign', undated; McDonald, 'Through Nez Perce Eyes', 224.

29. McDonald, 'Through Nez Perce Eyes', 237.

30. Lavender, *Let Me Be Free*, 245–49; Brown, *Flight of the Nez Perce*, 130–39.

31. McDonald, 'Through Nez Perce Eyes', 236.

32. Duncan McDonald Papers: Note in Angus McDonald's hand, headed 'Nez Perce Campaign', undated.

33. This and the following paragraphs depend

on Duncan McDonald Papers: Note in Angus McDonald's hand, headed 'Nez Perce Campaign', undated.

34. McDonald, 'Through Nez Perce Eyes', 260.

35. McDonald, 'Through Nez Perce Eyes', 260.

36. Lavender, *Let Me Be Free*, 282–84; Hampton, *Children of Grace*, 167–69.

37. Lavender, *Let Me Be Free*, 283–85.

38. Haines, *Elusive Victory*, 119, 135; Hampton, *Children of Grace*, 175.

39. Knowles Papers: A. McDonald to Knowles, 7 October 1877.

40. Lavender, *Let Me Be Free*, 285–310.

41. Brown, *Flight of the Nez Perce*, 13; M. Stevens, 'Chief Joseph's Revenge', *New Yorker*, 8 August 1994; R.M. Utley, *The Lance and the Shield: The Life and Times of Sitting Bull*, NewYork, 1993, 180–82.

42. Lavender, *Let Me Be Free*, 310–15.

43. Lavender, *Let Me Be Free*, 317–18.

44. R. Wooster, *Nelson A. Miles and the Twilight of the Frontier Army*, Lincoln, 1993, 65.

45. McWhorter Papers: D. McDonald to McWhorter, 1 February 1928; Lavender, *Let Me Be Free*, 318–21.

46. McWhorter Papers: Duncan to McWhorter, 30 May 1930; Duncan McDonald Papers, Note in Angus McDonald's hand, headed 'Nez Perce Campaign', undated.

47. Lavender, *Let Me Be Free*, 325–26; Hampton, *Children of Grace,* 307.

48. Trafzer, *The Nez Perce*, 88.

49. McWhorter, *Yellow Wolf*, 153; Hampton, *Children of Grace*, 299–300; Utley, *Lance and Shield*, 193; McWhorter, *Hear Me*, 509.

50. McDonald, 'Through Nez Perce Eyes', 272–73.

51. McDonald, 'Through Nez Perce Eyes', 244.

52. E.W. Said, *Culture and Imperialism*, London, 1993; Lewis, 'Boyhood Days'; Partoll, 'Angus McDonald', 138.

53. Decker Papers: Extract, *Ronan Pioneer*, 3 March 1927; M. Ronan, *Frontier Woman*, Missoula, 1973, 128–29.

54. McWhorter Papers: Extract, *Record Herald*, 11 August 1929; *Samuel Johns History: Volume I*, 155–56.

55. Knowles Papers: Knowles to A. McDonald, 2 November 1879.

56. *Samuel Johns History*: Volume I, 156; Knowles Papers: Knowles to A. McDonald, 2 November 1879.

57. For information on McGillivray, see, among many other sources, Morgan, *Wilderness at Dawn*; R.S. Cotterill, *The Southern Indians*, Norman, 1954.

58. See G.E. Moulton, *John Ross: Cherokee Chief*, Athens, 1978; S. Carter, *Cherokee Sunset: A Nation Betrayed*, New York, 1976; R.C. Eaton, *John Ross and the Cherokee Indians*, Chicago, 1921; Wright, *Stolen Continents*.

59. R. Thornton, 'The Demography of the Trail of Tears Period', in W.L. Anderson (ed), *Cherokee Removal: Before and After*, Athens, 1991, 79.

60. Thornton, 'Demography of the Trail of Tears', 77–93.

61. G.E. Moulton (ed), *The Papers of John Ross*, 2 Volumes, Norman, 1985. For details of the Highland famine, see Hunter, *Making of the Crofting Community*, 50–72.

62. McWhorter Papers: D. McDonald to McWhorter, 1 February 1928.

63. McWhorter Papers: D. McDonald to McWhorter, 1 February 1928 and 30 May 1930.

64. Knowles Papers: A. McDonald to Knowles, incomplete and undated. Duncan's articles have recently been reprinted in Loughy, *Pursuit of the Nez Perce*, and this reprinting of them is referred to here as McDonald, 'Through Nez Perce Eyes'.

65. McWhorter Papers: D. McDonald to McWhorter, 1 February 1928; McDonald, 'Through Nez Perce Eyes', 271.

66. Lavender, *Let Me Be Free*, 323–40; Trafzer, *The Nez Perce*, 88–90.

67. Knowles Papers: A. McDonald to Knowles, 1 May 1878; Duncan McDonald Papers, Note in Angus McDonald's hand, headed 'Nez Perce Campaign', undated.

68. Lavender, *Let Me Be Free*, 341–43.

69. Lavender, *Let Me Be Free*, 5–6.

70. Loughy, *Pursuit of the Nez Perce*, 298–99.

Chapter Six: As long as our songs are sung

1. J.G. Neihardt, *Black Elk Speaks*, Lincoln, 1932, 270. Also D. Brown, *Bury My Heart*

at Wounded Knee: An Indian History of the American West, London, 1975, 344–53.

2. Fahey, *Flathead Indians*, 202, 228.

3. McWhorter Papers: D. McDonald to McWhorter, 30 May 1930; Fahey, *Flathead Indians*, 198, 249–53.

4. McWhorter Papers: D. McDonald to McWhorter, 30 May 1930; Fahey, *Flathead Indians*, 203.

5. Fahey, *Flathead Indians*, 264.

6. Bergman, *Fabulous Flathead*, 45, 64, 71–72; Partoll, 'Angus McDonald', 145; Fullerton Collection: Extract article by C.K. Francis, 'Duncan McDonald', *Missoulian*, 21 June 1964; Samuel Johns History, I, 156; A.L. Stone, *Following Old Trails*, Missoula, 1913, 167–72.

7. Samuel Johns History, I, 35–36.

8. Decker Papers: Extract, *Ronan Pioneer*, 11 September 1925; Partoll, 'Fort Connah', 400; Charlie McDonald in conversation with the author.

9. Stone, *Following Old Trails*, 153, 167; McWhorter Papers: Extract, *Record Herald*, 11 August 1929.

10. Decker Papers: Extract, *Ronan Pioneer*, 11 September 1925.

11. From this point forward, quotations which are not otherwise attributed are drawn from the author's conversations with the McDonald family members mentioned in the text.

12. J.B. Katz (ed), *I Am the Fire of Time: The Voices of Native American Women*, New York, 1977, 118.

13. L.W. Towner, 'Introduction', in, D'A. McNickle, *The Surrounded*, Albuquerque, 1978, xi.

14. For a comprehensive assessment of the Dawes Act and its impact, see J.A. McDonnell, *The Dispossession of the American Indian, 1887–1934*, Bloomington, 1991.

15. Fahey, *Flathead Indians*, 264–70; D.L. Parman, *Indians and the American West in the Twentieth Century*, Bloomington, 1994, 14–16; McDonnell, *Dispossession of the American Indian*, 58–61; B.M. Smith, *The Politics of Allotment on the Flathead Reservation*, Pablo, 1995, 9–12.

16. Smith, *Politics of Allotment*, 25.

17. Smith, *Politics of Allotment*, 5–6.

18. J.C. Hale, *Bloodlines: Odyssey of a Native Daughter*, New York, 1994, 109.

19. For an assessment of these developments and their impact, see C.T. Brockman, 'The Modern Social and Economic Organization of the Flathead Reservation', Ph.D. Thesis, University of Oregon, 1968; R.L. Trosper, 'The Economic Impact of the Allotment Policy on the Flathead Reservation', Ph.D. Thesis, University of Harvard, 1974.

20. Angus P. McDonald Papers: A.P. McDonald to the Secretary of the Interior, 15 February 1914.

21. Goode Papers: C. Morrison (?) to A.P. McDonald, 27 October 1915.

22. Goode Papers: J. MacDonald to A.P. McDonald, 24 May 1907.

Bibliography

UNPUBLISHED SOURCES

In Montana Historical Society Library,
Helena, Montana:
    Hiram Knowles Papers
    William Fletcher Wheeler Papers
    Neil Fullerton Collection
    Angus McDonald Papers
    Duncan McDonald Papers
    Samuel Johns Collection
In University of Montana Library, Missoula,
Montana:
    Angus McDonald (Missoula) Papers
    Angus P. McDonald Papers
In Flathead County Library, Kalispell,
Montana, a multi-volume typescript history
of the Flathead Valley compiled by Samuel
Johns and others, here referred to as:
    Samuel Johns History
At St Ignatius, Montana, McDonald family
papers in the possession of Eileen Decker
and here referred to as:
    Decker Papers
At Niarada, Montana, McDonald family
papers in the possession of Maggie Goode
and here referred to as:
    Goode Papers
In Washington State University Library,
Pullman, Washington State:
    Lucullus V. McWhorter Papers
    Charles W. Wilson Diary
In University of Washington Library, Seattle,

Washington State:
    Clarence Bagley Papers
    Edward Huggins Papers
In Oregon Historical Society Library,
Portland, Oregon:
    Matthew P. Deady Papers
In Manitoba Provincial Archives, Winnipeg,
Manitoba, Canada:
    Hudson's Bay Company Archives
In Inverness Public Library, Inverness,
Scotland:
    Parish Registers and Census Returns
In Edinburgh University Library, Edinburgh,
Scotland:
    MacDonald of Dalilia Papers
In Clan Donald Centre, Isle of Skye,
Scotland:
    Macdonald of Castleton Papers

UNPUBLISHED THESES

Brockman, Charles T., 'The Modern Social
and Economic Organization of the Flathead
Reservation', Ph.D. Thesis, University of
Oregon, 1968.
Trosper, Ronald L., 'The Economic Impact
of the Allotment Policy on the Flathead
Indian Reservation', Ph.D. Thesis, Harvard,
1974.

212

PUBLISHED BOOKS AND ARTICLES

Adam, R.J. (ed), *Papers on Sutherland Estate Management*, 2 Volumes, Scottish History Society, Edinburgh, 1972.

Adams, Winona (ed), 'An Indian Girl's Story of a Trading Expedition to the Southwest about 1841', *The Frontier*, 10, 1930.

Alcorn, Rowena, *Nez Perce Indian Portraits*, Wenatchee, 1994.

Anderson, William L. (ed), *Cherokee Removal: Before and After*, Athens, 1991.

Anderson, M.S., *The War of the Austrian Succession, 1740–1748*, London, 1995.

Aoki, Harvo, *Nez Perce Texts*, Berkeley, 1979.

Armstrong, Virginia I. (ed), *I Have Spoken: American History through the Voices of the Indians*, Chicago, 1971.

Bachman, Ronet, *Death and Violence on the Reservation: Homicide, Family Violence and Suicide in American Indian Populations*, New York, 1992.

Ballantine, Betty and Ballantine, Ian (eds), *The Native Americans: An Illustrated History*, London, 1994.

Barron, James, *The Northern Highlands in the Nineteenth Century*, 3 Volumes, Inverness, 1903–1913.

Barrow, G.W.S., *Robert Bruce and the Community of the Realm of Scotland*, London, 1965.

Barrow, G.W.S., *The Kingdom of the Scots*, London, 1973.

Barrow, G.W.S., *Kingship and Unity: Scotland, 1000–1306*, London, 1981.

Beal, Merill D., *I Will Fight No More Forever: Chief Joseph and the Nez Perce War*, Ballantine Books Edition, New York, 1971.

Bergman, Sharon, *The Fabulous Flathead: The Story of the Development of Montana's Flathead Reservation*, Polson, 1988.

Berkhofer, Robert F., *The White Man's Indian: Images of the American Indian from Columbus to the Present*, New York, 1978.

Billington, Ray A., *Westward Expansion: A History of the American Frontier*, Fourth Edition, New York, 1974.

Billington, Ray A., *Land of Savagery, Land of Promise: The European Image of the American Frontier in the Nineteenth Century*, New York, 1981.

Black, Jeremy, *Culloden and the Forty-Five*, Stroud, 1990.

Blaikie, Walter B., *Itinerary of Prince Charles Edward Stuart*, Scottish History Society, Edinburgh, 1897.

Blaikie, Walter B., *The Origins of the Forty-Five*, Scottish History Society, Edinburgh, 1916.

Bordewich, Fergus M., *Killing the White Man's Indian: Reinventing Native Americans at the End of the Twentieth Century*, New York, 1996.

Bogue, Allan G., Phillips, Thomas D. and Wright, James E. (eds), *The West of the American People*, Ithaca, 1970.

Brogan, Hugh, *History of the United States of America*, London, 1985.

Brown, Dee, *Bury My Heart at Wounded Knee: An Indian History of the American West*, Picador Edition, London, 1975.

Brown, Dee, *The American West*, New York, 1994.

Brown, Jennie B., *Fort Hall on the Oregon Trail*, Caldwell, 1932.

Brown, Jennifer M. (ed), *Scottish Society in the Fifteenth Century*, London, 1977.

Brown, Jennifer S.H., *Strangers in Blood: Fur Trade Company Families in Indian Country*, Vancouver, 1980.

Brown, Jennifer S.H., 'A Parcel of Upstart Scotchmen', *The Beaver*, 68, 1988.

Brown, Jennifer S.H., Eccles, W.J. and Heldman, Donald P. (eds), *The Fur Trade Revisited*, Michigan, 1991.

Brown, Mark H., *The Flight of the Nez Perce*, Bison Books Edition, Lincoln, 1982.

Buchan, John, *The Massacre of Glencoe*, Edinburgh, 1933.

Burns, Robert I., *The Jesuits and the Indian Wars of the Northwest*, New Haven, 1966.

Cage, R.A., *The Scots Abroad: Labour, Capital, Enterprise, 1750–1914*, London, 1985.

Calder, Angus, *Revolutionary Empires: The Rise of the English-Speaking Empires from the Fifteenth Century to the 1780s*, London, 1981.

Cameron, Alexander, *Reliquiae Celticae*, 2 Volumes, Inverness, 1892–1894.

Campbell, John Lorne, *Highland Songs of the Forty-Five*, Edinburgh, 1933.

Campbell, Marjorie Wilkins, *The North West Company*, Vancouver, 1983.

Carlson, Leonard A., *Indians, Bureaucrats and Land: the Dawes Act and the Decline of Indian Farming*, Westport, 1981.

Carter, Samuel, *Cherokee Sunset: A Nation Betrayed*, New York, 1976.

Castile, George P. and Bee, Robert L. (eds), *State and Reservation: New Perspectives on Federal Indian Policy*, Tucson, 1992.

Catlin, George, *North American Indians*, Penguin Edition, London, 1989.

Chittenden, Hiram M., *The American Fur Trade of the Far West*, Fairfield, 1976.

Clark, Malcolm, *Eden Seekers: The Settlement of Oregon, 1818–1862*, Boston, 1981.

Clifton, James A. (ed), *Being and Becoming Indian: Biographical Studies of North American Frontiers*, Chicago, 1989.

Cline, Gloria G., *Peter Skene Ogden and the Hudson's Bay Company*, Norman, 1974.

Cole, Jean Murray, *Exile in the Wilderness: The Biography of Chief Factor Archibald McDonald*, Don Mills, 1979.

Coleman, Terry, *Passage to America*, London, 1972.

Cordier, Rick, 'My Son, My Son: Angus McDonald and Fort Connah', *Dovetail Magazine*, Ronan, I, 1973.

Cornell, Stephen, *The Return of the Native: American Indian Political Resurgence*, New York, 1988.

Cotterill, R.S., *The Southern Indians*, Norman, 1954.

Cowan, Edward J., *Montrose: For Covenant and King*, London, 1977.

Cox, Ross, *Adventures on the Columbia River*, 2 Volumes, London, 1831.

Crosby, Alfred W., *Ecological Imperialism: The Biological Expansion of Europe*, Canto Edition, Cambridge, 1993.

Davies, R.R. (ed), *The British Isles, 1100–1500: Comparisons, Contrasts and Connections*, Edinburgh, 1988.

Debo, Angie, *A History of the Indians of the United States*, Pimlico Edition, London, 1995.

Deloria, Vine, *Behind the Trail of Broken Treaties: An Indian Declaration of Independence*, Austin, 1985.

Deloria, Vine (ed), *American Indian Policy in the Twentieth Century*, Norman, 1985.

Dictionary of American Biography, 22 Volumes, New York, 1928–1958.

Dictionary of Canadian Biography, 12 Volumes, Toronto, 1966–1991.

Dippie, Brian W., *The Vanishing American: White Attitudes and US Indian Policy*, Middletown, 1982.

Doig, Ivan, *This House of Sky: Landscapes of a Western Mind*, New York, 1978.

Drummond, John (ed), *Memoirs of Sir Ewen Cameron of Locheil*, Abbotsford Club, Edinburgh, 1842.

Drury, Clifford M., *Chief Lawyer of the Nez Perce Indians, 1796–1876*, Glendale, 1979.

Dunbar, Seymour (ed), *The Journals and Letters of Major John Owen*, 2 Volumes, Portland, 1927.

Duncan, Archibald A.M. and Brown, A.L., 'Argyll and the Isles in the Early Middle Ages', *Proceedings of the Society of Antiquaries of Scotland*, 90, 1957.

Duncan, Archibald A.M., *Scotland: The Making of the Kingdom*, Edinburgh, 1975.

Dwyer, J., Mason, R.A. and Murdoch, A. (eds), *New Perspectives on the Politics and Culture of Early Modern Scotland*, Edinburgh, 1982.

Eaton, Rachel C., *John Ross and the Cherokee Indians*, Chicago, 1921.

Eckenridge, H.J. and Conrad, Bryan, *George B. McClellan: The Man who Saved the Union*, Chapel Hill, 1941.

Ehle, John, *Trail of Tears: The Rise and Fall of the Cherokee Nation*, Doubleday Edition, New York, 1989.

Elliott, T.C., 'Richard (Captain Johnny) Grant', *Oregon Historical Quarterly*, XXXVI, 1935.

Elwood, Henry, *Montana, and the Upper Flathead Valley*, Kalispell, 1980.

Fahey, John, *The Flathead Indians*, Norman, 1974.

Fahey, John, *The Kalispel Indians*, Norman, 1986.

Fairweather, Barbara and Cargill, D.C., *Pre-1855 Tombstone Inscriptions at Eilean Munda*, Highland History Society, Inverness, 1969.

Ferguson, William, 'Religion and the Massacre of Glencoe', *Scottish Historical Review*, 46–47, 1967–1968.

Ferguson, William, *Scotland: 1689 to the*

Present, Edinburgh, 1968.

Fergusson, James, *Argyll in the Forty-Five*, London, 1951.

Friesen, Gerald, *The Canadian Prairies: A History*, Toronto, 1987.

Frush, Charles W., 'A Trip from the Dalles of the Columbia, Oregon, to Fort Owen, Bitterroot Valley, Montana, in the Spring of 1858', *Contributions to the Historical Society of Montana*, 2, 1896.

Further Papers Relative to the Affairs of British Columbia, Parliamentary Publication, London, 1860.

Galbraith, John S., 'The British and Americans at Fort Nisqually, 1846–1859', *Pacific Northwest Quarterly*, XLI, 1940.

Galbraith, John S., *The Hudson's Bay Company as an Imperial Factor, 1821–1869*, Berkeley, 1957.

Galbraith, John S., *The Little Emperor: Governor Simpson of the Hudson's Bay Company*, Toronto, 1976.

Galloway, Colin G.(ed), *New Directions in American Indian History*, Norman, 1988.

Garcia, Andrew, *Tough Trip Through Paradise*, Abacus Edition, London, 1977.

Gibson, James R., *Otter Skins, Boston Ships and China Goods: The Maritime Fur Trade of the Northwest Coast, 1785–1841*, Seattle, 1992.

Gidley, Mick, *With One Sky Above Us: Life on an Indian Reservation at the Turn of the Century*, Exeter, 1979.

Gidley, Mick, *Kopet: A Documentary Narrative of Chief Joseph's Last Years*, Seattle, 1981.

Gildart, Robert C., *Montana's Flathead Country*, Helena, 1986.

Glengarry Historical Society, *The Glengarry Nor'Westers*, undated and unpaginated pamphlet.

Goetzmann, William H., *Army Exploration in the American West, 1803–1863*, Yale, 1965.

Goetzmann, William H., *Exploration and Empire: The Explorer and the Scientist in the Winning of the American West*, New York, 1966.

Goetzmann, William H., *New Lands, New Men: America and the Second Great Age of Discovery*, Penguin Edition, New York, 1987.

Goldring, Philip, 'Lewis and the Hudson's Bay Company in the Nineteenth Century',

Scottish Studies, XXIV, 1980.

Gordon, John (ed), *Papers Illustrative of the Political Condition of the Highlands of Scotland, 1689–1696*, Maitland Club, Glasgow, 1845.

Grant, Alexander, *Independence and Nationhood: Scotland, 1306–1469*, London, 1984.

Grant, Isobel F., *The Lordship of the Isles*, Edinburgh, 1935.

Grant, Isobel F. and Cheape, Hugh, *Periods in Highland History*, London, 1987.

Grant, Louis S., 'Fort Hall under the Hudson's Bay Company', *Oregon Historical Quarterly*, XLI, 1940.

Gunn, Donald, *Manitoba from the Earliest Settlement*, Ottawa, 1880.

Hafen, LeRoy R., *The Mountain Men and the Fur Trade of the Far West*, 8 Volumes, Glendale, 1965–1972.

Haines, Aubrey, *An Elusive Victory: The Battle of Big Hole*, Glacier, 1991.

Haines, Francis, *The Nez Perce*, Norman, 1972.

Hale, Janet C., *Bloodlines: Odyssey of a Native Daughter*, Harper Perennial Edition, New York, 1994.

Hampton, Bruce, *Children of Grace: The Nez Perce War of 1877*, New York, 1994.

Harmon, Alexandra, 'Lines in Sand: Shifting Boundaries between Indians and Non-Indians in the Puget Sound Region', *Western Historical Quarterly*, 26, 1995.

Hewitson, Jim, *Tam Blake and Co: The Story of the Scots in America*, Edinburgh, 1993.

Hill, J. Michael, *Fire and Sword: Sorley Boy MacDonnell and the Rise of Clan Iain Mor, 1538–1590*, London, 1993.

Hopkins, Paul, *Glencoe and the End of the Highland War*, Edinburgh, 1986.

Howard, Helen A., *Saga of Chief Joseph*, Caldwell, 1965.

Howard, Oliver O., *My Life and Experience Among our Hostile Indians*, Da Capo Press Edition, New York, 1972.

Hoxie, Frederick E., *A Final Promise: The Campaign to Assimilate the Indians, 1880–1920*, New York, 1984.

Hugo, Richard, *Making Certain It Goes On: Collected Poetry*, Norton Paperback Edition, New York, 1991.

Hunter, James, *The Making of the Crofting*

Community, Edinburgh, 1976

Hunter, James, *A Dance Called America: The Scottish Highlands, the United States and Canada*, Edinburgh, 1994

Hunter, James, *On the Other Side of Sorrow: Nature and People in the Scottish Highlands*, Edinburgh, 1995

Irving, Washington, *Astoria: Adventures in the Pacific Northwest*, KPI Edition, London, 1987.

Jackson, John C., *Children of the Fur Trade*, Missoula, 1995.

Jackson, W. Turrentine, *The Enterprising Scot: Investors in the American West after 1873*, Edinburgh, 1968.

Jennings, Francis, *The Founders of America*, London, 1993.

Johnson, Dorothy M., *The Bloody Bozeman: The Perilous Trail to Montana's Gold*, New York, 1971.

Johnson, Olga W., *Flathead and Kootenay: The Rivers, the Tribes and the Region's Traders*, Glendale, 1969.

Josephy, Alvin M., *The Nez Perce Indians and the Opening of the Northwest*, Lincoln, 1979.

Josephy, Alvin M. (ed), *America in 1492: The World of the Indian Peoples Before the Arrival of Columbus*, New York, 1992.

Judd, Carol M. and Ray, Arthur J. (eds), *Old Trails and New Directions*, Toronto, 1980.

Karamski, Theodore J., *Fur Trade and Exploration: Opening the Far Northwest, 1821–1852*, Norman, 1983.

Katz, Jane B. (ed), *I Am the Fire of Time: The Voices of Native American Women*, New York, 1977.

Kilgour, William T., *Lochaber in War and Peace*, Paisley, 1908.

Kirk, Sylvia Van, *Many Tender Ties: Women in Fur Trade Society in Western Canada, 1670–1870*, Winnipeg, 1983.

Kittredge, William and Smith, Annick (eds), *The Last Best Place: A Montana Anthology*, Seattle, 1991.

Kopper, Philip (ed), *The Smithsonian Book of North American Indians Before the Coming of the Europeans*, Washington, 1986.

Kroes, Rob (ed), *The American West as Seen by Europeans and Americans*, Amsterdam, 1989.

Lang, Andrew (ed), *The Highlands of Scotland in 1750*, Edinburgh, 1898.

Lavender, David, *The Penguin Book of the American West*, London, 1969.

Lavender, David (ed), *The Oregon Journals of David Douglas*, 2 Volumes, Ashland, 1972.

Lavender, David, *The Fist in the Wilderness*, Albuquerque, 1979.

Lavender, David, *Let Me Be Free: A Nez Perce Tragedy*, Anchor Books Edition, New York, 1993.

Leatherbarrow, Linda, *The Shadow on the Plain*, London, 1983.

Lenman, Bruce, *The Jacobite Risings in Britain, 1689–1746*, London, 1980.

Lenman, Bruce, *The Jacobite Clans of the Great Glen, 1650–1784*, London, 1984.

Leroy, Bruce, *Lairds, Bards and Mariners: The Scot in Northwest America*, Seattle, 1978.

Lewis, W.S., 'Archibald McDonald: Biography and Genealogy', *Washington Historical Quarterly*, 9, 1918.

Lewis, W.S. (ed), 'Christina M. Williams: The Daughter of Angus McDonald', *Washington Historical Quarterly*, 13, 1922.

Lewis, W.S. (ed), 'Boyhood Days at Old Fort Colville', *Spokesman-Review*, Spokane, 28 April 1929.

Lewis, W.S. (ed), 'Narrative of Benjamin MacDonald', *Washington Historical Quarterly*, 30, 1939.

Lewis, W.S. and Meyers, J.A., 'Life at Old Fort Colville', *Washington Historical Quarterly*, XVI, 1925.

Lewis, W.S. and Murikami, N. (eds), *Ranald MacDonald: The Narrative of His Life*, New Edition, Portland, 1990.

Linklater, Magnus, *Massacre: The Story of Glencoe*, London, 1982.

Linklater, Magnus and Hesketh, Christian, *For King and Conscience: John Graham of Claverhouse*, London, 1989.

Livingstone, Alistair, Aikman, Christian W.H., and Hart, Betty S. (eds), *Muster Roll of Prince Charles Edward Stuart's Army, 1745–46*, Aberdeen, 1984.

Lopach, James J., Brown, Margery H. and Crow, Richmond L., *Tribal Government Today: Politics on Indian Reservations*, Boulder, 1990.

Lothrop, Gloria R. (ed), *Recollections of the*

Flathead Mission, Glendale, 1977.

Loughy, Linwood (ed), *In Pursuit of the Nez Perces*, Wrangell, 1993.

McDermott, John F. (ed), *Travellers on the Western Frontier*, Chicago, 1970.

MacDonald, A. and MacDonald, A., *The Clan Donald*, 3 Volumes, Inverness, 1896–1904.

McDonald, Angus, 'A Flathead Tradition', *The New Northwest*, Deer Lodge, 24 May 1878.

McDonald, Angus, 'White Bird's Song', *The New Northwest*, Deer Lodge, 11 April 1879.

McDonald, Angus, 'A Few Items of the West', (edited by Howay, F.W., Lewis, W.S. and Meyers, J.A.), *Washington Historical Quarterly*, VIII, 1917.

Macdonald, Iain S., 'Alexander MacDonald of Glencoe: Insights into Early Highland Sheep Farming', *Review of Scottish Culture*, 1996.

MacDonald, Donald J., *Slaughter Under Trust*, London, 1965.

MacDonald, Donald J., *Clan Donald*, Loanhead, 1978.

MacDonald, Keith N., *MacDonald Bards*, Edinburgh, 1900.

McDonald, Walter, 'A Closer Look at Indian History', *Mission Valley News*, 8 July 1976.

McDonnell, Janet A., *The Dispossession of the American Indian, 1887–1934*, Bloomington, 1991.

MacDougall, Norman, *James IV*, Edinburgh, 1989.

McFeely, William S., *Yankee Stepfather: General O.O. Howard and the Freedmen*, New Haven, 1968.

MacKechnie, John (ed), *The Dewar Manuscripts*, Glasgow, 1964.

MacKenzie, Annie M., *Orain Iain Luim, Scottish Gaelic Texts Society*, Edinburgh, 1964.

MacKenzie, Cecil W., *Donald MacKenzie: King of the Northwest*, Los Angeles, 1937.

MacKenzie, William C., *History of the Outer Hebrides*, Mercat Press Edition, Edinburgh, 1974.

MacKintosh, Charles Fraser, *Antiquarian Notes: Second Series*, Inverness, 1897.

McLean, Marianne, *The People of Glengarry: Highlanders in Transition, 1745–1820*, Montreal, 1991.

Maclean, Norman, *A River Runs Through It and Other Stories*, Chicago, 1976.

McLoughlin, William G., *After the Trail of Tears: The Cherokee Struggle for Sovereignty, 1839–1880*, Chapel Hill, 1993.

McLynn, F.J., *The Jacobite Army in England*, Edinburgh, 1983.

McNickle, D'Arcy, *The Surrounded*, University of New Mexico Press Edition, Albuquerque, 1978.

McNickle, D'Arcy, *Native American Tribalism: Indian Survivals and Renewals*, Oxford Paperback Edition, New York, 1993.

MacPhail, J.R.N. (ed), *Highland Papers*, 4 Volumes, Scottish History Society, Edinburgh, 1914–1934.

McWhorter, L.V., *Yellow Wolf: His Own Story*, Abacus Edition, London, 1977.

McWhorter, L.V., *Hear Me, My Chiefs: Nez Perce Legend and History*, Caxton Printers Edition, Caldwell, 1992.

Malone, Michael P., *The Battle for Butte: Mining and Politics on the Northern Frontier, 1864–1906*, Seattle, 1981.

Malone, Michael P. and Roeder, Richard B., *Montana: A History of Two Centuries*, Seattle, 1976.

Matheson, Angus, 'Traditions of Alasdair MacColla', *Transactions of the Gaelic Society of Glasgow*, 5, 1958.

Mathiessen, Peter, *In the Spirit of Crazy Horse*, Penguin Edition, New York, 1992.

May, Dean L., *Three Frontiers: Family, Land and Society in the American West, 1850–1900*, New York, 1994.

Menzies, Gordon (ed), *Who Are the Scots?*, London, 1971.

Mercier, Laurie and Simon-Smolenski, Carole, *Idaho's Scots-Americans*, Idaho Ethnic Heritage Project, Boise, 1990.

Merk, Frederick (ed), *Fur Trade and Empire: George Simpson's Journal, 1824–1825*, London, 1931.

Merk, Frederick, *The Oregon Question*, Cambridge, Mass., 1967.

Meyers, J.A., 'Finan McDonald: Explorer, Fur Trader and Legislator', *Washington Historical Quarterly*, XIII, 1922.

Miller, Jay (ed), *Mourning Dove: A Salishan Autobiography*, Lincoln, 1990.

Milner, Clyde A., O'Connor, Carol A. and

Sandweiss, Martha A. (eds), *The Oxford History of the American West*, New York, 1994.

Mitchell, Arthur (ed), *Geographical Collections Relating to Scotland made by Walter MacFarlane*, 3 Volumes, Scottish History Society, Edinburgh, 1906.

Mitchell, H.T. (ed), *The Journals of William Fraser Tolmie: Physician and Fur Trader*, Vancouver, 1963.

Morgan, Dale L., *Jedediah Smith and the Opening of the West*, Lincoln, 1953.

Morgan, Ted, *Wilderness at Dawn: The Settling of the North American Continent*, New York, 1993.

Morrison, A.G., 'The MacDonalds of Glencoe', *West Highland Notes and Queries*, July 1995.

Moulton, Gary E., *John Ross: Cherokee Chief*, Athens, 1978.

Moulton, Gary E. (ed), *The Papers of John Ross*, 2 Volumes, Norman, 1985.

Mowat, Ian R.M., *Easter Ross, 1750–1850: The Double Frontier*, Edinburgh, 1981.

Munro, Jean and Munro, R.W. (eds), *Acts of the Lords of the Isles, 1336–1493*, Scottish History Society, Edinburgh, 1986.

Myers, William S., *General George Brinton McClellan*, New York, 1934.

Nabokov, Peter (ed), *Native American Testimony: An Anthology of Indian and White Relations*, Harper Colophon Edition, New York, 1979.

National Trust for Scotland, *Glencoe and Dalness*, Edinburgh, 1975.

Neihardt, John G., *Black Elk Speaks*, Lincoln, 1932.

Nelson, Robert M., *Place and Vision: The Function of Landscape in Native American Fiction*, New York, 1993.

Newman, Peter, *Company of Adventurers*, Penguin Edition, London, 1987.

Newman, Peter, *Caesars of the Wilderness*, Penguin Edition, London, 1988.

Nicholson, Ranald, *Scotland: The Later Middle Ages*, Edinburgh, 1974.

Nisbet, Jack, *Sources of the River: Tracking David Thompson across Western North America*, Seattle, 1994.

O'Baoill, Colm, *Gair nan Clarsach: An Anthology of Seventeenth Century Gaelic Poetry*, Edinburgh, 1994.

Oliphant, J.O., 'Old Fort Colville', *Washington Historical Quarterly*, XVI, 1925.

Overmeyer, Philip H., 'George B McClellan and the Pacific Northwest', *Pacific Northwest Quarterly*, 32, 1941.

Parker, Dorothy R., *Singing an Indian Song: A Biography of D'Arcy McNickle*, Lincoln, 1992.

Parkman, Francis, *The Oregon Trail*, Signet Classic Edition, London, 1982.

Parman, Donald L., *Indians and the American West in the Twentieth Century*, Bloomington, 1994.

Partoll, Albert J., 'Fort Connah: A Frontier Trading Post, 1847–1871', *Pacific Northwest Quarterly*, 16, 1925.

Partoll, Albert J., 'Angus McDonald: Frontier Fur Trader', *Pacific Northwest Quarterly*, 42, 1951.

Paton, Henry (ed), *The Lyon in Mourning: A Collection Relative to the Affairs of Prince Charles Edward Stuart by the Rev. Robert Forbes, 1746–1775*, 3 Volumes, Scottish History Society, Edinburgh, 1895.

Paul, Rodman W., *Mining Frontiers of the Far West, 1848–1880*, New York, 1963.

Perdue, Theda and Green, Michael D. (eds), *The Cherokee Removal*, Boston, 1995.

Pettus, Terry, 'Frolic at Fort Nisqually', *The Beaver*, 1960.

Phillips, Paul C. (ed), *Forty Years on the Frontier: As Seen in the Journals of Granville Stuart*, 2 Volumes, Cleveland, 1925.

Phillips, Paul C., *The Fur Trade*, 2 Volumes, Norman, 1961.

Porter, H.C., *The Inconstant Savage: England and the North American Indian, 1500–1660*, London, 1979.

Porter, Mae R. and Davenport, Odessa, *Scotsman in Buckskin: Sir William Drummond Stewart and the Rocky Mountain Fur Trade*, New York, 1963.

Powell, Peter J. and Malone, Michael P., *Montana: Past and Present*, Los Angeles, 1976.

Prebble, John, *Culloden*, London, 1961.

Prebble, John, *Glencoe*, Penguin Edition, London, 1968.

Report of the British and American Joint Commis-

sion for the Settlement of the Claims of the Hudson's Bay Company and Puget Sound Agricultural Companies, 7 Volumes, Montreal, 1868.

Rich, E.E. (ed), The Letters of John McLoughlin, 3 Volumes, Toronto, 1941–44.

Rich, E.E. (ed), Peter Skene Ogden's Snake Country Journals, 1824–26, London, 1950.

Rich, E.E., Hudson's Bay Company, 1670–1870, 3 Volumes, Glasgow, 1960.

Rich, E.E., The Fur Trade and the Northwest to 1857, Toronto, 1967.

Richards, Eric, A History of the Highland Clearances: Agrarian Transformation and the Evictions, London, 1982.

Richards, Eric, A History of the Highland Clearances: Emigration, Protest, Reasons, London, 1985.

Richards, Kent D., Isaac I. Stevens: Young Man in a Hurry, Provo, 1979.

Ridge, Martin and Billington, Ray A. (eds), America's Frontier Story: A Documentary History of Westward Expansion, New York, 1969.

Riley, P.W.J., King William and the Scottish Politicians, Edinburgh, 1979.

Robertson, Franc C., Fort Hall: Gateway to the Oregon Country, New York, 1963.

Ronan, Margaret, Frontier Woman, Missoula, 1973.

Ronda, James P., Lewis and Clark Among the Indians, Lincoln, 1984.

Ronda, James P., Astoria and Empire, Lincoln, 1990.

Rosenstiel, Annette, Red and White: Indian Views of the White Man, 1492–1982, New York, 1983.

Ross, Alexander, Adventures of the First Settlers on the Oregon or Columbia River, Lakeside Press Edition, Chicago, 1923.

Ross, Alexander, The Fur Hunters of the Far West, Lakeside Press Edition, Chicago, 1924.

Ross, Frank E., 'The Retreat of the Hudson's Bay Company in the Pacific Northwest', Canadian Historical Review, 18, 1937.

Ross, Raymond J. and Hendry, Joy (eds), Sorley MacLean: Critical Essays, Edinburgh, 1986.

Ruby, Robert H. and Brown, John A., The Spokane Indians, Norman, 1970.

Russell, Archie, The History of St Munda, Glencoe, Glencoe, 1990.

Ruxton, George Frederick, Life in the Far West, Edinburgh, 1849.

Said, Edward W., Culture and Imperialism, London, 1993.

Sale, Kirkpatrick, The Conquest of Paradise: Christopher Columbus and the Columban Legacy, Papermac Edition, London, 1992.

Saum, Lewis O., The Fur Trader and the Indian, Seattle, 1965.

Schultz, James Willard, Rising Wolf, The White Blackfoot: Hugh Monroe's Story of his First Year on the Plains, Boston, 1919.

Schwantes, Carlos A., The Pacific Northwest: An Interpretive History, Lincoln, 1989.

Scott-Moncrieff, Lesley (ed), The Forty-Five: To Gather an Image Whole, Edinburgh, 1988.

Sellar, W.D.H., 'The Origins and Ancestry of Somerled', Scottish Historical Review, 45, 1966.

Seton, Bruce G. and Arnot, Jean G. (eds), The Prisoners of the Forty-Five, 3 Volumes, Scottish History Society, Edinburgh, 1928.

Slickpoo, Allen P., Noon Nee-Me-Poo: We, the Nez Perces, Lapwai, 1973.

Smith, Allan H., 'The Location of Flathead Post', Pacific Northwest Quarterly, XLVIII, 1957.

Smith, Burton M., The Politics of Allotment on the Flathead Reservation, Pablo, 1995.

Smyth, A.P., Warlords and Holy Men: Scotland, AD80–1000, London, 1984.

Spence, Clark C., British Investments and the American Mining Frontier, Ithaca, 1958.

Spry, Irene M. (ed), The Papers of the Palliser Expedition, 1857–1860, Toronto, 1968.

Steele, Richard F., An Illustrated History of Stevens, Ferry, Okanogan and Chelan Counties, Spokane, 1904.

Steer, K.A. and Bannerman, J.W.M., Late Medieval Monumental Sculpture in the West Highlands, Edinburgh, 1977.

Stegner, Wallace, Wolf Willow: A History, a Story and a Memory of the Last Plains Frontier, Penguin Edition, New York, 1990.

Stevens, Hazard, The Life of Isaac Ingalls Stevens, 2 Volumes, Boston, 1900.

Stevens, Mark, 'Chief Joseph's Revenge', New Yorker, 8 August 1994.

Stevenson, David, *Alasdair MacColla and the Highland Problem in the Seventeenth Century*, Edinburgh, 1980.

Stevenson, David, *Scottish Covenanters and Irish Confederates*, Belfast, 1981.

Stewart, John H.J. and Stewart, Duncan, *The Stewarts of Appin*, Edinburgh, 1880.

Stone, Arthur L., *Following Old Trails*, Missoula, 1913.

Sutton, Imre (ed), *Irredeemable America: The Indian Estate and Land Claims*, Albuquerque, 1985.

Thomson, Derick S., *An Introduction to Gaelic Poetry*, London, 1974.

Thomson, Derick S., *Gaelic Poetry in the Eighteenth Century*, Aberdeen, 1993.

Thornton, Russell, *American Indian Holocaust and Survival: A Population History Since 1492*, Norman, 1987.

Tirrell, Norma, *Montana*, Oakland, 1995.

Tobie, Harvey E., *No Man Like Joe: The Life and Times of Joe Meek*, Portland, 1949.

Todd, A.C. and James, David, *Ever Westward the Land*, Exeter, 1986.

Trafzer, Clifford E., *The Nez Perce*, New York, 1992.

Turney-High, Harry H., *The Flathead Indians of Montana*, Menasha,1937.

Unruh, John D., *The Plains Across: Emigrants, Wagon Trains and the American West*, Pimlico Edition, London, 1992.

Utley, Robert M., *The Lance and the Shield: The Life and Times of Sitting Bull*, New York, 1993.

Vanderburg, Agnes, *Going Back Slow: The Importance of Preserving Salish Indian Culture and Language*, Pablo, 1995.

Versluis, Arthur, *Native American Traditions*, Shaftesbury, 1994.

Walker, Deward E., *Indians of Idaho*, Moscow, 1978.

Weisel, George F., *Men and Trade of the Northwest Frontier as Shown by the Fort Owen Ledger*, Missoula, 1955.

Welch, James, *The Death of Jim Loney*, Penguin Edition, New York, 1987.

Welch, James, *Killing Custer: The Battle of the Little Bighorn and the Fate of the Plains Indians*, New York, 1994.

West, John, *The Substance of a Journey During a Residence at the Red River Colony*, London, 1828.

White, M. Catherine, 'Saleesh House: The First Trading Post Among the Flathead', *Pacific Northwest Quarterly*, XXXIII, 1942.

White, Robert H., *Tribal Assets: The Rebirth of Native America*, New York, 1990.

Wild, Peter, *James Welch*, Boise, 1983.

Wilson, Derek, *The Astors, 1763–1992*, London, 1993.

Williams, Ronald, *Montrose: Cavalier in Mourning*, London, 1975.

Williams, Ronald, *The Lords of the Isles*, London, 1984.

Willson, D. Harris, *King James VI and I*, London, 1956.

Wishart, David J., *The Fur Trade of the American West, 1807–1840*, London, 1979.

Withers, Charles W.J., *Gaelic Scotland: The Transformation of a Culture Region*, London, 1968.

Withrington, Donald J. and Grant, Ian R. (eds), *The Statistical Account of Scotland*, 20 Volumes, Wakefield, 1983.

Womack, Peter, *Improvement and Romance: Constructing the Myth of the Highlands*, London, 1989.

Wooster, Robert, *The Military and United States Indian Policy, 1865–1903*, New Haven, 1988.

Wooster, Robert, *Nelson A. Miles and the Twilight of the Frontier Army*, Lincoln, 1993.

Wormald, Jenny, *Court, Kirk and Community: Scotland, 1470–1625*, London, 1981.

Worster, Donald, *Under Western Skies: Nature and History in the American West*, New York, 1992.

Wright, Ronald, *Stolen Continents: The Indian Story*, London, 1992.

Youngson, A.J., *After the Forty-Five: The Economic Impact on the Scottish Highlands*, Edinburgh, 1973.

Index